FILMMAKERS SERIES
Anthony Slide, Editor

Straight from the Horse's Mouth

Ronald Neame, an Autobiography

Filmmakers Series, No. 98

Ronald Neame
with Barbara Roisman Cooper

The Scarecrow Press, Inc.
Lanham, Maryland, and Oxford
2003

SCARECROW PRESS, INC.

Published in the United States of America
by Scarecrow Press
A Member of the Rowman & Littlefield Publishing Group
4720 Boston Way, Lanham, Maryland 20706
www.scarecrowpress.com

PO Box 317
Oxford
OX2 9RU, UK

British Library Cataloguing in Publication Information Available

Library of Congress Cataloging-in-Publication Data

Neame, Ronald.
  Straight from the horse's mouth : Ronald Neame, an autobiography / Ronald Neame with
  Barbara Roisman Cooper.
    p. cm. — (Filmmakers series ; no. 98)
  Includes index.
  ISBN: 978-0-8108-4490-2
  1. Neame, Ronald. 2. Cinematographers—Great Britain—Biography.
  3. Cinematographers—United States—Biography. 4. Motion picture actors
  and actresses—Great Britain. 5. Motion picture actors and actresses—United
  States. I. Cooper, Barbara Roisman, 1941– II. Title. III. Series.
  TR849.N43 A3 2003
  791.43'0233'092—dc21   2002008702

To my wife Donna and my son Christopher, without whose tenacity, loyalty, and daily creative input this book would never have seen the light of day.

Photo by Cornel Lucas

Contents

Foreword

by Michael Caine

$\mathscr{I}$'d been to New York to publicize a movie before, but *Gambit* was my first visit to Hollywood. What happened was that Shirley MacLaine had the right to choose her leading man in her contract and so that was me. She'd seen me in *The Ipcress File*. I was in awe of everything, sunshine and swimming pools. I was there in the Beverly Hills Hotel and I made friends with John Wayne in the lobby.

My first meeting with Ronnie was in his office at Universal just before we started filming. He put me at ease immediately. He wasn't a Hollywood character at all, not in the least. You'd expect to find him in one of those gentleman's clubs in England, asleep with *The Times* over his face.

It's a very nerve-wracking thing making your first big movie in a foreign country, when you're a British actor with a big American movie star. If I'd had some kind of yelling and screaming director it would have been terrible. Instead I had this extremely kind, very sensitive English gentleman, and I thank God to my dying day he directed that picture with me.

In a way Ronnie and I go back to my childhood. Among the few pleasures in my neighborhood were visits to cinema. As I grew up, my fascination with movies intensified. I couldn't help but recognize in the title cards of many films the name Ronald Neame. His credit always seemed to be changing, cinematographer, screenwriter, producer, director. He's one of the best "all rounders" in the business.

He started out as Alfred Hitchcock's assistant cameraman on *Blackmail*, the first sound motion picture made in England. The fact that his career lasted over seventy years is testament to his multi-faceted talent.

David Lean, Anthony Havelock-Allan, and Ronnie formed a company known as Cineguild. Working with them, and often with Noël Coward, he photographed some of the best films to come out of England, including *Major Barbara*, *In Which We Serve*, and *Blithe Spirit*.

The Academy of Motion Pictures Arts and Sciences has honored him with three nominations: as writer on *Great Expectations*; for screenplay on *Brief Encounter*; and for special effects photography on *One of Our Aircraft Is Missing*.

Ronnie is credited for guiding the career of Alec Guinness with whom he made six pictures, including *The Horse's Mouth* and *Tunes and Glory*. He also got to know John Mills pretty well, having made five pictures with him.

As director, his choice of material has been as varied as the actors with whom he has worked. Whether it's *The Prime of Miss Jean Brodie*, in which Maggie Smith won an Oscar for best actress, or the vanguard disaster film, *The Poseidon Adventure*.

I could never have imagined that my first movie in Hollywood—Universal's *Gambit*—would give me the opportunity to work with Ronnie. He started me on the road to becoming a better actor than I realized I could be.

This book is a personal autobiography about Ronnie's relationship with his family, associates, and friends, but it highlights many of the things a director should know before commencing production—the reader will discover what it takes to make a motion picture from script conception to delivery.

Thank goodness he has finally put his memories down so that those who aspire to the industry can learn from a master. His revelations about his contemporaries and himself make not only interesting reading, but chronicle a time that will never come again: The Golden Age.

Ronnie as a "Brit" you know that in cricket ninety is not enough; you've got to make a century, and I am sure you will. Thank you for your friendship, kindness, and everything else you have done for me. God bless you.

Foreword

by Alan Parker

This is a true story. I was fourteen. I'd just been to the Odeon Upper Street, Islington and sat transfixed whilst watching a most curious movie which, without the help of illegal substances or *Sight and Sound*, had simply possessed me. I ran home along Florence Street to Canonbury Court, the block of flats where I lived. It would be a good hour before my mother came home from work and, standing on a chair, I opened the top cupboard, where my father kept his paints. It was half tins of Dulux, mostly, and his old brushes kept moist in jam jars of moldy turps. On my bedroom walls I started to paint like a madman. To be exact like Gulley Jimson, the crazy genius played by Alec Guinness in *The Horse's Mouth*, directed by Ronnie Neame, a fact unknown to me at the time as I filled my walls with giant closeups of the soles of men's feet. Just like in the movie. Those demented murals in floor-tile red, bathroom green, kitchenette blue, and bedroom pink stayed there for most of my teenage years. When I returned home one day and found that my father had repapered with Sanderson's "garden rose on beige" I knew it was time to leave home.

Although I didn't know it, this wasn't the first time that Ronald Neame had entered my life. After school we would dash to the Odeon, Carlton, Savoy, Marlborough, or Bluehall, and for half-price, watch the afternoon re-runs of the dreadful British "quota quickies" which Ronnie cut his teeth on and which influenced us so profoundly. Films that don't make the history books stay clearly in my brains, *The Four Just Men, I See Ice, Feather Your Nest* and *Drake of England*.

As I grew up and endeavored to understand the crafts of writing and directing, *Great Expectations*, the greatest Dickens film ever, became the touchstone of everything we did. So beautiful, so concise, so dramatic, so powerful—each frame of Neame's and Lean's brilliant masterpiece remains emulsified in the back of my head and regurgitates every time I make a movie.

Writing a few words like this, I realize that Ronnie Neame has permeated my entire cinematic life, from *Major Barbara* to *In Which We Serve* to *Blithe Spirit* to *Brief Encounter*, from *Oliver Twist* to *Tunes of Glory* and to *The Prime of Miss Jean Brodie*. It was Ronald Neame who filled my head with Herbert Pocket, Henry Machin, Jean Brodie, and Shelley Winters swimming in her underwear. It was Ronnie Neame who was the assistant cameraman as Alfred Hitchcock tentatively shot his first talkie, *Blackmail*. Yes, he was actually there! It was Ronald Neame who, with David Lean, Noël Coward, and Anthony Havelock-Allan formed Cineguild, creating a magnificent template for the British film industry which my generation still stumbles and stutters to emulate. Why, it was Ronald Neame who even received a pair of gold cuff links from George Formby for photographing the well-known miserable bastard with such sunshine sympathy that fooled us all.

If this were a movie, we would be fading in old George's ukulele about now " . . . I'm leaning on a lamppost at the corner of the street . . . "

Ronnie, oh how you've touched all of our lives and for so long. Oh, how we treasure you.

Introduction

$\mathscr{I}$t was a very special birthday—my ninetieth. The British Academy of Film and Television Arts, Los Angeles (BAFTA/LA) hosted a party at the Four Seasons Hotel in Beverly Hills, inviting three hundred friends for the occasion, which ended up being one full of happy surprises and memories. Donna, my second wife, helped organize the event. Not least among the surprises, my son and grandson flew over from England and our dear friend, Bill Saunders, came in from Monte Carlo to play the piano.

Father Joe Fenton put together a collection of sequences from many of the pictures I have worked on. The lights dimmed, and suddenly they were all there. Each one vibrant and alive, captured in a moment of time: Noël Coward addressing the crew of *The Torrin* from *In Which We Serve*, Judy Garland singing "By Myself" in *I Could Go On Singing*, John Mills' famous outburst as Colonel Barrow in *Tunes of Glory*, Alec Guinness as the outrageous Gulley Jimson in *The Horse's Mouth*, dear Walter Matthau conducting Mozart in *Hopscotch*, and Maggie Smith riding her bicycle in *The Prime of Miss Jean Brodie*. There was Shelley Winters saving Gene Hackman in *The Poseidon Adventure*, Michael Caine and Shirley MacLaine living it up in *Gambit*, Deborah Kerr arguing with Hayley Mills in *The Chalk Garden*, Albert Finney singing in *Scrooge*, and so many others.

The myriad components that go into making a motion picture filled my mind as I watched—the laughter, the stress, and the apparently insurmountable problems on the set and behind the scenes. But above everything else, I recalled the undiluted excitement.

When the lights came up, one thought was stuck firmly in my mind: thanks to the moving images on the screen, these characters are still with us exactly as they were in bygone days, and the people behind those characters and movies still have such wonderful stories to tell. In an instant the rough shape of an idea took form. By writing a book about my life in film, I hope to bring back many talented colleagues, those who have gone and those who are still very much with us.

Although I have filmed in both America and Europe, I have spent my life, for the most part, making British films. Many that were financed in America were either filmed in Great Britain or starred British actors.

Hopefully, writing down these experiences will result in a kind of cinematic journey on paper. If I have failed to paint vivid pictures of the people I saw on the screen at my birthday party, the fault is mine alone because I am the one who knew them all.

• 1 •

Miss World

$\mathscr{I}$vy Lillian Close was a pretty, blue-eyed, eighteen-year-old blonde raised in Stockton-on-Tees with her parents, sister, and two brothers. With her slender figure and natural grace, she made an ideal model for her father, an amateur photographer, who took many snapshots of his lovely daughter with a primitive camera. One day on a kind of dare with her, he sent a picture to the *Daily Mirror*, the reigning tabloid, which in 1908 was about to launch the first World Beauty Competition.

Elwin Neame, at twenty-three, was probably the youngest and certainly the most successful photographer in London. Apart from his commercial business, he also ran a profitable portrait studio. Placed prominently on every station platform of London's underground were larger-than-life photographs of gorgeous women, beneath each was the caption: If It's A Neame, It's You At Your Best.

Actresses and debutantes came to his Bond Street studio, located in the smartest shopping center in town and a mecca for the young and the beautiful, as well as women and men of a certain age, who were convinced that Elwin Neame could restore their youth, at least photographically!

Knowing of his keen eye for beauty, the *Mirror* offered him an assignment he couldn't possibly have turned down—to photograph the twenty-five finalists in the beauty competition, and, in so doing, help the judges choose the winner. As a result of the submitted photo, Ivy was to be one of the contestants.

A few weeks earlier, she would never have dreamed she'd shortly be on her way to London and walking into the young photographer's studio. In a storybook ending, Ivy won the competition and in the spring of 1910 married Stuart Elwin Neame.

My parents-to-be became the toast of the town, with the same media spotlight on them as royalty today. Whoever they visited, wherever they

1

dined, it was reported on the front page of the tabloids the following morning. Almost overnight Ivy became a major celebrity. In fact, a well-known artist, Arthur Hacker, was commissioned to paint her portrait for exhibition at the Royal Academy.

It was the era of the picture postcard, always featuring women in idealized poses. They would be exchanged in the same way as we send contemporary greeting cards. My mother, photographed by my father, appeared on thousands of them, many still in existence. She was also pictured in several commercials including Pear's soap, Enoline toothpaste, perfume, shampoo, and the like.

When Ivy became pregnant she continued working right up to the time I was born on April 23, 1911. So eager was she to get back to the set that she took me there with her from the age of six weeks onwards.

My father left his photographic business for a while to try his hand at the new art of cinema. He made a film with Ivy in 1912 entitled *The Lady of Shalott*. Most of it was shot on location and what few interiors he used were filmed in a daylight studio at Walton-on-Thames, near London. With the help of a couple of assistants, he'd built the sets himself and cleverly mounted them on a revolving platform so the sun would always come from the same direction.

The Lady of Shalott ran for a mere eight minutes, but was received with some acclaim. It was sold for the princely sum of seventy pounds to the Coronet Theater in Notting Hill Gate, one of the first movie houses in London. Before long, my father returned to his photographic studio, but a few years later, under the banner of Ivy Close Films, he again directed and photographed my mother in *The Haunting of Silas P. Gould* in 1914.

When Broadwest Productions signed Ivy, she was catapulted to film stardom alongside her good friend Violet Hopson, an actress also under contract to the company. Vi was a brunette and often played the villainess to my mother's blonde heroine. They appeared together in such films as *The House Opposite* and *The Ware Case*, both in 1917, and *The Irresistible Flapper* in 1919.

When I was a kid, we seemed to move houses a great deal. One or both of my parents must have been unusually restless, my father I suspect. I was born in Hampstead Garden Suburb, and then it was off to Walton, then Esher, followed by Golders Green, then, much later Finchley. All of these were middle-class suburbs around London.

Prior to the Great War, my mother contracted to make films for the famous Kalem Company in America, working in a series of slapstick comedies at its studio in Jacksonville, Florida—Hollywood had not yet been invented! Always doing her own stunts, one in particular had her sliding down a rope from a tall building. This she told me later, left her with rope burns on both hands. There is another sequence in which she actually lies beneath a train as it races over her!

Ivy Close: I made twelve comedies for Kalem. We had Oliver Hardy. It was before he teamed up with Stan Laurel. He was the top boy; we called him "Babe." Also Bert Tracy, Louise Fazenda, and Robert Ellis. I initially didn't want to go because of my family, but my husband said to go for six months. We had it put in the contract that I could come back at the end of that time if I wanted to. The management agreed to that stipulation adding one of its own. I couldn't go to any other company. I had marvelous offers, one from Famous Players; however, because of the contract I couldn't accept.

"Annie the Nanny" (Whitaker), who was to become an indispensable member of our family, was hired at the Esher house. I adored her and couldn't wait to go for our morning walk together. In the fall I loved shuffling through dead leaves that had accumulated on the sidewalk, hearing the scrunching sound under my feet. Annie often stopped and chatted with other nannies who were out strolling with their charges, or we would watch a neighbor playing with his dog. We were still in Esher when the war began.

When I was four, Annie told me if I looked in the dining room sideboard cupboard every morning, I might find a little brother or sister inside. Each day when we returned from our walk, I would go straight to that cupboard, but, alas, no baby. Then one morning, I heard crying coming from my mother's bedroom. Someone had gotten to the cupboard before me and hidden my little brother named Derek.

My favorite meal without question was Sunday dinner of roast beef, Yorkshire pudding, roast potatoes, and treacle tart. On Monday, we would have cold roast beef; Tuesday, Annie put the leftovers into the mincer to prepare cottage pie. And, if the joint of beef was large enough, it was served as Wednesday's lunch.

In 1916, when I was five, we moved to 11 Rotherwick Road, Golders Green, where we had several interesting neighbors. The Ackermans and the Yanish families had come to England from Germany two years before the War; Natalie Yanish was my first girlfriend. Caroline Hatchard, the opera singer, lived across the street, and I remember hearing her practicing musical scales as I played with young friend Jack Davies who years later would work with me at Elstree as a screenwriter.

"Milko!" "Milko!" was the cry of a man driving a dray horse and cart that clip-clopped towards our house. There he would stop and fill our pewter canisters from an enormous container. Every two weeks, another man would ask in a singing voice if we wanted our knives sharpened. With awe, I used to watch the sparks from his revolving wheel explode into the air. There was also an elderly lady who traipsed up the street with a basket, singing, "Who will buy my blooming lavender, sixteen bunches for one penny?" It was an era when merchants came to neighborhoods, announcing their wares with a rhyming tune, sometimes a bit off key, but always colorful. These were the sights and sounds of the streets!

My friends and I had dug a pit in my back garden, where we would roast potatoes taken from the larder on an old discarded grate. While we were feasting, there were times we would hear gunfire nearby, signaling German planes were coming, and we would run into the house. One night there was tremendous excitement. My parents, who had been to the theater, awakened me to watch a German Zeppelin lighting up the night sky, spiraling to earth with black smoke trailing behind it.

A few months later, my father was called up. I recall him in uniform knocking over my toy soldiers with his big army boots as he crossed the living room to kiss my mother goodbye. And all the while there were films starring Ivy Close, including *The House Opposite* and *Kissing Cup's Race*, produced by Cecil Hepworth and Walter West, well-known British filmmakers of their day.

Elwin Neame was an ordinary "Tommy" never to become an officer—he just didn't bother; he hated the whole idea. Even the army uniform was cumbersome to him. He could never manage the puttees, which were supposed to be wound around from ankle to calf to finish below the knee. "Senny," as his friends called him (from his initials, Stuart Elwin Neame), could photograph people and make them look more beautiful than they were, but he himself wasn't very pulled together, either as a civilian, or as a soldier. He had empty cigarette packs, with other crumpled papers, stuffed in his pockets, and he was constantly reprimanded for not having done up his uniform jacket properly or for not having the requisite shiny buttons.

An officer asked him, "Private Neame, do you call yourself a soldier?"

My father replied, "I'm afraid not, sir."

He was shipped out to France, where he would have preferred carrying a camera to a rifle. Instead, he was based in a trench behind the lines, but not far enough behind to be out of range of the infamous Big Bertha. This colossal cannon fired forty or fifty rounds every night over the heads of my father's unit, the shells falling several miles behind them. As the gun became hot, its range became shorter. He told me, "I was certain one day Big Bertha's shells would fall so short, they would land on us."

The war ended in 1918, and my father returned. I was seven when Britain began to recover and enjoy the peaceful years that followed. King George V was on the throne with the dignified Queen Mary at his side.

British women, who had spent four years in munitions factories, took pride in becoming feminine again. But the remnants of war cast its shadow, little boys with their toy guns still tried to shoot imaginary Germans.

I was very much the older brother at this time. Inheriting Ivy's classic features, Derek was a bit of a nuisance who had to be tolerated. Annie loved him and would say, "He's at an awkward age." For me, he was always at "an awkward age."

About a half mile from where we lived was an enormous stretch of woodlands and grassy slopes known as Hampstead Heath. It was here I had my first brush with the law. Although we knew it was against the rules, we loved to climb trees. I made it to the uppermost branches, while my friends were playing several branches below.

We heard a deep voice at the base of the tree, "What do you think yer doing up there? Come down 'ere at once!"

My chums slipped to the ground and, surprisingly, were allowed to scatter, but I was not so fortunate. A constable grabbed my collar as I jumped down, and said in a gruff voice, "Don't yer know that climbing trees on the 'eath is forbidden?"

I knew only too well. "No sir," I replied, "I'm afraid I didn't."

He was towering over me. "Yer gonna 'ave to come along with me. Boys like you 'ave to be taught a sharp lesson."

"Are you taking me to the police station, sir?"

"I wouldn't be a bit surprised if I was." Then, "Can yer think of any reason why yer shouldn't be goin' to prison?"

"No, sir," I was contrite.

"Where d'ye live, sonny?"

I told him.

To my amazement and relief, instead of carting me straight off, we started towards my home, eventually walking up the path of my front garden. The policeman knocked. Annie answered,

"What's he done?" she asked in a tone suggesting I'd robbed a bank.

"'E's been climbin' trees on the 'eath, ma'am. Ye'd better see 'e doesn't do it again, or 'e'll be in real trouble."

Did I see him give Annie a wink as he turned to leave?

There came a moment when I recognized my father as a person. Up until then his image was more the remote head of the family. Prematurely graying, he was a handsome man of average height, with pale blue eyes beneath fair, bushy eyebrows, which I have inherited as well as his prominent chest. A determined man, with a winning smile and a great sense of humor, who had little tolerance for petty matters and none for careless minds—upon occasion, he could make his opinion felt by all around him.

He and I were walking down Hampstead High Street one Saturday when he noticed my interest in a toy soldier in the shop window. "Oh yes," he said, "he looks very attractive and he's well crafted, but he isn't real and he doesn't have a soul." I thought about it for a moment and then inquired, "Having a soul is good isn't it?" He assured me it was.

Suffering from claustrophobia, he couldn't bear to be in an enclosed space of any kind, not even a car. When we went on picnics, my mother drove her Humber coupe, and my father followed on his Harley-Davidson, with sidecar. He enjoyed this mode of transportation. Rain or shine, he donned his goggles, climbed aboard his bike, and drove off to his studios, about twenty minutes from home.

In 1921, we relocated to our fourth house, the Orchard on Long Lane, Finchley. Perhaps my father felt he and my mother should have a larger home, more befitting their success. It stood on ten acres, which included a hundred-year-old asparagus bed, an apple orchard, and a greenhouse. Warm-hearted, indispensable Annie came with us.

Senny loved this house, my mother did not. She was unhappy from the start. The Rotherwick Road house had been cheerful, the Orchard imposed its gloomy presence on our family and rather than drawing my parents together, it seemed to pull them apart.

My mother remained a big film star and towards the end of 1920, she received the most important offer of her career—a French film that placed her firmly in the archives forever, *La Roue (The Wheel)*.

Its director was the famous Abel Gance, the D. W. Griffith of France. His techniques and use of the camera were years ahead of their time. A large part of the film was shot in the mountains above Chamonix in France where my brother and I spent our school summer holiday, although for some reason we didn't actually visit the set.

Elwin Neame: I'm going out to visit my wife in Chamonix. Our two boys are with her—as lively a pair of youngsters as you could imagine. Ivy is the most adaptable girl in the world, able to motor, no mean fisherman, and an accomplished dancer. She is rather too venturesome where flying is concerned, but knowing my sentiments, she curbs her ambitions in that direction.

While I was attending University College School in Hampstead, I began to realize my parents were having problems. Although my father respected my mother's independence and, in fact, had encouraged her career, the long separations resulting from war and film production were affecting their relationship. Abel Gance had taken nearly two years to make *La Roue* and finally my father presented my mother with an ultimatum—he now wanted a wife, not an actress as his partner, so he asked Ivy to stop working for a while and stay at home. She complied, but the relationship did not improve because she resented her sacrifice and he felt guilty for having asked her to make it.

Discovering my growing interest in photography, Senny bought me a camera, took me shopping for developing dishes, printing paper, and a red lamp for the darkroom, which he helped me to construct in a closet under the stairs.

Pleased with the idea that his son might want to follow in his footsteps, he taught me one of his photographic secrets. "It's the 'S' line that is beautiful. Always think of a large 'S' turned at any angle, and your photographs will flow."

He went on to show me what he meant with a series of photos entitled "Classic Myth and Legend." Another series, published as a calendar, featured a girl beautifully draped, with the caption, "Once in a Blue Moon." Pictures at that time were in black-and-white but my father had a talented colorist, Miss Oates, a spinster lady, who hand tinted these photos in shades of blue. My father was a dreamer and his photographs reflected those dreams.

With London now more or less relaxing into peacetime, my parents were able to return to their active social engagements, and pursue their love of the theatre and the music hall. But increasingly their glamorous life became a way of escaping their growing unhappiness. My father, who had always enjoyed a drink, began doing so more heavily and in the summer of 1923, something occurred which altered our lives forever.

My mother went up to London to see an oculist having prearranged a place to meet him after her appointment, their intention being to ride home together. She went to what she thought was the designated location and waited an hour. When Senny didn't arrive, she came home by train.

My father went to the spot he thought had been agreed upon and also waited an hour before returning home. When he arrived at the Orchard he was upset and my parents had words. Later, their quarrel seemed to have abated and he asked my mother and me to ride with him to Appenrodt's, a restaurant-cum-delicatessen, to collect some food for a late supper.

Ivy climbed into the sidecar and I took my usual place on the pillion. Although my father usually drove with great caution, this night was different. I was scared and held on to him with all my might. We pulled up in front of the deli, purchased a roast chicken, diced potatoes, and bread, then headed home. I'm not sure why my parents asked me to go with them. Perhaps they felt I would be a calming presence.

The argument began again a few minutes after we got back home. Half an hour later my father stormed out of the house and sped away. Annie tried to comfort my tearful mother, as I went sadly to bed. I was old enough to know what was happening, but too young to do anything about it. It is a dreadful thing for a child to hear his parents behaving in such a way towards one another.

I knelt to pray as I did every night, always the same: "God bless Mummy, Daddy, Annie, Derek, my uncles and aunts. Amen." That night, my prayer was not memorized, but from my heart: "Please God, stop my mother and father from quarreling."

I fell asleep. Sometime later, the sound of the telephone awakened me. My mother answered it on the landing near my bedroom, where we had an extension.

I could tell she was talking to my father. I went to my bedroom door and listened.

"Oh darling it's so silly," I heard her say. "I love you, too."

There was a pause.

"We've got to stop hurting each other."

Another pause.

"Yes, of course, I'll wait up for you."

I couldn't believe how quickly my prayer had been answered. Everything was going to be all right again. I went back to bed and fell happily asleep.

I was awakened again. There was a strange voice coming from downstairs. I slipped out of bed and crossed the landing to the stairwell. Peering between the banisters, I could see my mother, Annie, and a policeman, who was writing in his notebook.

My mother stood silently. Annie was crying.

Annie turned and came towards me as I started down the stairs.

"What's happened?" I asked. I knew it was something dreadful.

"Your father has been in an accident," she said.

Looking directly at her, I asked, "Is he dead?"

"I'm afraid he is," she said.

On his way home, he had hit a car, parked illegally on a tree-lined road in Hyde Park. In those days people didn't wear helmets. The motorcycle and sidecar had flipped over. His head hit the road. His neck was broken.

When the policeman left, the three of us clung to each other; it was impossible to believe something so terrible could have happened.

It was three in the morning when we finally went to bed. I slept in my mother's bedroom because I was afraid to sleep alone. That night I was forced to grow up—at age twelve I became the man of the family.

The next morning I woke to see my mother putting on a black dress, which was still the custom in 1923. It seemed everyone knew about my father's death. That Thursday, August 15, a newspaper was delivered to our house showing a photo of my family accompanied by the caption: "Famous photographer killed in Hyde Park crash."

At breakfast, as my eight-year-old brother came downstairs, Annie cautioned him, "Be a good boy because there has been an accident."

"I want my breakfast," he demanded, still too young to fully comprehend.

My father's coffin was brought into the house and put on pedestals in the dining room; we looked at it in silence for several moments and then my mother collapsed.

At the funeral, we stood together at the graveside holding hands. My Uncle Willie was there, being kinder than usual. He didn't much like Ivy. I never knew why, perhaps because she was an actress, or from a less elevated background. Maggie O'Brien, my father's personal secretary, and Miss Oates attended the service with thirty members of his staff.

Afterwards we all returned to the Orchard where I assumed the role of host, doing everything I thought my father would have wanted me to, including showing the mourners the darkroom he had helped me organize.

My mother never forgave herself, although she was no more at fault than my father. As for myself, I had lost someone I loved dearly, who was just beginning to become my best friend. For a long while, I could not believe he was dead. In the evenings, especially, I would listen for the sound of his motorcycle coming into the drive.

· 2 ·

Blackmail

*M*y mother took Derek and me to Margate—in its heyday an exclusive seaside resort—where we stayed a couple of weeks in a Victorian hotel overlooking the English channel. I remember sitting at a window seat, thinking about what the priest had said at my father's funeral. "Look across the water," he instructed, "and watch a boat as it becomes smaller and smaller heading over the horizon. Just as the boat is still there even though you no longer see it, so is your father still part of you, always."

Once we had returned from Margate reality hit sharply. Without leadership, Elwin Neame, Ltd., started to slide. Uncle Willie, who had been looking after my father's finances, gave us the bad news. Apparently Senny had not believed in life insurance, never for a moment considering he would die at thirty-six. If this wasn't bad enough, we had gone further into debt suing the people who had illegally placed their car in my father's path the night he was killed. We had lost the case, and, therefore, had to pay all legal expenses.

Another lethal blow—our beloved Annie died of cancer. Only towards the end did we realize she had been ill and knowing her, I would not be surprised if she had been aware of her terminal condition for a long time without breathing a word about it to a family already in distress.

Ivy attempted to revive her career, but the once sought-after Ivy Close was no longer a star. She did, however, enjoy some success on the stage, touring in a variety of leading parts including the musical *Going Up*, which played at the Shaftesbury Theatre in London's West End. We were forced to sell the Orchard, a truly unhappy home, and my mother found a flat over a shop in Golders Green. It was merely a place to live without warmth or character, but it was close to familiar landmarks and having our same friends near helped us feel more at home.

Another advantage was that it was right across from the Ionic Cinema. Even though I was the man of our family, I couldn't help sometimes being a little boy. And so, on Saturdays, my friends and I would pay four pence to sit in the first four rows to watch a twenty-minute silent serial, *The Man in the Iron Mask*, always ending in a life-threatening predicament—followed by the title card "To be continued." In the next week's installment the same boulder, plane, or train that had been inches away from killing our hero, suddenly veers off in another direction. And in the final episode after weeks of suspense, the masked man was unmasked—and turned out to be a woman!

Since my mother's stage career forced her and Derek to travel, she felt that a boarding school would provide me with a more stable life. According to Uncle Willie, there was just enough money left for me to attend. I was sent to a British public school at age thirteen. Public schools in England are the equivalent of private schools in America.

Life for a new boy at Hurstpierpoint College in Hassocks, Sussex, wasn't easy. There was a good deal of bullying, and school monitors were permitted to punish young offenders in their own way. This was usually six hefty kicks up the backside. I was terribly homesick and on more than one occasion I silently cried myself to sleep.

Most students knew my mother was famous and during my first week, a kid named Gorman made an insulting remark about her, "Ivy Close wears no clothes." Egged on by other boys, I challenged him to a fight behind the gym. I had never hit anyone in my life and I suspect Gorman hadn't either. If it hadn't been for the forty or so boys watching, we might have called it off. Once the fight started, I realized he wasn't protecting himself, and I bashed his nose, which bled profusely. Someone "threw in the towel." We shook hands and from then on, became best of friends with an added advantage—after the fight, I was no longer a "new squit." The second term went much better—I'd earned my colors and was even allowed to do a little bullying of my own.

I had a reasonably good treble voice, thus I joined the choir, considered one of the best in southern England. Although we appeared saintly as we made our way up the aisle in our cassocks and surplices, the choir was not what it seemed. Most members, including myself, had joined for reasons far removed from religion; we were allowed to miss class work and were given a one day extra holiday each term.

At Christmas, the choir enjoyed The Boars Head Stodge, leading the entire school along the cloisters to the dining room, carrying aloft a large wooden platter with the roasted head of a boar. My favorite was Ascension

Day when all the students climbed to the top of the South Downs for a choral service and every choir member was given an extra five shillings.

Sometimes we broke the rules and ventured into the local sweet shop in the village. One boy would stand outside, making certain no prefects or masters would spot us. We would hide these candies in a "tuck box," under lock and key. At my previous school our headmaster's name was Bernard Lake and we referred to his children as " the puddles." The headmaster at Hurstpierpoint was a Mr. Towers and thus we called his children "the turrets." How witty we thought ourselves!

My claim to fame came in the winter of my third and last term—I played the lead in the school production of *Romeo and Juliet*. Believe it or not, I was cast as Juliet—the hardest bit was walking in high-heeled shoes.

My Uncle Willie told me at the end of the third term I would have to leave college and go to work. There was no longer enough money. It was a big setback but had to be faced. He found me a job as an office boy with the Anglo-Persian Oil Company where I worked for an unmemorable six months. Then miraculously my mother managed to get me an appointment with Joe Grossman, the studio manager of British International Pictures.

We had moved from Golders Green and were now living in a flat in Notting Hill Gate with my maternal grandmother. By this time, we began to know the anxiety of near poverty. *The Daily Mirror* learned of our circumstances and ran the headline, "Ivy Close, The Famous World Beauty Is Destitute." It was humiliating for my family to receive a check for a hundred pounds from a lady well-known for her charitable works—I became more resolved than ever to make my own way.

The next morning I set out from Notting Hill Gate for Elstree, an hour by bus and train. Once at the studio, Grossman kept me waiting for two hours and I began to wonder if he had decided not to see me, maybe I wasn't destined for a film career after all. But when I ultimately met Joe, I was completely won over by his Cockney accent and friendly manner, and to his eternal credit, he offered me a handsome fifty shillings a week, a substantial improvement on what I had been receiving at Anglo-Persian. He told me to report the following Monday.

My impressions remain as vivid as if they were happening today:

It is a typical English winter day in 1927 and heavy rain is falling on the corrugated roof of Elstree studios. It is noisy, but this is of no consequence because the four features being made in the shed are silent. The structure is large, divided down the middle lengthwise by a thin, non-soundproof wall. I am sixteen and this is my first working day in a movie studio. I am a messenger boy, a tea boy, a callboy, a you–name–it boy.

I am assigned to a thriller called *Toni*, starring theater matinée idol Jack Buchanan, located at the far end of the studio on the right-hand side of the dividing wall. There are two other films being shot on this side of the wall. The one in the middle is *A Little Bit of Fluff*, (released in the US as *Skirts*), starring Betty Balfour, a well-known comedienne. Charlie Chaplin's brother Syd is directing. Much later, I regret to say, Syd will be asked to leave England for becoming, to put it mildly, involved with an underage girl! The production closest to the entrance is *The First Born*, starring Madeleine Carroll.

On the other side of the dividing wall is a fourth production, a very important film because it occupies the whole length of the left side of the studio and only those who are part of the unit are allowed to enter.

As I walk from the camera room to my set I pass by each production. Madeleine Carroll's film has a small four-piece orchestra playing mood music. The musicians on the Betty Balfour movie are playing something more lighthearted. Silent films used music to set a mood for the actors and help them get into character.

Each set is flanked by banks of mercury vapor lights, long tubes that give off a weird green luminosity to the whole area. These banks, I soon find out, supply a basic soft, all over light, to which are added arc lights, creating a source light, giving shape to both actors and set.

Being a keen amateur photographer, it is the camera that draws my attention. In between fetching cups of tea I watch it being reloaded. I see it is turned by hand. The assistant cameraman, Gordon Dines, tells me it shoots sixteen pictures per second and that each second is two turns of the handle.

I am probably overeager, because someone on the crew sends me to fetch the "sky hook." It seems Elstree has only one of these much sought after, complicated pieces of equipment, and we, on the *Toni* set, are scheduled to use it this afternoon.

Gordon tells me it's in the property room, but the property master says, "Dines should know better. The 'sky hook' is kept in the metal shop."

The metal shop people tell me *The First Born* unit used it yesterday, "It's probably still there."

I am unable to get close to the Madeleine Carroll set because the lovely actress is filming a bath scene. The set is very much closed, but a young assistant emerges from the protected area telling me, "The 'sky hook' is on *The Farmer's Wife* set. They were using it this morning." *The Farmer's Wife* is the film being shot on the other side of the dividing wall, forbidden territory. But I have been told to get the "sky hook," and this I am determined to do.

Somewhat timidly I slip through the door winding my way through a number of farmyard sets towards a lighted area at the far end. Then I discover why this production is so special. The director, busy rehearsing his actors, is the rather plump twenty-seven-year-old Alfred Hitchcock.

It only takes a few moments for me to realize this is a man in complete control. For several minutes I forget the "sky hook" as I watch this great director at work. Then I come sharply down to earth and approach Jack Cox, Hitchcock's cameraman.

This kind man lets me down gently. "What's your name?" he asks.

"Ronnie Neame," I reply.

"And this is your first day here?"

I nod.

"Well Ronnie, you've been given a sort of initiation. You see, there's no such thing as a 'sky hook.' They've been pulling your leg. Why don't you go back to your set and tell them it was sold last week because nobody was using it!"

This fictitious hook turned out to be a blessing in disguise. Because of it, I was able to watch Hitchcock at work, and I met Jack Cox, someone I would work with again.

It was a pleasurable day but it was also disappointing because I learned there really wasn't a job for me, at least not on the camera. *Toni* had been shooting for three weeks, and they had a full crew.

Ivy Close: After Senny died, Joe Grossman asked how my boys were doing. I told him Ronnie had to leave school, and he responded, "Send him along to me." He phoned after meeting Ronnie, "You know, I don't really have a job for him. It's up to him to make one." And Ronnie did.

Utterly determined to make a niche for myself, I started by cleaning the equipment and I practiced turning the camera at the correct speed. One afternoon, *Toni* used two cameras, and for a few wonderful hours, I became an assistant cameraman.

As part of my job, I was asked to carry a large still camera to the set. My father had taught me how to handle tripods. As I confidently lifted the tripod to my shoulder, the lens slipped and crashed to the floor!

"Looks as though you're out before you're in, Mate." Gordon Dines, assistant cameraman, said. On inspection, however, the lens was intact and so was my job.

Remembering back decades later, I find it extraordinary to think how modest my ambitions were compared to young aspirants of today. My great hope was to be a top assistant cameraman.

Nowadays, when an inexperienced person comes to me seeking advice about how to get into films, he or she invariably starts off by saying, "I'm going to be a director." But not everyone is suited to this craft and it is arrogant to think it can automatically happen.

I'm glad I went through the business from the bottom. I wouldn't have missed those early days for anything!

As the weeks passed, I became more involved, carrying magazine boxes and running errands. When the American director, Scott Sidney died while working on a comedy at Elstree, I was assigned to photograph his funeral with George Pocknall, a cameraman in his late thirties who had known my mother in the early days. This footage was destined for Hollywood to be used in a newsreel. We arrived at the crematorium and filmed without incident, and then hoping to sell footage to Gaumont-British News, we positioned ourselves to shoot the second funeral that afternoon as well for the famous, well-loved Dame Ellen Terry. What we hadn't counted on was the massive crowd of mourners who suddenly appeared, shoving their way in, knocking over our tripod. Looking more like Laurel and Hardy than filmmakers, George and I fell over ourselves, trying to salvage our equipment and ultimately considered ourselves lucky to escape alive.

I worked on several pictures with Pocknall. The only one worthy of mention starred Monty Banks, the Italian comic, well-known in silent films, (later he was to marry music hall star Gracie Fields). *Adam's Apple* was directed by Tim Whelan.

Whelan and Banks were great friends and complemented each other. Tim was soft-spoken and charming while Monty was volatile and more crass. Between takes they would roll dice on the floor, money changing hands as the unit gathered around to laugh and root for one or the other. If a game became heated, we simply delayed shooting. Imagine that happening today!

The still man on *Adam's Apple* was Michael Powell, who subsequently went on to produce and direct such landmark films as *The Red Shoes* and *The Life and Death of Colonel Blimp.*

Girls were beginning to become an important part of my life. It was a thrill when the stunningly beautiful Gillian Dean, *Adam's Apple's* leading lady, joined the camera department for lunch in the canteen. She had obviously noticed me noticing her and asked if I would like to take a walk with her on the studio backlot. She kissed me and, even more wonderfully, asked me to dinner at her flat in Maida Vale. When I arrived, a brunette, who was helping Gillian prepare dinner, greeted me at the door. Two glasses of wine at age sixteen goes straight to the head. The ladies, who had also been drinking, began giggling. They made a provocative suggestion that would involve all three of us. Young and lacking experience, I made my apologies and left.

My mother had just celebrated her thirty-fifth birthday. Beneath her outward self-confidence, there lay a certain kind of self-doubt caused by her fear of growing older and losing her beauty and fame to time. She had never adjusted to life without my father and she missed the adoration she had received in her twenties. She was a free spirit, trapped indelibly within the intangible limits of her nineteenth-century upbringing and she now had the added responsibility of having to support herself and Derek. Some women age gracefully. This was not the case with Ivy and I became aware of a bitterness that was to grow more pronounced in her later years.

Towards winter, she and my brother left for the south of France. A wealthy gentleman, Mr. Madlina, asked them to join him for a three-month holiday at the Negresco Hotel in Nice where he maintained a permanent suite. I never understood this relationship because the man seemed more interested in Derek, who was only twelve, than in Ivy. My mother saw this tall, dark, Italian benefactor as a gentleman and would have been too naive to comprehend any ulterior implications. It has remained a disturbing episode for me, which, as a family, we never discussed, but somehow I feel it set my brother on a lifelong path of unhappiness and self-destruction and I have always wished I had been old enough to have been more protective.

After ten months at Elstree, I replaced Jack Cox's assistant cameraman, who had left for another assignment. The film I was about to start had already been shooting a few weeks and was the most important production at the studio, *Blackmail*, directed by Alfred Hitchcock. It was a wonderful opportunity for me.

Blackmail was, of course, a silent film. Just a few weeks before completion, however, we began to hear rumors that John Maxwell, head of British International Pictures (BIP), was considering the addition of sound. Talkies had recently arrived in Britain from Hollywood and Maxwell wanted to be the first to make one in England. In preparation, a large property room and a plaster shed were hastily converted into sound stages. The original writers, Charles Bennett, who had written the stage play, and Benn Levy, were brought in to write dialogue to replace titles used in the silent version.

Hitch must have had more than a hint of what was about to happen. Instead of completely dismantling the sets as we finished shooting on them, he had them "pack struck." So they could be quickly reassembled.

Most of the footage already shot on *Blackmail* could be transferred to the new version. We had fortunately used motorized cameras, which ran at twenty-four pictures a second, the essential speed required for talkies.

Once we began shooting on the primitive sound stages, we had dozens of seemingly unsolvable problems. Jack and I, with our noisy camera, were installed in a sealed soundproof booth with a large glass window for the camera to shoot through. When it was necessary for the camera to track, two men had to push the booth backwards and forwards on rails. They also had to pivot the booth if we had to pan more than three feet to avoid filming the frame of the window.

The only good thing about this claustrophobic box was it was big enough to install a hot plate and a table to make tea and it became a type of club—the camera people had one, the sound people had another. Their booth was larger because it didn't need to pan or track.

The members of this new sound department thought they were the most important people on the set, and perhaps they were; after all this was the first "talkie." But the difficulty was, that unless the microphone, an enormous contraption, was practically touching the top of the actor's head, the sound was unusable. Also, the hum from our arc lights drove them into a frenzy. In an attempt to be helpful, we switched to incandescent lamps, not really powerful enough for the slow film stock.

The mike and its cumbersome boom cast heavy shadows on the walls of the set, wreaking havoc with Jack Cox's lighting. Several times a day, both crews would emerge from their padded booths with friction in the air—it would go something like this:

> Soundman: "We can't put the mike any higher. We cannot record sound unless the mike is close to the actors."
> Cameraman (Jack Cox): "I've already ruined my lighting for you. You've got to compromise too."
> Soundman: "We're getting a hum from somewhere."
> Cameraman: "Well, there are no arcs, so it's not coming from the lights."
> Soundman (irritated): "But nonetheless there is a hum."

After an extensive, time-consuming search, they found the hum was caused by a sound cable on the floor crossing a light cable. Another time it was caused by our booth panning. On more than one occasion there was an impasse and we would retreat into our respective booths uttering expletives.

Hitch took all this in his stride. Rather than create another level of anxiety, he resolved it. Technical problems brought out his gift as an innovator. I don't think anything ever ruffled him, not even the heat on the set. Dressed in his invariable black suit, white shirt, and dark tie, he never seemed to perspire. The rest of us, also in suits and ties, were dripping, especially when sealed in our booths.

Adding to these technical problems was our leading lady, Anny Ondra. She was not British and she spoke with a heavy Czechoslovakian accent, which didn't matter for the silent version. To overcome this problem Hitch devised the first form of "dubbing." British actress Joan Barry was engaged to be Anny's voice. They rehearsed the dialogue together to get in synch. When it came time to shoot, Joan stood just outside frame, with a separate microphone, and as she spoke the lines, Anny mouthed them.

One day Hitch handed me his 16 mm camera and asked me to film some behind-the-scenes footage. I shot a version of the murder the audience doesn't see. In the film the Artist, Cyril Ritchard, drags Alice (Anny Ondra), through drapes into an alcove the viewer assumes is a sleeping area. The curtains move indicating a violent struggle. Alice's hand comes out from between the curtains, grasping for a knife on a table. A few moments later, the Artist's hand flops down from between the drapes; he has been fatally stabbed. Alice comes through the drapery into the picture, the bloody knife in her hand.

I filmed what really happened on the other side of the curtains. A prop man ruffled them to give the impression of a struggle. At the right moment Alice stepped forward to reach for the knife and bring it behind the curtains. A second property man smeared "blood" on it. The Artist dropped his hand through the curtains to simulate his death.

The next scene takes place the following morning at breakfast with the family seated at the table. A neighbor is discussing the murder, saying, "What a terrible way to kill a man, with a knife in his back. If I had killed him, I might have struck him over the head with a brick, but I wouldn't use a knife." The talk goes on becoming a confusion of noises which the girl no longer hears—except for the word "knife," . . . "knife," . . . "knife." This was typical of Hitchcock's skill. He used sound on this first British talkie with more imagination than his peers would do for years to come.

There is a scene where Alice walks around London all night after she has murdered the Artist. For this, Hitch asked second cameraman, Freddie Young, to shoot a long shot of Trafalgar Square. I was asked to go with him. Since he didn't want to see any signs of life, except for pigeons, Hitch told us to be in the Square at dawn on the following Sunday when the Square would be empty.

We figured we'd get the shot within a few minutes of setting up but each time we started, something or someone would cross the Square, a milk wagon, a pedestrian, a taxi. An hour later, three minutes before the sun came up, just as we were about to admit defeat, we struck lucky.

Freddie later became one of the greatest and most respected lighting cameraman in the world, winning three Oscars for cinematography (*Ryan's Daughter*, *Dr. Zhivago*, and *Lawrence of Arabia*) and other honors, including being awarded an OBE.

On one of many good days associated with *Blackmail*, the Duke and Duchess of York visited the set—the Duke became King George VI, after his brother Edward abdicated and the Duchess became our Queen Mother. Hitch and the Duchess went into the sound booth, while the Duke joined Jack Cox and me in the camera booth. I saw Hitch ask the Duchess to take off her hat in order to wear earphones as she and the Duke waved at each other.

Without a doubt, Hitch was a cinematic genius. But he had a penchant for practical jokes that were more cruel than funny. The brunt of his humor on *Blackmail* was Harry, the prop man. Hitch used part of the set, a gas bracket with a live flame, to heat up a coin with a pair of pliers. After the coin was hot he dropped it to the floor and asked Harry to pick it up.

His practical jokes went beyond the crew. He invited Sir Gerald du Maurier, one of England's most important actors, to a dinner party at the Café Royal in Regent Street, along with 200 other guests. Sir Gerald was told that the evening was a fancy dress party, meaning he should wear a costume. The poor man arrived in Shakespearean garb. To his great embarrassment, and Hitch's sheer delight, everyone else was in formal evening attire.

There was another surprise courtesy of Hitch that same evening. During dessert, the restaurant door opened and in walked a naked girl who crossed the room and sat down on Sir Gerald's lap.

I have little memory of my home life during this period—probably because like everyone else on production I didn't spend much time there. Hitch preferred to work late, never finishing before eleven P.M., and more often than not, we were still working at midnight. At about eight P.M. when the unit broke for supper, Hitch, a gourmet, and his actors, and sometimes Jack Cox, would go to a rather special pub, the Plough, about three miles from the studio, where they ate an excellent meal. The rest of us were allowed to charge the company one shilling and sixpence for a sandwich and a glass of beer.

If we worked after the last train, we were taken home by car, but this was not a direct route. As best he could, the driver figured out how to deliver home three or four people who lived in opposite directions. Even if I arrived at my flat at one or two A.M., I was always back on set next morning by eight.

It was these long hours that eventually brought about a meeting one Saturday in 1928. About a dozen of us on the unit met at a pub in Elstree, to discuss the formation of the Association of Cine Technicians. For many years, technicians felt studio management had treated them unfairly. However, it took two or three years for the ACT to become a reality.

Much later, at the height of the union's power, it took its revenge against the bosses along with other unions across the country. The pendulum swung too far and before long it became impossible to get an efficient day's work. The unions' grip remained firm until the 1980s when Thatcher's government put an end to so-called restrictive practices.

· 3 ·

Beryl

$\mathcal{T}$he studio had now become my life. Along with Gordon Dines, Phil Grindrod, and Bryan Langley, I became a permanently employed assistant cameraman. Bill Haggett, head of the camera department, would allocate us to various productions and knowing that Hitch was fond of me, I had every reason to hope I'd be on his next film.

But everything changed when Uncle Willie asked to see me. With my father's secretary, Maggie O'Brien, he had taken over the running of Elwin Neame Ltd. And now he wanted to make a last attempt to get my father's business back on its feet. As I had learned how to take photographs, the plan was for me to take over from an elderly Mr. Joyce, who was retiring.

Senny had been an artist with a great talent and drive, but no head for financial matters, whereas his brother was a more conventional, solid businessman—for years, he had been a manager at the National Provincial Bank. On the portly side and a bit pompous, he had always been cold towards my mother, yet to me had shown affection. I thought a lot about his offer. It was a tough decision because I loved my job at Elstree, but it seemed right to help my father's business and the six pounds a week my uncle offered was a fortune!

I explained the situation to Bill Haggett who was extremely understanding, and after weighing the pros and cons, told me it sounded like a great opportunity. We shook hands, and optimistically I walked away from one world into another.

The Bond Street Studio was located above the Embassy Club, one of the smartest venues in London and where several Elwin Neame photographs were on display in the foyer. Uncle Willie greeted me and gave me the tour of the premises: a spacious daylight studio, dressing rooms, fully equipped darkrooms, and a beautifully furnished reception area, complete with a pretty brunette receptionist, Beryl Yolanda Heanly (pronounced Henley), who became a lifesaver, protective of both the Neame image and me.

Beryl scheduled the appointments for "Mr. Neame," showed potential clients their photographic options and explained the price: five guineas for six half plates or ten guineas for a half dozen whole plates; they were also offered the small, carte de visite, for three guineas. When clients arrived, she introduced me.

"We expected to be photographed by *the* Mr. Neame."

"This is *the* Mr. Neame," Beryl said, with as much dignity as possible.

Reluctantly the clients accepted me.

The camera, a cumbersome affair, had a cap on the lens that acted like a shutter, so initially I would try to relax the sitter and when I felt they were ready, I would take off the cap and start counting, "One,"—the slow speed of film emulsion required a long exposure, "Two . . . "—their stiff smile held, and "Three . . . "—and I'd put the cap back on the lens hoping they hadn't moved.

Then an alternative pose—shoulder turned, a lock of hair pushed back, a cape adjusted "just so." In all I took six different setups exactly as my father had done.

Dreams of photographing beautiful girls like those I'd seen on the underground quickly faded. Round, middle-aged men and women with extra chins, crows' feet, and paunches made up the bulk of our clientele.

I used the same lighting techniques as my father had, the lovely north light that is so flattering for portraits. But daylight is capricious, changing hourly so after six months I suggested to Uncle Willie that in order to bring our company into the future we should modernize the operation by using controllable incandescent lights. I'm sorry to say it turned out to be an unfortunate move, not because it didn't make sense, but because I wasn't experienced enough to use the lights correctly.

The business went from bad to worse when Kodak brought out a simple camera with which anyone could take pictures, perhaps not with the claimed Neame quality, but at a fraction of the Neame cost.

There were a few bright days. Beryl and I gave a party for our friends. Everyone brought a bottle and something to eat; someone brought a record player. This was the first time I began to think of her as more than a working companion. We danced together to Noël Coward's memorable song:

> I'll see you again
> Whenever spring breaks through again
> Time may lie heavy between
> But what has been is past forgetting.

This song became our signature tune. One day, a short man in a long over-coat with his bowler hat held respectfully at his side, arrived and announced he was the bailiff assigned by the bankruptcy court to protect the interests of creditors—just in case we tried to take anything away. He was an odd fellow with a precisely aligned, but very bad wig, who turned out to be a benevolent presence. During the fourteen days of his residence, he kept out of the way allowing us to attend to our few remaining clients.

Finally, on a drizzly Monday morning, removal men arrived and took my father's treasured photos, dressing tables, couches, chairs, reception desk—everything except the camera and some lights! It seems creditors have to leave behind the "tools of the trade." But what good was a giant camera by itself in an empty studio?

Beryl and I wrote a brief message that we pinned to the studio door: "Closed until further notice."

My career as a West End photographer had apparently ended. I began to deeply regret having left Elstree and the comradeship of the many people I had worked with. I was about to try to get my old job back when a man named Joshua Harris stepped forward—he was the accountant who had handled the closing down of Elwin Neame Ltd.

Astonishingly he suggested, "Why not go into partnership together, Ronnie, and open our own studio?"

I had the name, he had the two hundred pounds we needed. With Beryl's help, we took our equipment, bought a little furniture, and opened Ronald Neame, Ltd., Portrait Photography, a studio in Beauchamp Place, just a couple of blocks from Harrods. We were able to pay the rent with a few pounds a week left over. But after a few months, this new enterprise encountered the same fate as Elwin Neame, Ltd.

Leslie Olive—one day to become an important executive of Technicolour, England—had a relative, Mrs. Frewer who was about to open a color photographic studio in Ealing. Badly in need of a partner, she offered me a job—representing my last attempt as an independent photographer.

As there was no position open for Beryl, she accepted a job in Northhampton with Jeromes, a chain of studios with branches throughout the country. This meant we could only see each other on weekends. Even so, she was a great support to me, representing sanity and offering me the warmth that had been sadly missing from my life.

Her father, a retired Army colonel, had spent a good deal of his life in Burma, serving as private secretary to the Governor of Rangoon. Her mother had been left to raise seven children—hers, his, and theirs. Quite a handful, made worse by lack of funds. I was extremely fond of Mrs. Heanly who made a wonderful sloshy trifle, laced with sherry, and more to the point, she took my side if Beryl and I had a disagreement.

My family still kept the flat in Notting Hill Gate, but my mother was away most of the time, touring with one play or another. When my grandmother became ill and died of cancer, we decided to give up the flat and without that financial burden, my mother was able to save enough from her actor's pay to send Derek, now fourteen, to Hurstpierpoint.

My brother's early life had been vastly different from mine. Whereas I had a chance to know my father, and enjoy many of the luxuries money had offered, Derek was dragged along from one town to another with Ivy. Yet somehow, without any real formal background, he had become the better educated of us.

He was moody though, even from a very young age. One terrible day while we were still living at the Finchley house, he had climbed onto the roof, and threatened to jump into a rainwater tub, shouting at the top of his voice, "You'll be sorry when I'm dead."

I was glad to move from Notting Hill into my own place because I wanted to find a way to be with Beryl. For twenty-five shillings a week, I rented a furnished bedsitter in a big house on Mattock Lane, Ealing, and bought myself a Dutch oven, which could be hooked onto the gas heating element in the fireplace. The asbestos bars on the oven heated to red-hot, enabling me to roast lamb chops or sausages for supper.

Beryl, as the daughter of a conventional Victorian father, was expected at her parents' home on Claygate Road at the weekends. What he didn't know was that she would occasionally take an early Friday evening train from Northampton to Ealing where I would collect her. She would come to my room for the night and we would prepare a meal together. Later, I would gallantly give her my bed, while I tossed and turned on the sofa. It wasn't a comfortable arrangement, but it was the 1920s and morality was stricter than it is today.

Neame & Frewer would have succeeded had it not been for the exorbitant cost of color laboratory work. The highlight of this final venture came at the request of the Richmond Ice Rink proprietors, who wanted some pictures of one of their young instructors for display—a gorgeous, seventeen-year-old who was destined to become a figure skater, an Olympic gold medallist and later, an international film star, Sonja Henie.

Almost three years had slipped by since I'd left Elstree. They had been wasted years, except for Beryl.

I telephoned Bill Haggett at Elstree to ask what the chances were of getting back in.

After several seconds that seemed an eternity, he said. "You're in luck, Claude Friese-Greene needs an assistant. I can give you a job, but I can't pay you six pounds a week. The best I can do is four pound ten (shillings)."

Needless to say, I accepted!

The journey from Ealing to Elstree took ninety minutes; the Underground to Acton, a bus to West Hampstead, a train to Borehamwood and a ten-minute walk to the studio. Any misgivings I might have had during the lengthy journey immediately evaporated. I had made the right decision! The hustle and bustle of a busy film studio, the smell of a sound stage. This is where I wanted to be. "Why on earth," I thought, "did I ever leave?"

In my absence, my contemporaries in the camera department were now all in positions senior to me. I was welcomed back into the group with handshakes and slaps on the back. At age nineteen, I was home again, and I was going to be assistant to the son of the famous William Friese-Greene.

William Friese-Greene—along with Edison in America and the Lumière brothers in France—share credit for the invention of the motion picture camera. We, in Britain, claim Friese-Greene came first. Years later, I was to produce a film called *The Magic Box* for The Festival of Britain with Robert Donat, one of our finest actors, playing William Friese-Greene.

"Friese," everyone's nickname for Claude, was a short, balding, and rather plump gentleman of about forty. I was very fond of him. When he laughed, which was often, his stomach bounced. But unfortunately, like his father, he became a heavy drinker, which would soon get out of control and nearly destroy him.

Working as only an assistant cameraman, I did not pay much attention to the stories of the films, but I did understand the importance of the camera and the camera lenses. Let us suppose we are taking a shot of an actor walking towards camera from a full figure into a large close-up. If we put on a 100 mm or long focus lens, the actor would have to start his walk fifteen paces from the camera. He would take many seconds to come into close shot. This creates suspense. If, on the other hand, we put on a 25 mm or short focus lens, the actor would be in large close-up after only three paces, thus creating surprise.

I also learned more about setups and tracking shots, how to keep the camera on the move without allowing it to become self-conscious. We did our best to conceal the mechanics of a shot in order not to take attention away from the actor and his performance. Today, perhaps with the influence of commercials and pop videos, the camera overplays its role, too much frenetic movement, too many quick cuts. The story is lost in overly clever camera work.

McGlusky, the Sea Rover is about Arab gunrunning, taking place in and around Tripoli (a French protectorate). It was one of many films I would work on with Friese and it was my first trip to an overseas location. We traveled by train through France and part of Italy to Genoa, where we embarked on a slow Italian manned boat across the Mediterranean, making several stops before finally reaching Tripoli four days later. The intense heat mixed with the smell of garlic was so strong, it seemed to have seeped into the woodwork.

As well as film equipment, we had 200 rifles, which we intended to dole out to Arab extras for the shoot-out scenes. The Tripoli customs officials took one look at these lethal weapons and promptly confiscated them, saying in *patois*, "What in Allah's name do you think you are doing bringing in guns?"

"We are making a film," explained the production manager.

They obviously thought we were completely insane, "Nobody gives guns to Arabs. They will disappear into the desert, never to be seen again." To emphasize their concern, they confiscated the offending weaponry as well as our cameras.

The unit, about thirty of us, checked into a hotel, cabled our predicament to the studio, then settled in with nothing to do but wait for further instructions. Each passing day became so boring that I have forgotten most everything that happened—other than an episode involving Skeets Kelly's regularity.

The most junior member of the unit, Skeets was our clapper boy and film loader. He was somewhat gawky and shy, about sixteen, and this was his first trip outside England. Where most people on location would suffer from "gyppy" tummy, Skeets encountered the opposite problem.

The news of his plight spread though the unit. Skeets' movements—or lack thereof—became the main topic of conversation. Before long, the friendly hotel landlady heard about it and went to talk to the pasty-faced worried lad. On her return she told us there was only one thing for it—"he must have an enema."

Skeets was nervous and uncertain about undergoing this procedure, but with each passing day, his condition worsened and so finally he agreed.

At six o'clock that evening, Friese, with a large scotch firmly in hand—for himself, not Skeets—followed by a half a dozen supporters from the camera and sound department—ascended the stairs to Skeets' room. The landlady walked in carrying the necessary equipment on a tray.

The operation was a mighty success. Not five minutes after it was performed, Skeets beat all records to the "loo." The next day he was as bright as a button leaving the rest of us to resume our boredom.

Skeets gained more confidence through the years and grew up to become one of the world's leading aerial photographers, filming from bombers, fighters, and helicopters, anything that flew. Sadly, he was killed in the early seventies when he was shooting from a helicopter, which was accidentally rammed by an adjacent aircraft. We all miss him.

Without local cooperation the film never went into production and eventually the authorities agreed to return our cameras, but not the guns, on condition that we leave Tripoli immediately.

In 1932, I sailed aboard the *SS Corona*, a P&O liner with Friese and the unit to Port Said and then onto Cairo where we chartered a paddle-wheeled steamer to take us up the Nile. We filmed *Fires of Fate* in Egypt for eight weeks, and this time, since the British Empire owned the country, the production was completed without incident.

On these early films I learned that traveling is integral to filmmaking. Location work allows us to see the world in a special light, getting to know locals in ways not possible for tourists. And the knowledge one picks up through these encounters can only add to the film's reality.

Back in England, I was again teamed with Friese on the comedy *For the Love of Mike*, with Bobby Howes, a well-known comedian, and father to Sally-Ann Howes. Halfway through, Beryl and I decided to get married. We thought that rather than going to a Registry Office, we would have a religious ceremony at St. Stephen's Church, a hundred yards from where I was now living on Westbourne Park Road. We couldn't afford to ask a lot of people to a wedding breakfast, so we decided it was best to ask no one, not even our parents. There were just the two of us, the clergyman and a witness. The wedding took place, Saturday, October 15, 1932, at 9:30 A.M. I was twenty-one, Beryl a few years older.

Beryl Neame: The minister wanted to know if we would like the church bells to ring. "How much would that cost?" I asked. "Ten shillings," he replied. "We don't need bells," I told him. We were saving money in those days, and I had already bought a new dress and shoes and goodness knows what. After we were married and were leaving the church, a bell started ringing! Ronnie said, "They've given us the bells for nothing." "Don't be silly," I said, "it's the church clock striking ten!"

We left by train to spend our honeymoon in Brighton. Although we couldn't afford it, we stayed at the best hotel, the Grand, in a sunny room overlooking the sea. On Saturday evening, after dinner, we danced the foxtrot, the one-step, the old-fashioned waltz, and, of course, the Charleston. On the Sunday morning, we walked along the pier and had our fortunes told. "You will never want for money," the turbaned Indian gentleman predicted. Considering our financial situation, it sounded far-fetched.

By Monday I was back at Elstree and Beryl had I settled into our flat, which consisted of one bedroom with a combined bathroom and kitchen—when it was not being used as a bath, we could cover the tub and use the area as a worktop. And we had a gas geyser, an intimidating device, which went off with a loud bang on ignition. The rent for the place was one pound, ten shillings a week.

Beryl became pregnant, which was slightly worrying since only a few months earlier she had been diagnosed with a thyroid deficiency and the medication she was given to correct this condition caused her to become weak and much too thin. When she was into her sixth month, she had to be admitted to a public ward in St. Mary's Hospital, Paddington. She was frail and for some reason had a dangerously high pulse.

Every evening after I left the studio, I would go straight to the hospital, arriving at around nine P.M. Afterwards, I went home, made bangers and mash, and flopped into bed, getting to work the next morning at eight A.M.

The doctors eventually found out that Beryl didn't have a lack of thyroid, but rather an excess. Therefore, the medication she received could have killed her. Labor was induced at the beginning of the eighth month—but the baby boy was stillborn.

When I had first heard I might become a father, I thought we were too poor, I was too young, the responsibility would be too great. We should have waited longer before we got married. But the loss of my little son was very sad for me, and for Beryl it was heartbreaking.

The Elstree Fire

$\mathscr{I}$'d always regretted that my formal education had been curtailed so early on, but now there were compensations—most of my friends were just finishing their university studies and wondering what they would do with their lives. Meanwhile I'd already established a career for myself in the film industry and had gained considerable experience.

I continued working with Claude Friese-Greene for two more years, receiving a weekly salary from Elstree, whether in production or not. If there was no set to report to we played cards—usually "nap" (a form of whist). We all complained when we weren't on a picture, but while we were in the middle of a game, we complained even more if we were interrupted with some insignificant studio errand.

Often an extended lunch would be taken at a restaurant known as the Manx Cat, about a half a mile from the studio. It was here I first met E. M. Smedley-Aston "Smed," a young, second assistant director, who would later become a producer. In fact, many years down the line, he and I would work on a film together.

Smed used to drive to lunch in his small, sporty MG. One day, as a practical joke, we switched the wires from one sparking plug to another so nothing connected. He repeatedly cranked the handle to try and start his car, but the more he tried, the more frustrated he became, until finally in a rage he tossed the starting handle over a hedge and into a field, spending the next half hour trying to find the rotten thing.

We considered Smed too naïve to have a girlfriend so a group of us started the "1932 Smedley-Aston Fuck Fund." But as the saying goes, "Watch out for the quiet ones." Smed in his own inimitable, upper-crust style had already discreetly found himself a girlfriend, whom he later married without assistance or interference from his chums.

My next film with Friese, *Mr. Bill the Conqueror,* was shot on location in Sussex—not the William of 1066, but the story of a young farmer played by popular actor, Henry Kendall. Neighboring farmers are determined to run Bill out of business but he is equally determined to stand his ground.

Considered to be a large unit, there were thirty of us staying at a six-teenth-century hotel that was said to be haunted. On several occasions, in the middle of the night I did actually hear ghostly footsteps creaking along the corridor. It turned out to be Friese, slipping stealthily along to continuity girl Connie Newton's bedroom—a relationship that continued many years.

Unusual for those days, I had a bedroom *with* bathroom, an amenity af-forded me in order to convert the latter into a darkroom, which was easily accomplished by sealing up the windows and the door. I put plywood across the bath to make a bench and here I could unload the day's work into film tins to be sent back to the lab at Elstree.

After filming one evening, as I took a roll of film out of the magazine, the center core fell out and fifty or sixty feet spiraled into the bath, which, unfortunately had a half-inch of water in it. Tearing off the wet bit, I man-aged to save the rest. Although certain at least one shot was spoiled, I re-strained myself from telling Friese. What could I have said? I didn't want to lose my job. Luckily no one ever mentioned anything and I can only assume the damaged negative was not on the list of takes to be printed.

On completion Beryl and I managed a brief motoring holiday in my 1925, four pounds and fifteen shillings, unreliable, two-seater Peugeot, fondly named "The Peanut."

When we returned I was assigned to *Happy,* a comedy starring music hall star Stanley Lupino (Ida's father) and several other talented performers, including young ingénue Dorothy Hyson with Gus McNaughton playing her lecherous father. His lines were difficult to deliver with straight-faced professionalism, "I've been looking for you nowhere and couldn't find you all over the place."

The film, directed by Fred Zelnik, gave me my first screen credit, al-though it was shared on a rather crowded card with Friese, second camera-man, Bryan Langley, as well as the screenwriters, the editor, the supervising art director, and the sound recordist. Nonetheless, it was a career landmark.

Part of my education as a cameraman included learning how to make each shot visually interesting. To this end, Bryan Langley and I would place what we christened "jingleberries" in the foreground of the picture—a lamp, a bowl of flowers, anything to enhance the composition. For exteriors we hung branches of leaves or berries that would dance in the wind to dis-tract from a bald sky. Through Friese, I met Arthur Woods, a talented young director, who was to become paramount to me as a friend and to my career. He was a keen observer and an energetic daredevil, always looking to get away from the crowd. Our first film together was a musical, *Radio Parade.*

At the weekends, Arthur, who owned a small aircraft, a rarity in 1933, would take me flying, and do I mean *flying!* We would position ourselves high above the enormous reservoirs between Shepperton Studios and Staines (now the busy approach to Heathrow) and indulge in stunts.

We would dive at the water below, pulling up at the very last moment. Then loop-the-loop—bringing my stomach to my mouth. We became a falling leaf, the plane twisting and turning as it fell to earth. Unquestionably we were quite mad!

Arthur was signed to direct BIP's most important film of 1934, *Drake of England*, with Friese as cinematographer, and me, as usual, as his assistant. The story portrays Sir Francis Drake, the British Vice-Admiral, who insisted on finishing his game of bowls before engaging the Spanish Armada. Matheson Lang, a Scottish-Canadian matinée idol, was cast as Drake, but his fifty-five years and overly generous girth flew somewhat in the face of the slim, historical figure he was portraying.

Friese was drinking more heavily. As soon as he arrived on the set in the morning, he asked the property man to bring his "medicine," either whiskey or gin. It was difficult to tell which because he kept his hand firmly round the glass. He never gave the impression of being drunk, although he always wore dark glasses to hide his bleary eyes. It was amazing to me how he managed to judge the lighting in tinted glass. Then after lunch he would drop off to sleep in his chair and that was when I had to take over, virtually becoming the lighting cameraman and generally keeping things going until he awakened.

While he was sleeping, the rest of us would finish the shot and then move onto another setup, leaving him behind. Someone cruelly placed a cardboard sign at the side of his chair that read "A Penny for the Blind." When he awoke, he would become angry with me for taking over, but I had no other choice.

The situation changed dramatically one afternoon when he collapsed and had to be rushed to hospital—*Drake of England* was without a cameraman!

"You know you can do it," Arthur Woods was the first to suggest it.

"I don't think I've got the experience," I said.

"Nonsense! You've been doing it for the last three weeks haven't you?"

"I suppose so, but Friese was there."

"Was he?"

This conversation took place during the lunch break when Arthur and I were sitting with the new studio boss, P. C. Stapleton, who settled the matter. "I want you to take over from Friese," he stated emphatically. "There are eight weeks of shooting left. I won't give you a raise in salary, but we'll give you a bonus at the end of production. What do you say?"

"Thank you, sir."

With tremendous support from Arthur and a great deal of help from Ernie, the chief electrician, I got through to the end with reasonable success and learned at lot more about lighting along the way.

As promised, Stapleton gave me the bonus, forty pounds, or five pounds a week more than I'd been earning up until then. So by twenty-four I'd become the youngest director of photography in England and the cheapest!

But my career was launched!

I quickly learned how to photograph beautiful women on *Invitation to the Waltz*, a ballet film directed by Paul Merzbach. Wendy Toye, who subsequently made her own directorial debut in 1952 with the wonderful *The Stranger Left No Card*, was the leading dancer, as well as choreographer.

Lillian Harvey starred. She would arrive at the studio dressed in white accented by an enormous diamond ring on her finger, escorted out of her white limousine by her chauffeur also dressed in white. She was gorgeous and naturally it was my job to make her look good. The secret is the correct placing of the all-important key-light, and the careful use of diffusion. Good advice to a cameraman in those days was "hitch your wagon to a star" and I suppose it still applies today.

I made several more pictures at Elstree as a fully-fledged director of photography. Some that linked with my childhood days at Golders Green—my talented former neighbor Jack Davies had written the screenplays. This current association reinforced our long-term friendship and I would also eventually make a film with Jack's as yet unborn son, John.

Beryl and I had always lived in or around London, but now that I had achieved my dream of earning ten pounds a week and was hopefully on my way up, we agreed it was time to realize our ambition and move to the country. So to begin with we rented a little house in Radlett, a village only four miles from Elstree. Number 20 Rosewalk had three bedrooms and a pretty garden—paradise! At the first real home I had lived in since my father's death, we'd be woken in the morning by birdsong and in the evening there was the stability of Beryl waiting to greet me.

I sold "The Peanut" for five shillings profit and bought a brand new eight horsepower Ford for a hundred pounds, plus an extra ten for a sunshine roof—beginning a lifelong affinity for top-of-the-line cars.

One night, long after we'd gone to bed, the phone rang. It was my next-door neighbor, Hector Coward, the manager of British and Dominion Studios, which ran alongside BIP. He sounded distraught.

"Look out of the window," he said.

The night sky was lit by a great red glow.

"What is it?" I asked.

"It's the studios . . . not yours, mine! My bloody car won't start. You've got to get me there, fast!"

I pulled on some clothes and we both jumped into my new car, reaching Elstree in record time. The flames were already bursting through office windows and one of the stages and part of the roof were well on their way to collapsing.

Joe Grossman, the studio manager who had given me my first job and was by this time a little larger round the middle, was in charge of the studio fire brigade. He and some of his men had run out six hoses and were valiantly fighting the inferno, but alas, there was little water pressure—certainly not enough to reach the flames. Talk about a piss in the ocean! Joe was frantic, shouting orders left, right, and center, to no avail.

My God! I thought. We ought to be filming this. At that moment I ran into Jack Cardiff, a young colleague cameraman, and now internationally famed cinematographer of *The Red Shoes*, and *The African Queen*. Together we broke into the camera room of BIP and in no time had the equipment set up in front of the burning building. But the camera was newly designed and I didn't know how to load it.

"Jack! For heaven's sake, lace up this wretched thing!" I shouted over the commotion. I was scared stiff the fire might go out before we could start filming. Joe's hoses still weren't functioning, but the real fire brigade had arrived. Jack looked at me in dismay.

"I can't!"

"Oh, my God, what can we do?"

Then we noticed a young lad standing nearby. He was the clapper boy on my current production.

"Hey, Bob! Can you load this camera?"

"Of course," he said, rather cockily.

In a couple of minutes we were shooting away like crazy. I operated, Jack pulled focus, and Bob lugged the equipment. We got some of the best fire footage I have ever seen—in black-and-white, of course.

That night, February 10th, 1936, the studios of British and Dominion were completely destroyed and never rebuilt, but British International survived.

The next day we became temporary heroes. *The Daily Express* sent a photographer down to Elstree to get pictures of the charred remains. After watching the footage we had shot, the reporter stated, it was "a masterpiece of realism."

Jack Cardiff: It was like a mad dream because there were girders and things falling down and flames everywhere. We gasped and ran back. The firemen ordered us out because they thought the film would explode. By that time, the other stage had caught fire and was blazing. Ronnie somehow appeared and in the midst of the excitement, we went all over the place photographing the blaze. It was my first bit of publicity in a very peculiar way because the next morning, it was quite loudly proclaimed in the newspapers, "Terrible Fire Destroys Film Studio," and the story said something like, "Mr. Ronald Neame and his tripod carrier, Jack Cardiff, got shots of the fire." I thought, *tripod carrier*! As if I were his slave. But I realized any publicity is better than no publicity. That was my first mention in a paper.

• 5 •

Quota Quickies

$\mathcal{I}$n the 1930s, as today, British cinemas were dominated by American product. The small budget British producer could not compete with the large-scale epics coming from Hollywood. By 1936, the situation had reached a point of crisis. No one was watching British films. Stages were empty, studios were closing down. Finally, out of work film technicians organized a large-scale lobbying effort in front of the House of Commons, which belatedly brought about much needed help from the government.

An Act of Parliament made it mandatory that by the end of the 1930s twenty percent of all films shown on British screens had to be made by British companies and employing British talent.

Naturally we were delighted. Even if our films were on a smaller scale than those from Hollywood, with an assured market, we would be able to spend more and improve quality. We might even be able to re-equip our studios with up-to-date cameras and modern lighting.

At first we ignored the screams of fiscal pain heard from across the Atlantic. Studios in America were not pleased with these new requirements. The films that began to be made under this system started to become known by the derogatory term of "quota quickies."

We underestimated the determination and the ingenuity of our American cousins who busily went about searching for loopholes in British law. In no time, major US film producers formed their own subsidiary British film companies. International marriages of convenience were performed in lawyers' offices. Suddenly there was Fox-British operating out of studios in Wembley; Warner-British at Teddington; and Paramount-British based at the brand-new Pinewood Studios in Fulmer, Buckinghamshire.

The plan was simple; the gentleman in charge of Fox-Wembley would hire a British producer and pay him six thousand pounds for a six thousand foot movie—in other words, one pound per foot of finished film. The producer would then, within a seven-day schedule, make a film as economically as possible and put the balance of the cash in his pocket. Some of these fly-by-night characters would make as many as ten pictures a year and get comparatively wealthy on the proceeds. Needless to say, most of the pictures were horrendous, but who cared—neither the American executives, nor the British cinema owners in which these "masterpieces" were screened.

London's West End theaters would open at eight A.M. to admit the cleaners and while they were tarting up the place for the day's filmgoers, the projectionist would show the British product, running it twice. The film would then be put on a shelf at the back of the projection room until the following morning leaving the day free for the more popular product from Hollywood.

Quota quickies were bad films, and, therefore, bad for our industry, but the immediate effect was a godsend to British craftsmen. Plasterers, carpenters, electricians, camera assistants, soon found themselves with more job offers than they could handle and more money than they'd ever made before.

While Edward VIII was abdicating so he could marry Wallis Simpson, I was leaving Elstree, for the second time, to accept a job with Fox-British at Wembley. They were shooting two pictures simultaneously and needed a cameraman for each. One was Roy Kellino, the other was me. Roy and I became friends at once and through him I met his wife, Pamela Ostrer, a beautiful, dark-haired British starlet, later married to James Mason.

Under Edward Black's leadership, Gaumont-British, a company based in Shepherd's Bush, was trying to build a roster of British stars, similar to the American studio system. Gaumont didn't make quickies. Determined to be more up-market they put a number of young people under contract and some important names emerged; Pamela, Phyllis Calvert, Margaret Lockwood, and Patricia Roc.

There were not many alternatives available for a young filmmaker in England during this time. One couldn't wait around for a good film because very few were being made. Therefore I got caught up in a whirlwind of production, not minding too much about the content of the film. I wanted to get more lighting experience behind me and save money, and towards this end, it seemed time to find an agent. I approached Christopher Mann, the doyen of British agents, who immediately managed to get Wembley to pay me twenty-five pounds a week.

Chris was a genius, but somewhat difficult. He was quite brilliant about the law and financial matters, but he was very much a recluse, perhaps because he had a speech impediment. It was rare to see him in person.

His assistant, Anne Hutton, went on to become an artist's manager and another lifelong friend.

Quantity not quality counted with quickies. There was a permanent street set on the lot behind Wembley Studios, which was used on practically every film. One sequence I shot called for a man to come out of a house, cross the road, and go into a phone booth. The next day, after he had seen the rushes, the producer stormed onto the set in a great rage asking me why I hadn't put the phone booth at the far end of the street. He yelled, "You idiot, it would have taken the actor ten more seconds to walk there. That's fifteen feet and that's an extra fifteen pounds to me." He did have a point!

On another film, *Against the Tide*, director Alex Bryce was promised a bonus of three hundred pounds if he came in on schedule. At the end of two days he was half a day behind—at the end of four days, he'd lost over a day. He eventually solved the problem by simply cutting ten pages of script and tossing them into the waste bin. We finished a day ahead of schedule and only after he had left town, with his check, did the producers discover their film was considerably shorter than had been contracted.

Maurice Elvey, who had directed my mother in *Nelson* nineteen years before, came to Wembley in 1937 and I had the pleasure of working with him on *Who Goes Next?* starring Jack Hawkins. It was a better than average quickie, because it followed a successful formula: People in jeopardy, overcoming impossible odds to save themselves from disaster—in this case, World War I prisoners digging an escape tunnel. Tension is created when characters are trapped in any enclosed space, an aircraft about to crash, a submarine on the bottom of the sea or an ocean liner turning over—the latter theme I would get involved with much later on with *The Poseidon Adventure*.

Having the opportunity to work on so many films, I developed my own style of lighting, which was to use one single source. It was copying nature; after all there is only one sun.

Ossie Morris: Ronnie experimented a lot trying to get just one light to cover four people as against the usual two. This he did by introducing a spill ring into the beam to even the spread. He continued with that system until we were able to get Mole Richardson lights from America. I copied him when I started out as a cameraman.

Some while after my father's death, my mother started going out with a few men. In 1938 she met extremely friendly Curley Batson, a slim, athletic, Australian who did stunts for the movies. I was glad she had found someone, it had been fifteen years since Senny's accident. She was forty-seven when she and Curley were married, and shortly afterwards, they decided to move to America, arriving first in Toronto. Curley had always loved Buicks, so they bought an old one, drove it across Canada, and then down to Los Angeles. Although he had a great deal of trouble getting a work permit, Curley, now too old to do stunts, eventually became an American citizen and joined the film makeup artist's union.

Because of the fullness of my life and where we lived, I was unable to see very much of Derek. After leaving public school he had rented a small flat in London and went into the camera department of Gaumont-British, subsequently switching to the script department. He certainly had the brains and talent for that kind of work. A few months later, in 1938 he wrote a screenplay for a quickie produced by Anthony Havelock-Allan and then left to go to Cassis, in the South of France. He joined up with a group of young literati including playwright Christopher Isherwood and his companion W. H. Auden. My brother had struggled for years with his homosexuality and in this liberal community, he felt more at home.

To celebrate my increased income, I bought yet another new car, a maroon convertible MG. I certainly enjoyed what money could buy, but remembering my father's negligence, I took out life insurance.

Beryl and I went on a proper honeymoon, taking a two-week break in Monte Carlo where we ate in elegant restaurants and gambled at the casino. We figured out a mathematical formula that I couldn't remember today if my life depended on it, but somehow by playing only on red or black, we won sufficient francs to cover the cost of our holiday.

We had lunch with Derek during this trip, walking with him through Le Jardin Exotique, in Monaco. He seemed to have little ambition to work, preferring to sit in cafés, drinking with friends. Somehow he maintained himself, perhaps from royalties he received from writing poems. I sent him money, but he rarely cashed my checks. I was ambitious, like my father, also practical, like Uncle Willie, but Derek didn't seem to concern himself about where he was going or how he would get there. He worried me and always left me wondering how different his life might have been if I had been more able to help him when he was younger.

When we returned from France, I went straight back to work. Every now and then there was a lull in production at Wembley and the company would loan me out to another studio for forty pounds more a week than I was earning. Mr. Garfield, head of Wembley, was generous and split the profit with me.

For the next two years, my existence becomes a blur: Wembley four weeks, Shepperton three, and a few days at Pinewood. I filmed about ten quickies a year. It really was all work, but for me work was play.

At Pinewood I met a future partner, Anthony Havelock-Allan. He asked me to shoot *The Scarab Murder Case*, to be directed by Michael Hankinson, and to star Wilfrid Hyde-White.

Tony's good friend at that time was the chief executive running Pinewood, the Honorable Richard Norton, who had recently inherited the title Lord Grantley. Tony and Richard went into the gents on their way to the stage where I was shooting. On the wall in bold letters was scrawled, "Richard Norton is a Bastard." According to Tony, the newly titled studio head took a pencil from his pocket, carefully scratched out "Richard Norton" and in equally bold letters wrote "Lord Grantley."

Pinewood was and is my favorite studio. Situated on the grounds is a beautiful period mansion, Heatherden Hall with its carefully manicured gardens and lake, all of which we used in many films. Initially the house was converted into a residential country club for producers and actors as well as other wealthy outside members. It had an indoor swimming pool, a squash court, and a generous bar and wine cellar.

I had enjoyed my brief experience there and would have loved to stay, but quickies were being phased out. Wembley loaned me more often to Ealing. As was the case with Gaumont-British, Ealing had always made pictures of high standard, spending more on their productions than other studios. Soon I began working there exclusively arriving shortly after Michael Balcon took over from Basil Dean for his twenty-year tenure.

Balcon, believing wholeheartedly in British films and talent, was prompted to use an end title on all his productions—superimposed proudly over a fluttering Union Jack was the patriotic statement "A British Picture." Some thought this was slightly over the top!

Throughout the next three years I photographed more than twenty films for the studio, including six George Formby comedies.

Tremendously popular at the box office, Formby was an unattractive guy with a crazy smile and big teeth. But he always got the girl in the end. That's what people enjoyed seeing. He was what in farming terms would be called a "yokel," and the girls were sophisticated young women. It wouldn't have been funny if he had a relationship with a shop assistant who wasn't attractive. The stories were always the same more or less, with the expectation of laughter. This type of comedy is something of the past. George will never happen again!

We almost froze to death making *I See Ice* as George gets on the ice rink, plays hockey, and trips over everyone. We shot through the night at the Richmond Rink (where my photographs of Sonja Henie had been displayed) after it was closed to the public. Wearing woollies, overcoats, and thick boots and drinking copious amounts of tea fortified with rum, we accomplished the sequence in three nights before, mercifully, moving to the warmer ground of the studio.

Jack Kitchin, an American executive, who also happened to be one of the best editors in the business, complained that "Kay Walsh didn't look so good in yesterday's rushes" and asked whether I was lighting her in a different way. I assured him I wasn't. We eventually found out from someone in the cast that she'd been seen out late each night at the Dorchester with a young editor by the name of David Lean.

The Air Ministry decided to use comedy as a recruitment vehicle, agreeing to feature the RAF in *It's in the Air*. George becomes a reluctant test pilot, flying loops, and then starts to free-fall, performing every conceivable aeronautical stunt imaginable. It ends with him landing the aircraft upside down through a hangar, achieved by combining live action with rear projection. The film was a major commercial success when it was released in 1939 and was reissued twice.

Formby's wife Beryl was very jealous, particularly of his leading ladies. On *Trouble Brewing*, she stayed on the set all day watching him like a hawk. Googie Withers and George had to play a dialogue scene in an enormous vat of beer. The beer was supposed to come up to their shoulders but the vat wasn't deep enough, so George sat on a chair and Googie sat on his lap. George kept giggling and remarking in his North Country accent that he was "'avin' a loovely time." Each time Googie laughed, Beryl became so angry she nearly jumped into the vat.

Googie Withers: We couldn't use beer in that scene, so they used pyrene, the frothy stuff used to put out fires. George and I very nearly choked to death on it. Because we were in water, my skirt had ridden up and I was sitting with my knickers on his lap and he had his hand on my bare thigh. No one could see this, of course, because of the stuff. We had a big kiss at the end of the scene and then Mrs. Formby screamed, "Cut! Cut!" The poor man really didn't have any fun at all.

When Mrs. Formby was stricken with appendicitis and whisked off to hospital, I have never seen George look so happy. For a whole week he was a changed man, laughing and joking with everyone.

Let George Do It and *Girls Will Be Boys* were directed by the admirable Marcel Varnel. Every Formby film has a scene where the story stops to allow him to serenade a lady with his ukulele. In the latter film, Phyllis Calvert plays a spy, and she sits entranced while George sings four songs, amongst them "Count Your Blessings and Smile."

Phyllis Calvert: When Googie knew I was going to work with George, she called me and said, "He'll be in your dressing room telling you how much he loves you." Well, he didn't come near me. I thought, "Thank goodness." It was Christmas time and just before we finished shooting, Beryl left the set to do some shopping. I was in my dressing room, waiting to be called. There was a knock at the door and in comes Mr. Formby, saying, "Baby, I'm crazy about you."

In Radlett, Beryl really seemed to be thriving in the country. I had never seen her healthier and although she and I didn't have enough time to spend together, she had lots of friends, including film critic Maude Miller.

At parties, while many of us gossiped about one actor or another, some of my film chums thought her on the quiet side. That's because she would never enter into any form of gossip—if there was nothing nice to say about a person, she found it easier to remain silent.

Grateful beyond belief when she became pregnant again, we started preparing one of our bedrooms, buying toys and baby clothes. She was in her seventh month when I received a call at the studio from a neighbor saying she had been taken to hospital in St. Albans. We lost our second child, this time a little daughter. Resigned never to having a family, we tried to carry on as cheerfully as possible—Beryl had a tremendous strength whereas I simply went on making one film after another.

I made three films with the quietly self-assured, director, Robert Stevenson. *The Ware Case* featured a cast that turned into a sort of stock company used on many subsequent films: Jane Baxter, Barry K. Barnes, Clive Brook, Athene Seyler, Francis L. Sullivan, John Laurie, and Peter Bull. Also there was charming and eccentric Ernest Thesiger who between setups knitted woolen scarves for the rest of us.

A Young Man's Fancy starred Stevenson's wife, Anna Lee, playing a circus performer who is shot out of a cannon. Insisting upon doing her own stunt, she was stuffed down the cannon feet first and shot out by a catapult causing her to leap into her leading man's lap.

Also starring Anna Lee, *Return to Yesterday* was shot on location in Torquay, Devon. In between takes, I jokingly asked Stevenson if he would mind if I took his wife out to dinner?

"Yes, I would!" he said emphatically.

Anna, who was within earshot, was amused at both my question and his answer. That night, when I went to my hotel room, there in the bed was a large bolster dressed in her costume. On set the next day, she told me she had put it together with the wardrobe lady and although it wasn't as good as a dinner with her, I was, nonetheless, paid a compliment.

Making Anna look good on camera was easy, she has the perfect oval face. She and I have remained best friends and close neighbors for decades. For over twenty-two years she has appeared on the daily soap opera, *General Hospital* in the role she made famous—Mrs. Quartermaine, a wealthy, powerful matriarch.

Anna Lee: I fell in love with Ronnie when I was twenty-six never knowing how he felt about me. He had a wonderful laugh and a wonderful voice. He used a little light on me called an "inky dink." I never looked better.

At a time when American cameramen were considered superior to us British, Michael Balcon gave me all the films I could manage. I made four of them with director Walter Forde and his wife Culley, including *The Four Just Men*. My salary was now a steady forty pounds a week and I began to believe the fortune-teller Beryl and I had visited on our honeymoon—but the future was not to be plain sailing.

· 6 ·

Major Barbara

$\mathcal{D}$uring the summer months of 1939, we in Britain began to realize that something pretty horrendous was about to happen. Hitler was no longer a funny little man with a Charlie Chaplin moustache, but a maniac about to lead Germany and Austria into a catastrophe that would nearly destroy Europe and Russia not to mention the rest of the world. Chamberlain's attempts at appeasement were met with Hitler's hostile takeover of Czechoslovakia, and on September 1st, the invasion of Poland.

Although it was clear war was inevitable, Beryl and I took a short respite in North Wales at Portmeirion, a seaside resort overlooking an estuary. But upon hearing the declaration was to come at any moment, we immediately started to head for home.

Nearing London we passed streams of cars coming in the opposite direction. Thousands of people had decided to leave the city for what they presumed would be the safer north. Back in Radlett, we found government issued gas masks left on our doorstep. The Germans used poison gas at the end of World War I and it was generally assumed this war would commence with the Nazis dropping huge quantities over large areas of Great Britain.

The following morning, at exactly eleven o'clock, Chamberlain made his memorable announcement on the wireless:

> I am speaking to you from the Cabinet Room at 10 Downing Street. This morning the British Ambassador in Berlin handed the German Government a final note stating that unless we heard from them by eleven o'clock that they were prepared at once to withdraw their troops from Poland, a state of war would exist between us. I have to tell you now that no such undertaking has been received and that consequently this country is at war with Germany.

Within minutes air raid sirens warned us Armageddon was imminent. We waited! Nothing! We waited more! At noon, we phoned our neighbors in the twelve houses on Rosewalk, suggesting they bring a bottle and celebrate our survival. We ate and drank heartily. Several hours later, thoughts of destruction seemed less frightening. In reality, it was months before the Germans made up for lost time.

The day after war was declared, Derek made his way to the West Coast of France and secured passage on the last ship to leave for England—Christopher Isherwood and W. H. Auden had already left for America. When he arrived at our house, he was in utter panic, "Hitler is going to invade us and we are defenseless." He had always been convinced Germany wanted to take over Britain and now he feared it would happen in a matter of weeks. We tried to persuade him to join his friends in America or perhaps stay with Ivy and Curley, but he would have none of it. He seemed afraid of going there. Instead, he moved into a flat, just off Oxford Street only a few steps from the White Tower Restaurant where I'd meet him for lunch as often as possible.

Our country had to find a way of protecting herself. Normality disappeared as we slowly pulled ourselves together. Air Raid Wardens patrolled through towns and villages to insure blackout rules were enforced. Signposts were removed throughout England, sometimes replaced with misleading ones. Maps were carefully guarded or destroyed. We were reminded that "Walls have ears" and "Careless talk costs lives."

Apart from the conscription of young men into the armed forces, there was the formation of the Home Guard, mostly elderly veterans from World War I, who took back their ranks, and formed companies and platoons. There weren't many rifles so they marched with walking sticks or broomsticks, proudly reliving their old days as comrades-in-arms, knowing only too well they were no match for the Nazis.

Concrete gun posts were installed at either end of most small towns and villages, but there were no guns to put in them. The piers at all seaside towns had a fifty-foot section removed from the center to stop an invading force from coming ashore. Iron railings protecting parks and gardens began to disappear, as factories demanded more metal for armament manufacture.

Men under thirty, such as myself, believed that within weeks we would be in uniform. My friend Ossie Morris was one of the first to be called up. I was prepared to serve my country, but wondered if I would be any better at soldiering than my father. While my colleagues and I waited with uncertainty, the Ministry of Information concluded that films were good propaganda, and those of us working at the studios were advised to remain in our present jobs until we received further instructions.

In early 1940, I was assigned to Ealing's first war picture, *Convoy*, the story of a cruiser designated to escort a convoy of merchant ships across the North Sea that is ambushed by a German battleship.

Kodak had recently released a new fast film stock called Type 2. Always interested in the latest innovations, I tried it. Tests should have been done first, but I trusted what the Kodak boys had told me. Using my usual lighting system, I ran into trouble getting far too contrasty results. The film, though fast, suffered from severe emptiness in the shadow areas. Neither Denham Film Labs nor I had properly learned how to cope with it. It was difficult to accept after filming more than two dozen films, that I could run into this kind of problem. I tried putting extra light into the shadows to no avail. There was dark mahogany furniture on the set and this furniture appeared on the screen to be black. I sprayed gray paint into the dark areas to lighten them and pumped in more light. The light in the shadow area became almost as bright as on the highlight side, quite wrong. Then came panic! I was so distressed I couldn't think straight. Each day the rushes got worse and my confidence disintegrated.

Finally, I went to Balcon with my predicament asking him for a leave of absence explaining I was possibly overanxious and tired. Already aware of the problem, he was sympathetic and granted my request. Gunther Krampf and Roy Kellino were assigned to take my place and they returned to the old film stock. Thus everything, except me, was back to normal. In hindsight, I should have employed the same obvious remedy, but by this stage I was on the point of breakdown.

With my career and future in question, it seemed fortuitous that my three-year contract with agent Christopher Mann was coming to an end. I called him, explaining I would not be renewing our association.

"Quite honestly," I said, "I don't think a cameraman needs an agent." He hadn't been influential in finding jobs for me, but to be fair, he was responsible for obtaining a higher weekly salary. I was paying him ten percent as called for by the contract. We said goodbye amicably on the phone, and that, I thought, was that!

Knowing how on edge I was, Beryl suggested a temporary solution. We joined the Radlett Golf Club—exercise, fresh air, no other responsibility but to hit the ball. Although the sport helped me tremendously it was short-lived—I just wasn't good at it. I like to think because golf balls were in short supply, thus my main concern centered on not losing one. I tended to look up to see where it was going before completing a stroke, resulting in a slice or a hook.

Since I was not working on a picture there was a high probability of being called up. Deciding to face the inevitable, I was on the verge of enlisting when I received a call from P. C. "Sammy" Samuels, production manager for Gabriel Pascal, asking me to come to Denham Studios and photo-graph makeup tests of Wendy Hiller. She was set to star in Pascal's big budget production of George Bernard Shaw's *Major Barbara*.

Three years earlier, Gaby had visited Shaw at his home in Ayot St. Lawrence. Without a penny in his pocket, through sheer force of personal-ity, he had persuaded Shaw to give him the rights to his plays.

Pascal hadn't lost any time in taking advantage of Shaw's generosity and had already successfully produced *Pygmalion* with Leslie Howard and Wendy Hiller.

I'd first worked with this infamous character at Shepperton making quota quickies. Born in Hungary in 1894, he had come to England in the early thirties. A maverick producer-director, he was a swashbuckling pirate prepared to scuttle anyone who got in his way. While others were spending five thousand, the quickies Gaby made cost fifteen. I photographed one he directed called *Reasonable Doubt* and I remember him coming out of rushes effusively declaring, "Ronald Neame is a genius!" Unfortunately, he would be less supportive in the near future!

Major Barbara wasn't exactly a war picture, but its theme included ar-mament, and equally importantly, it was considered to have the potential of being a much needed dollar earner for Britain.

Pascal was away in Cornwall the day I arrived at Denham, thus an up-and-coming filmmaker, David Lean, whose name I had heard connected with Kay Walsh, was left to supervise. Evidently he and Gaby were having some sort of disagreement, not an uncommon occurrence, and as a result Gaby had requested that David leave Cornwall for a few days and direct Wendy's makeup tests back at the studio.

Bearing in mind my recent experience, I was slightly apprehensive. But I went back to the old film stock, and, thank goodness, the tests were excel-lent. In fact, David told me how pleased he was with the results.

Sammy called again.

David was assigned to shoot a montage of a steel factory in Sheffield and had asked if I would photograph it.

From the first moment we worked together we found a rapport. While I had started out at Elstree, David had been a junior in the wardrobe de-partment at Gaumont-British. He lost his first job over a pair of trousers, ac-cidentally giving an actor the wrong ones. The director, Walter Forde, was so upset he had David fired. Someone took pity on him and moved him into the newsreel department. From there he went to the cutting rooms and by 1940 was acknowledged as one of the best editors in the country.

Photographing molten steel in Sheffield was a challenge; the white-hot liquid flared the lens, and the background would go black. Once again I had to throw extra light in to compensate for the steel's brightness. I solved the problem by using enormous arc lights known as "brutes."

While we were there, word reached us that the principal cameraman, Freddie Young—my colleague from *Blackmail*—wasn't too happy with Gaby and had arranged to be called away to another picture. Having no other ally, David was suddenly back in favor and with a strong recommendation from him and Freddie, I was asked to become the director of photography on *Major Barbara*.

Even though there was no written contract between Ealing and me, I owed it to Michael Balcon to ask his permission to move on. He was extremely gracious, as he had been when I'd asked for a leave of absence, "It's a good opportunity for you, Ronnie, take it." But when he heard Gaby was giving me eighty pounds a week, he phoned complaining that paying technicians such high wages would ruin the British film industry!

Major Barbara had a distinguished cast. In addition to Wendy in the title role, there was Rex Harrison, eighteen-year-old Deborah Kerr, Robert Newton, Robert Morley, Donald Calthrop, and eminent stage actors Emlyn Williams and Sybil Thorndike.

Set Designer John Bryan, who had trained under Vincent Korda (Alexander's brother), was also experiencing his first big production. Originally Gaby had wanted Vincent, but by the time he'd gotten his finances together, Vincent had moved on to other things.

Working with John, it became clear to me that this was a remarkably talented man. He fully understood that his sets had to follow the needs of the script, but also they had to help the cameraman achieve good pictorial composition. When you talked about a layout with him, he would take a sixteen by twelve drawing pad and, with a few deft strokes in charcoal, give you exactly what you had in mind. It was from the instant John began his sketches that a film started coming to life.

Quickly he and his wife, Janie, became Beryl and my closest friends. We were cast from the same mold, equally unsophisticated, yet curious enough to want to learn more.

David, John, and I became inseparable.

David was dedicated to film more strongly than anyone I've ever known—a perfectionist who believed if he had to shoot something twenty times before he got it right, so be it. Years later, he was a bit shirty with me because I said, "If necessary, David will hold up shooting for hours until he's satisfied the cloud formation in the background is in the right place." I simply meant that he wouldn't settle for very good, it had to be great.

A handsome man, he was destined to break hearts more than once. His strict Quaker roots left him in conflict between his sense of morality and his more bohemian spirit, thus he never quite escaped the repressive demon inside him. Women and film were his ways of breaking loose from an austere and demanding upbringing. When he fell in love he felt he must marry and when he was married he felt restricted. Therein lay his unhappiness.

My former agent, Christopher Mann, called out of the blue and asked why he wasn't receiving commission on my salary. I reminded him of the phone conversation we'd had canceling our agreement. He then reminded me of a clause in the contract stating that unless I gave him three months' notice in writing, it would remain valid for another three years!

He was using a technicality unfairly. He knew perfectly well we had severed our relationship. I told him so, adding that I'd no intention of giving him a commission on a film he had neither found nor negotiated. Within twenty-four hours, I received a letter from Bulcraig & Davis, the law firm representing him, demanding payment immediately.

I explained my problem to Sammy, who advised me not to take this situation lying down—I put myself in the hands of the lawyer he recommended.

During the shooting of *Major Barbara*, the war got underway in earnest; the Germans had invaded Norway and Denmark, subdued Holland, Belgium and Luxembourg, and occupied France. The British Army, rescued by the evacuation from Dunkirk, got home almost intact, but lost all its equipment. When Hitler occupied the Channel ports, Ostend, Boulogne, and Calais, and had the nerve to invade and capture the Channel Islands, we believed it was only a matter of weeks before our island would also be overcome.

Endlessly the planes came across the Channel, dropping a few bombs on the south coast, then flying to London, their primary target—we were at the end of their run. After returning to their base, sometimes they would fly past London to wreak havoc further north.

The Blitz went on every night. Just as it was getting dark the take-cover sirens would start up and continue until midnight, an irregular wail followed almost at once by gunfire and soon afterwards the screaming whine of bombs.

Driving the forty minutes to Denham in the mornings, I was frequently confronted with the previous night's devastation; streets blocked with rubble; people digging in debris, searching for what few possessions they could retrieve; stretchers carting away the wounded and the dead.

We tried to finish work early before it all started up again, but this was not always possible. After packing up and discussing the next day's agenda, it was often already dark, and seldom did I travel back to Radlett without the accompanying sound of distant and sometimes nearby explosions. Once there I would remove the rotor from my car's distributor to prevent the enemy from stealing it!

As did our neighbors, Beryl and I took precautions against the bombings by building a small reinforced concrete air raid shelter in our back garden where we would go after dinner to sleep. It had four bunks and was supposed to protect us from all but a direct hit. But when we heard some friends of ours had been killed by a direct hit on their shelter, ours turned into a shed for garden tools.

Harold French, our codirector, had rented a small flat near the studio to avoid the long drive back to London. He and his wife used to chat with each other on the telephone at the end of the day. One evening he called, no answer. He tried continuously through the next day. That evening he drove to London to find his wife dead in a pile of rubble that had once been their home.

Filming became even more precarious when Germany started sending an aircraft over every hour, on the hour, and each time it would set off the sirens and force us to go to the shelters. We called them "nuisance raids." It was a clever idea, the aim being to disrupt industry. But Gaby Pascal wasn't about to let Adolf Hitler get in the way of *Major Barbara*. The cast and crew didn't run to shelters every time we heard a warning. Instead the studio placed "spotters" on the roof, protected by sandbags, watching for the enemy. Even if it was cloudy, they could identify their planes by the quite different engine sound they made to British aircraft. In order to confuse our radar system, the Germans flew with their propellers out of synch, "mmm-wah-mmm-wah-mmm."

A large fire bell was fixed to a wall of the stage, which, if one of them came too close, would be rung by the "spotters," and then we'd drop everything and run for cover. It all seemed ingenious, but there was an immediate outcry from the Electrical Trade Union, many of whom worked above the set on spot rails. "It's all very well for you lot," they said, "but how are we supposed to get down in time?" The difficulty was overcome by giving each man his own personal escape rope.

For three weeks we carried on without interruption and, even though the "nuisance raids" continued, the bell wasn't rung once. We had just moved to an enormous set on Denham's largest stage—the courtyard and buildings of the Undershaft Armament Factory—when it suddenly broke its silence. Everybody started running and in the panic the camera was left running. The next day in rushes we saw it all over again.

A medium shot with Rex Harrison about to take Wendy Hiller in his arms as one or two extras cross the courtyard in the background. Suddenly "Clang! Clang! Clang!" Everyone freezes. . . . The set is full of running figures. . . . Rex looks around. . . . Wendy looks around. . . . Ropes drop into picture from above. . . . Electricians of all shapes and sizes slide down and run to safety. . . . Rex is off like a streak of lightning. . . . Wendy is left standing all by herself wondering what on earth has happened. . . .

She hadn't been on call the day the warning system had been arranged and nobody had told her about it. And there it was for all to see. Rex hadn't given a moment's thought to his leading lady's safety. We teased him for weeks, "Women and children first Rex."

Not every actress has the perfect oval face. Wendy's, although attractive, needed careful attention when it came to lighting—for each person there is a particular direction the light should come from to be the most flattering. In her case, one placed slightly above and off-center—which threw the side of her face closest to camera into soft shadow—was the way to go. To make the most of this, I invented a little lamp which I could hold and move in any direction, always keeping it in the right place. Because it was used specifically for Wendy Hiller, it became known as the "Wendy Light."

Even in the quota quickie days it had been apparent that Gaby could not direct. He had taste, he loved film, but he had no idea where to position a camera, or anything else. His real strength was being clever enough to sur-round himself with two talented codirectors, Harold French and David. Harold, a theater director, was in charge of working with the actors while David was responsible for advising Gaby how to design sequences.

The raids, along with more ordinary problems, caused us to fall behind schedule. Who was to blame? With a candor that might have cost him his job, Harold said the main reason was down to Pascal's inability to make up his mind; shooting far too many takes and generally interfering with everything.

Gaby needed a scapegoat, so he reported to C. M. Woolf, the distribu-tor who had put up part of the finance, that "Ronald Neame is a young man, very good but very slow."

I knew I wasn't slow having photographed God knows how many quickies. Sammy told David I might be removed from the picture. In re-sponse, he, and the entire unit, threatened to walk off if that happened. While David and Harold confronted Gaby, Sammy insisted I go and see Woolf to defend myself in person.

He heard my point of view and fortunately grasped the situation. I was reinstated, secure with his backing and the warm support of the unit.

A further delay occurred when Gaby fell out with Robert Morley. Feeling Morley's character should smoke Churchill cigars, and being a great smoker himself, Gaby supplied the Monte Cristos. Robert, a nonsmoker, was required to select one from a humidor, savor, clip, and light it. Take af-ter take was cut, by Gaby, "Non, non, non. You are not putting enough love into it."

"But Gaby, dear," Morley replied, "I'm doing exactly what you've asked me to do."

Ten cigars and an hour later we were in a pit of disaster. Angrily, in his thick Hungarian accent, Gaby said to David, "Tell to Robert Morley, he is stupid and a fool and I cannot any longer talk with him."

From that day on until the end of the picture Gaby would only give directions to him via David. "Tell to Robert Morley. . . ." he would say even though Morley was no more than five feet away. And David would respond, "Did you hear that, Bob?"

Added to the other difficulties affecting *Major Barbara* were the drinking habits of Robert Newton and Donald Calthrop. If Bob didn't have a drink before shooting, he was dull. If he had a couple too many, he was impossible. In Donald, he had a more than willing drinking partner. A slight, gentle man with discernment and charm, he liked drinking Port and lots of it. In the evenings, the two would go from pub to pub on Bob's motorbike and drink themselves into oblivion. The whole thing became too much for Donald and, a couple of weeks before the end of shooting, he had died of a heart attack.

Gaby called for a two-minute silence on the set and made an emotional speech. One wasn't sure if the tears he shed were for Donald or for the unfortunate fact that there were still several more scenes that should have been shot with him. This was overcome by using a double, seen only from the back and using the voice of an impersonator.

One evening, as the film was nearing completion, we got a nasty shock. We were on the backlot of Denham checking out a set built on a rostrum for the following day when we heard a German aircraft approaching. The entire unit, Gaby included, jumped off the set and dived beneath it—breaths held for thirty seconds—and the bomb exploded fifty yards away.

Any individual's instinct with bombs is firstly to duck, then, once safe, to laugh in relief. I can tell you we laughed a lot. Astonishing how quickly we got used to it all and went on with life much as usual. Later on, when the Battle of Britain was raging in the skies above southern England, games of cricket were being played on the village greens below.

Shaw had seldom visited the set, but he joined us on location at the Albert Hall, where we did the Salvation Army revival meeting, one of the big sequences. He even sat with the crowd of five hundred extras while I had the daunting task of lighting this enormous building.

One important scene remained after principal photography was completed, Shaw speaking a prologue he had written for himself. On September 12,

1940, he arrived at the studio in usual GBS attire, Norfolk jacket, plus fours, brogues, and knee-high socks.

His remarks that day were directed to the American audience and cut from the British version:

> Citizens of the United States of America. . . . I am sending you my old plays, just as you are sending us your old destroyers. . . . The German Humorist, I think his name is Dr. Goebbels, tells the rest of the world that England has sold her colonies for scrap iron. Well, why shouldn't we? We are in very great need of scrap iron. I am within forty minutes' drive of . . . London, and at any moment a bomb may crash through this roof and blow me to atoms, because the German bombers are in the skies. . . . I can't absolutely promise you such a delightful finish to this news item. If it does happen, it will not matter very much to me. . . . I am in my eighty-fifth year. I have shot my bolt. I have done my work. . . But if my films are still being shown in America, my soul will go marching on and that will satisfy me. . . . Look after my plays and look after my films. . . . That is all I have to say. And so farewell.

As he speaks the camera moves in from a medium to a close shot. His hands are folded at first; then he shakes an admonishing finger at the audience and places it thoughtfully at his temple. With his last words, he raises his hand to his brow in a salute.

Once he had read his material, we filmed an insert of him signing his name. He was meticulous about his signature and wrote it on several pieces of paper. Displeased, he dropped the pages onto the floor. At last he chose one that satisfied him, but by the time we had finished there were a dozen George Bernard Shaw signatures scattered around the room. I'm sorry to say they ended up in the dustbin. If only I had them today!

Shaw came for the screening of the completed film; there were only a few of us in the theater. He sat through the whole performance in complete silence and when the lights came up, Gaby, David, and I waited in suspense for the great man's verdict. It seemed like an eternity before he finally rose slowly to his feet.

He turned to face Gaby who was sitting next to him. "Gaby," he said, "You astonish me!"

Without another word, he left the theater.

Did he hate it? Did he like it? We never found out.

While plans were being laid for the premiere of *Major Barbara* in the Bahamas, scheduled for March 20, 1941, I found myself, with my attorney, at the Old Bailey, as the plaintiff in the lawsuit brought against me by my former agent. I was convinced, when the judge saw the evidence, he would render the verdict in my favor. I was wrong. Chris won and I had to pay three years commission, as well as the costs.

A week later Chris phoned me at home.

"Ronnie," he said, "the commission you owe me is approximately the same amount as the court costs which you have to pay."

"That's right." I replied.

"Now that I've proved my point, I want to be fair. You pay the costs, and I will waive the commission."

Under the circumstances I felt he was being generous so I agreed.

"It's unlikely, Chris, but if I ever leave the technical side of film, to become a director or producer, I'll ask you to be my agent, but no more contracts, we'll do business with a handshake."

During the making of *Major Barbara* our small home in Radlett became more crowded. Beryl's father, a retired Army colonel, had a stroke and by now Mrs. Heanly was too old to care for him, so we felt they would be safer living with us. My downstairs study was converted into a bedroom for the colonel and Beryl's mother had an upstairs room next to Curly's sister who had also moved in to help us care for the patient.

One day Mr. Baker, the then chief executive of Twentieth Century Fox in London, phoned to tell me Darryl Zanuck was about to produce a picture in Hollywood entitled, *A Yank in the RAF,* a sequel to *A Yank at Oxford*—the stars were to be Tyrone Power and Betty Grable. He asked if I'd be willing to shoot the potentially dangerous flying sequences involving dogfights between the British and Germans in the skies over England (as it transpired Scotland). I accepted and was also promised my first full screen credit. At the same time Michael Powell offered me his upcoming production, *One of Our Aircraft Is Missing.* Provided *A Yank in the RAF* kept on schedule I could do both.

Filming was made possible courtesy of the Air Ministry, who gave a few of us special clearance. Joining me was a small but efficient team, including assistant cameraman, Guy Green, who was later to become one of Britain's best cameramen and a leading director; Jack Hildyard, also to become a prominent cinematographer; assistant director Stanley Haynes, one day to be a producer; and director Herbert Mason (who never flew with us). Since our camera plane, an old Anson, was only just big enough to carry the camera crew, Herbert, fortunately for him, spent all of his time on the ground.

Our plane had to take off from the airfield well ahead of the Spitfires we were using because it took us twelve minutes to get above the cloud level, the fighters could make it in just two minutes. Once up at the required altitude, our machine, with one door removed for us to shoot from, was just capable of keeping up with a Spitfire, if the fighter pilot held back to just above stalling point.

Guy Green: On a couple of occasions I had the privilege of going up with Ronnie, though mostly I stayed on the ground, loading the camera and being a general dogsbody. I was the second assistant, having been demoted from being a camera operator at BIP when they closed down after the outbreak of war. But at least I was able to begin again.

The Spitfires were more or less at our disposal, nevertheless sometimes the fighters would suddenly vanish, when there was a "flap on," they went off to shoot down the real enemy and left us alone in an empty "shark-infested" sky.

The boys who flew for us, fearless young daredevils of about twenty, decorated for bravery with Distinguished Service Orders and Distinguished Flying Cross medals, from the Battle of Britain, lived life to the full. And women loved them. Very sadly many of them, once the war was over, and when the glamorous uniforms were gone, had trouble coming to terms with ordinary life. Yet for those moments when they streaked across the heavens in their tiny, but deadly machines to feud with equally daring young Germans, they were heroes. Too often one of them would not return from a sortie. His name was never mentioned again. This was the rule.

There was a big snag as far as the film was concerned. Several scenes, requested by Zanuck, called for the fighters to fly in "V" formation. Now everyone, except for the hierarchy at Twentieth, knew fighter planes in wartime do not fly in formation. The whole idea is to be invisible, keeping as far away from each other as possible to avoid becoming targets for enemy planes. On the ground, fighters were hidden under trees or other hideaways in remote corners of an airfield.

We explained these details to the company, but the reply from Darryl Zanuck, now Colonel Zanuck and a very influential man, read: "We want formation flying, so please see that we get it."

I was embarrassed to mention such a ludicrous request to the pilots and for the first two weeks managed to avoid it. We took all kinds of shots: air to air, ground to air; takeoffs, landings, high-speed "peel-offs" with the aircraft diving straight at the camera, then whipping away again at the last fraction of a second.

When behind a camera, one tends to forget the danger in front of it for the sake of perfection. "Come in closer before you turn away," I found myself shouting on the intercom. These aircraft were coming towards us at three hundreds miles an hour and I was yelling, "Come closer!" I must have been out of my mind.

Finally, I had to give my fighting friends the Colonel's instructions. Quite unexpectedly the young men, having never flown in formation, were exhilarated by the idea and wanted to give it a try. I shouted into the walkie-talkie, "Up a little, number three. . . . Left a bit, number seven. . . . Number four, get your wing tip closer to the wing tip of the fellow ahead."

We were running over schedule and only about three-quarters of the way through when Michael Powell's production manager called to say he expected me to start preparation on *One of Our Aircraft Is Missing* pretty well immediately.

Understanding my commitment to Powell, Twentieth released my crew and me two days after the start of the formation flying sequences. Otto Kanturek, who was already under contract to the company, and who I well knew to be a good cameraman, had recently returned from Hollywood and was available to take over.

On their first morning Otto and his team began filming a complicated shot in which ten Spitfires, flying in tight "V" formation, slowly pass the camera plane. . . . Keeping as close as possible, each pilot's concentration is on the aircraft ahead. . . . Wingtip to wing tips. . . . No one's eyes on the camera plane. . . . The lead Spitfire is too close as it flies past. . . . The last near-side plane in the "V" is left in a fatal position. . . . With a fearful rending sound it slices through the tail fin of the camera plane.

The fighter pilot bailed out safely, but the Anson plummeted into the ground. Otto and his entire crew were killed instantly. The news of this was shocking to us all.

Twentieth Century Fox's publicity department released a false report:

> England's censors relaxed their strictness recently to permit details to reach Hollywood about the death of two cameramen, who were filming footage over the British Isles for *A Yank in the RAF*, which Darryl F. Zanuck is producing. . . . The Studio's London executives advise that cameraman Otto Kanturek went up in a commercial plane with several English Spitfires over the Bristol region. Kanturek had asked studio heads to allow him to get actual shots of dogfights over England. London advised that the Spitfires ran into a convoy of German fighters. One Spitfire brought down a Jerry while Kanturek filmed the scene. A German made a hit on a Spitfire, but the pilot bailed to safety. Another German fighter bore down on the tail of Kanturek's plane, which was unarmed, and riddled it with machine-gun fire. The ship crashed to earth, killing Kanturek, [along with his assistant], and the pilot. . . .

The studio distorted the incident and exploited the deaths of three people.

In the end, very little of our footage was included in the film, nothing more than a few rear projection shots and a couple of long shots of pilots running for their aircraft. Strictly speaking, it should have been me who was killed in 1941. I have been a fatalist ever since.

Facing the dangers and heartaches associated with a film like *Yank in the RAF* made *One of Our Aircraft Is Missing* seem uneventful.

The film is a product of one of the best British filmmaking teams of the 1940s, Powell and Pressburger, nominees for an Academy Award for their screenplay.

The script begins dramatically with the crash of an RAF Vickers Wellington bomber, then flashes back to the events leading up to it. As it transpires, the six members of the crew had actually bailed out of their burning machine prior to the crash and landed in Nazi-occupied Holland where the Dutch covertly help them in their attempts to return to England.

David Lean, the editor, allowed me to spend many hours with him in the cutting room where I began to learn more about this fascinating stage of filmmaking. An editor can make or break a film; he is as much of a storyteller as the director. The "cuts" need to carry out the intention of the narrative, while showing the characters to their best advantage. Perhaps that's why so many directors remain in the cutting room throughout the editing period. How fortunate I was to be learning from one of the best there has ever been.

· 7 ·

Noël Coward

*W*e were all so deeply involved in making movies that we tended to forget what was happening in the real world. Germany attacked Russia. The battle for Libya opened the British Army's first offensive in North Africa. Japan attacked Pearl Harbor forcing America to join the Allies. And Britain, while continuing to defend herself, prepared for the Second Front.

With America as our partner we began to feel more confident about the outcome of the war. Hitler was still on the attack, but, probably because he was also fighting the Russians, he held back from attempting to cross the Channel.

When Mussolini joined forces with Germany, the British-based Italian producer Filippo Del Giudice, was automatically interned on the Isle of Man for a brief period. On his release, he became a resident alien and moved into an expensive house with his glamorous girlfriend, actress Greta Gynt. It was at one of his parties I met this smooth, flamboyant, larger-than-life character.

He had openly expressed a desire to make films to aid the British war effort and aiming at this goal, he formed Two Cities Films.

Del Giudice admired Noël Coward's work in the theater and knew of his patriotism. With the same bravado that Gaby Pascal used when he confronted George Bernard Shaw, Del Giudice approached Coward, suggesting that the latter should write, produce, and act in a major propaganda movie.

Coward was not enthusiastic at first, having had some negative experience with people attempting to adapt his plays for the screen. But his attitude started to change one night at a social gathering.

Lord Louis Mountbatten, shortly to become Chief of Combined Operations, invited him to a dinner at his and Lady Mountbatten's home. During the course of the evening Mountbatten started talking about his destroyer HMS *Kelly*, which the Germans had torpedoed and sunk. Listening to the story, Coward decided this might be the patriotic subject Del Giudice was looking for. And he would write himself in as the Captain, basing the character on his host.

Coward—an accomplished playwright, composer, lyricist, actor, producer, and director—realized that if he was going to transfer his talents from theater to film, he would need to surround himself with an experienced team. Turning to the husband of an actress friend, Valerie Hobson, Noël asked him to set the wheels in motion.

Anthony Havelock-Allan: Noël told Del and me "The man I want to photograph my picture is a fellow called Neame. I've seen a film of his and I liked it very much." So, Ronnie was actually Noël's choice and we told him it was a very good one.

As it happened, I'd worked with Tony on my last quota quickie. And David Lean also knew him. A meeting was arranged for the three of us at Coward's Gerald Road flat, just off Eaton Square.

It was 9 P.M. and the weather was chilly as Noël, immaculately dressed in a silk dressing gown, warmly welcomed us. Tony made the introductions, and we were at once given drinks. The room was actually a large studio with a picture window and a grand piano on a dais at one end, plus a minstrels' gallery, which led to the bedrooms. At the other end was a fireplace; the heat emanating from it suggesting that Noël had not yet started to feel the shortage of coal. We relaxed into comfortable armchairs, David to my left, Tony to my right, and Noël by the fire.

Anthony Havelock-Allan: That evening, there were two other people present, Gladys Calthrop, who Noël relied on for ideas about sets and things like that, and Mrs. Lorne Lorraine, sitting by the fireplace, the most important "other woman" in his life, the one on whom he relied totally. She had been his secretary from about 1921.

He had already written an original screenplay entitled *In Which We Serve* from a well-known naval quotation, "the fleet in which we serve." None of us being familiar with it, we tentatively asked whether a nonmilitary audience might understand the title.

Noël replied, "Even if they don't, that's what it's going to be."

Walking away from the fire, he settled into a chair and said; "I will read it to you." And he did, for nearly four hours.

While we listened, we had a couple more drinks and we most certainly had one afterwards. It was the story of a destroyer from the laying of its keel to its demise at the bottom of the Mediterranean. The script also detailed the lives of every member of the crew, from the captain, to the most junior able-bodied seaman, his wife, lovers, children, animals. It was an astonishing piece of work, but very, very long.

One of us said, "It's brilliant, but it goes everywhere and does everything." A pause.

Then a testy reply. "I thought that was the whole point about a film. You can do anything and go anywhere!"

Tony suggested we take the manuscript away with us, to absorb it and figure out how to turn the whole into a manageable shooting script. Noël thought it an excellent idea.

"So I take it you're with me," he said matter-of-factly.

We agreed we were.

Before we left, Noël insisted on discussing credits. The film should be produced, directed, written, and photographed, by Noël Coward, David Lean, and Ronald Neame all on one title. David balked at this because after his experience with Gabriel Pascal, he felt he should be given proper recognition as director. Someone else had always snatched the credit when he had actually done the work. It was decided that David and Noël would share director's credit, and on the same title card it would read "Photographed by Ronald Neame." Noël's insistence on including my name with theirs was highly unusual and a great compliment. Anthony Havelock-Allan was to receive credit as associate producer.

It was after one A.M. when we shook hands and walked from the opulent apartment back into the streets of war-torn London. Tony, who didn't drive, hailed a taxi. David and I got into my MG and headed towards the country.

Further readings of Noël's screenplay revealed how much first-rate material he had written, but how could we tell this complicated story within the framework of an acceptable length? It was David who came up with the solution by highlighting the essential parts of the individual's lives, revealing exposition by way of flashback. By doing this for each of the major characters, we were able to use the best from Noël's original document and still have a final script that wouldn't run forever.

It made sense to start the film with the laying of the keel of a ship already close to wartime. Almost the day that it's ready to be commissioned, war breaks out. It hardly hits water and it's in battle. It ends when it sinks in Crete. Noël liked the idea immediately.

Havelock-Allan, Lean, and Neame became a good team. We used to joke that together we made at least one first-rate mind. While David and I adapted the script, Tony split his time between working with us and organizing preproduction. Presumably Del was accumulating the necessary financial backing.

Knowing somewhat more about this side of film production than Noël, David and I were responsible for story construction. "Father," as he began to call himself, nearly always wrote the dialogue. Occasionally, though, David and I would write a few lines.

When Noël read over our notes, he would ask, "Which of my little darlings wrote this brilliant Coward dialogue?"

Sometimes embellishing or adding to it he would say, "Get out your little pencils." Pacing back and forth, his dictation reflected his fast mind.

He told me the reason he was able to write character-perfect dialogue quickly was that before he started a script, he gave all his characters backgrounds, where they were born, where they went to school, who they married, and who their friends were. He would then know them and understand how they would behave and how they would react to a particular situation.

The genius that would make David one of the world's top directors was clearly apparent even then. He had the ability to observe and then convert what he had seen into brilliant visual images. However, as an introvert, it wasn't always easy to know what he was thinking and he wouldn't make up his mind about anything until he had looked at it from every angle. Everything was written in longhand and he'd agonize over whether a phrase should be "a big explosion," "a huge explosion," or "an enormous explosion." He disliked interruption of any sort and when he worked he was totally unaware of time. By early evening Tony and I would be tired and suggest calling it a day, but David, who didn't come alive until around eleven A.M., would happily work until midnight.

Tony had the education and the background. His father had inherited a title, which eventually would pass to his son. He was more intellectual than David or me, ready to discuss Ming Dynasty, or pre-Columbian Art, as easily as saying good morning. He was a good executive and contributed a lot.

David and I would read him what we had written each day. He listened carefully and then gave his opinion with confidence. No matter what he said, David and I were convinced he was right. He explained precisely how what we had written needed to be altered and we would quickly rewrite according to his suggestions. The frustrating part was next morning he would come in and just as convincingly explain why he had been completely wrong in what he had suggested.

Noël called me "Old Feet-on-the-Ground," saying he trusted my instincts. We had plenty of healthy arguments about one thing or another, often over some detail in the script and sometimes we would have such a go at each other one might think our friendship was coming to an untimely end. Minutes later we'd be laughing completely unaffected by the momentary temperament. David couldn't grasp this; it didn't compute with his more private nature.

John Mills: Out of the three of them, Noël absolutely loved Ronnie best. He admired David, but he didn't have the warmth. He respected Tony. But in Ronnie, Noël recognized a very sweet man. They all worked frightfully well together.

Noël, at age 42, was already a world-renowned celebrity. There's been a great deal written about him, but I haven't read anything that captures the full essence of this creative talent. Few have clarified that underneath a frivolous veneer was a man who cared desperately about his work. He was a great enthusiast with a splendid sense of the ridiculous, but he was also a perfectionist in everything he touched. If he thought you cared too, he was a true and loyal friend.

Intolerant of stupidity, I remember when we were having a casting session; he said of a certain actor, "He has the eagle eye of the inefficient."

He told me people never bored him, "Only the boring are bored." He detested sentimentality, emphasizing, "someone isn't 'resting peacefully,' or 'passed' away. . . . He's dead."

The witty and stylish songs he wrote will be sung forever. He was a consummate stage director who was able to tell his actors what was wrong with their performance, as well as how to put it right. But what Noël really wanted was to excel as an actor. In the theater he was good, sometimes great. On screen, however, he could be self-conscious and unrelaxed perhaps because of the camera.

Always a decisive person himself, he told me, "Indecision is disastrous. You must make up your mind and then stay with it. If you are right six times out of ten, you'll be a success." He also said, "Never try to create something you think will please others. Create it to please yourself. If the others don't like it, then you've chosen the wrong profession."

Underneath a brittle facade was a man of great strength of character.

In less than two months we had a screenplay that made the four of us happy.

Upon completion, Noël and I went to Plymouth by train on a recce to visit some of his high-ranking naval friends. We visited several ships and were grandly entertained by top brass. It was a kind of a pub-crawl; cruisers and destroyers were the pubs. At each stop we drank pink gins, the "tipple" most favored by the British Navy.

A young officer, entering one of the wardrooms we visited, said in a loud voice, "Where on earth does that stink of scent come from?"

Noël replied, "It's from me, so much nicer than sweat, isn't it!"

Two ships and two pink gins later, we were escorted aboard a cruiser and found it hard to walk straight. Then, as we entered the captain's cabin, Noël suddenly veered off and fell into an electric fireplace. He was astonished. So was I. So was the captain. We found out we were not as inebriated as we had thought—the ship was in dry dock leaning at a fifteen-degree angle.

During our recce and the long train journey back to London, I learned a lot about Noël and I suppose he learned a lot about me. Looking away from the passing scenery, he turned to me and quietly related how he feared one day waking up to find his talent had disappeared. He was concerned that time was running out, and he hadn't yet fulfilled his potential. This humility was quite unexpected from one so successful.

With the production date nearing, Del Giudice had rented two stages at Denham. One was the largest sound stage in the country and on it we were to build our main set, an exact replica of Lord Mountbatten's destroyer.

John Bryan was under contract to Gaumont, therefore unable to join the team. Instead we hired David Rawnsley, who remarkably got hold of the original drawings of the *Kelly*. The plan was to mount the whole vessel on a large steel hydraulic platform, which would enable us not only to roll the ship from side to side, but also to pitch and toss it. This set was to be two hundred feet long, sixty feet wide, and weighing in at one hundred tons. Even in peacetime it would have been an enormous undertaking. In wartime, it seemed impossible. There was no steal and almost everything we needed was either in short supply or not available.

There were other hurdles as well. When we first embarked on *In Which We Serve*, we faced powerful opposition from the Ministry of Information and the Ministry of Defense. And when reports circulated that Noël Coward was to star in a war film as the captain of a British ship, a torrent of journalistic vitriol appeared from Lord Beaverbrook. "The Beaver," as he was called, was not only a Fleet Street mogul—publisher of the *Daily Express* and the *Evening Standard*, two of the most powerful newspapers in the country—but he also had great influence in government circles. Churchill had appointed him Minister of Aircraft Production. Worst of all, he wholeheartedly disliked Noël Coward!

On Monday, the *Evening Standard* demanded to know how an effete matinée idol could possibly play such a role. One Wednesday, John Gordon's column in the *Daily Express* read, "The trouble with us British is that we're so busy discussing whether or not clever Mr. Noël Coward can play a captain that we've completely forgotten we're supposed to be fighting a war. . . ."

Beaverbrook, as well as "The Establishment," felt that our film was the absolute opposite of what was needed as propaganda. They wanted to see the British defeating the enemy, rather than watching one of our ships being sunk by them. What they hadn't realized was that portraying people in jeopardy would actually inspire patriotism. We British are at our best when we're up against it. The tragic defeat at Dunkirk, the devastating Blitz and the Battle of Britain were some of our "finest hours." *In Which We Serve* is a story of the devotion and affection of men for their ship and for their country.

Noël didn't seem to take any notice of the scathing press other than to comment, "I don't care what they say about me as long as they go on talking about me." But beneath the sarcasm, he was bruised. Beaverbrook's negative campaign was completely unjust and so we decided to devise a way to give The Beaver his own back.

Tony remembered in January, 1939, the *Daily Express*, published the headline, "No War This Year." When less than eight months later war was declared, this statement was ridiculed and caused great embarrassment to the newspaper and to Beaverbrook. Noël gave us the general layout and told David and me to write a new sequence for the script:

Large close-up: the *Daily Express*. Cut to medium shot: enormous explosion, bombs hit and destroy buildings. Cut to long shot: the London docks filled with warships. Cut to tracking shot: the *Daily Express* headline "No War This Year." With bits of excrement clinging to the newspaper's edges, it floats slowly downstream in the filthy waters of the Thames.

We took pleasure knowing this addition would be sent to the various government agencies, including Beaverbrook's office at the Ministry of Aircraft. Noël had taken his time to savor the perfect retaliation.

Predictably, someone from Beaverbrook's camp read our script and tried to thwart our efforts. Wherever we tried to locate one of the back copies of the newspaper we were informed none existed. We heard there was a single copy among some evacuated research material that had been shifted out of London to a safe library in the north of England. A stillsman was sent to photograph the front page and then we enlarged the 35 mm negative to newspaper size.

Bad press, various antagonistic ministries, and the complications of war nearly destroyed us, but with Mountbatten's support and his willingness to use his influence, hurdles were overcome. He liked the story, not only because it was about his ship, but also he genuinely felt the film would be important propaganda for the war effort and help recruiting for the Royal Navy. He was one of a handful of men who held the destiny of our country in his hands. He believed in Noël Coward and, through him, he believed in us.

Coming down to the studio, he literally took over the supply arrangements, assuring us somehow he would get the steel for our gargantuan set and we would be given full cooperation from all departments, the Navy in particular. Our destroyer would be manned not by film extras but by real sailors—his personal batman seconded to take care of lower deck procedures. Through him we secured a retired naval commander to advise on upper deck activities, such as how the officers should conduct themselves.

Given his position, Lord Mountbatten's assistance had to be sought with great tact as he was also overseeing Combined Operations. We were truly grateful to this remarkable man.

John Brabourne: My father-in-law [Lord Mountbatten] first met Ronnie during the production of *In Which We Serve*, a film about the exploits of his wartime destroyer, HMS *Kelly*. This production will always be remembered as a milestone in British film history. I remember how thrilled Lord Mountbatten was by the film and he was always full of praise for the tremendous technical ability of everyone concerned with the production. He became very friendly with Ronnie, and I know was always delighted to see him.

During the following weeks, we assembled an extraordinary cast including John Mills, Celia Johnson, Kay Walsh, Bernard Miles, eighteen-year-old Richard Attenborough, Michael Wilding, and Johnnie Mills' daughter Juliet, who was just a few weeks old. As our production manager we hired Norman Spencer, who was to play an important role in our subsequent films, eventually joining David as his producer.

There were endless casting sessions; even the smallest part was important. We interviewed at least six people for each role, giving each aspirant a full thirty minutes of our time.

Two weeks before filming, Filippo Del Giudice gave a lavish cocktail party at the Savoy Hotel. Everyone was there, including the press. We received a great deal of good publicity, however the *Daily Express* and the *Evening Standard* continued to opine failure and disaster.

With further influence from "Lord Louis," as we affectionately called him, Tony and I, along with a small camera crew, were able to shoot footage for the opening montage of the building of a destroyer in Newcastle. There were several vessels being assembled at the same time, and we mixed and matched them for the documentary-like opening of the film. Utilizing David's editing expertise, this compilation of shots is woven together so that it looks like the building of a single ship.

Makeup and hair tests got underway—concentrating mostly on Noël, who could be very touchy about how he looked. He never forgot he had an appearance and reputation to maintain. As the lighting cameraman, the responsibility for this fell to me. He had a slightly receding hairline, which could be camouflaged by throwing a soft shadow across the top of his head shooting slightly down on him. In any case, he was in his captain's uniform a lot of the time, with a splendid braided cap loaned to him by Lord Louis.

On February 5, 1942 shooting began. The first week went well. HMS *Torrin*, our script's name for HMS *Kelly*, rocked and rolled beautifully on its hydraulic platform. The scenes played as intended. We had one glitch with an actor who arrived late and didn't know his lines. Noël fired him on the spot. He wanted a happy ship, but he was a taskmaster who expected total dedication. This applied to himself as well.

John Mills: The scene we were viewing in rushes was the one in which Noël [the captain] is giving Kay Walsh and me his good wishes in a train carriage. When we were shooting it the day before, I was desperately nervous. But strangely, Noël was also. At the end, they printed take seven or eight. Noël was sitting between David and Ronnie, and I was behind Noël with my wife Mary. The scene came on. Noël was not good. When it finished, the lights came up. There was a pause. Noël turned 'round towards me and said, "All right, dear, Daddy knows." And they reshot it. He was marvelous about it, very quick.

Each afternoon in the studio restaurant, Noël, David, Tony, and I always sat together. It wasn't that we were antisocial, simply totally engrossed in the production.

One gets a feeling about how good or not a film is going to be and by the second week, the vibrations were excellent. After shooting and screening the previous day's work, David, Tony, and I would join Noël in his dressing room for a nightcap. Sometimes Gladys Calthrop, now a high-ranking officer in the Auxiliary Territorial Service (later named the Women's Royal Army Corp.), and actress Joyce Carey would join us. These women and Lorne Lorraine, his private secretary, represented Noël's entourage.

On Wednesday of our second week, we received an urgent phone call from Del Giudice. He said he needed to see us in his office that evening, but "Don't tell Noël!"

"Close the door," he said after we'd entered. We knew trouble was afoot when he picked up his feather duster—he always swept his desk with it when he was worried.

Finally he sat down, saying rather dramatically, "It is a major disaster!"

"What is?" David asked, perhaps thinking Del didn't like the rushes.

"We've run out of money."

"*What!?*" we replied in unison.

"There is no money to make the film, and only a miracle can save us."

We were absolutely flabbergasted!

"But Del, what about the studio rent? What about the cost of set construction? What about the party and the cost of everything else?"

"A little front money, my own savings to pay salaries, and a lot of credit from everyone else," Del admitted.

"There is one more problem. . . . I can't leave the Savoy. I'm virtually a prisoner until I pay for the party." As an afterthought he added cheerfully, "But they're still giving me room service."

This couldn't be happening. Del had conned Noël, Denham, and everyone else involved with the production—including himself. He had launched the biggest propaganda film since the beginning of the war on nothing more than optimism and petty cash.

He'd maintained that British Lion, a distribution company, was behind us and we'd believed him. Looking back, if we hadn't been so stunned, we might have held a secret admiration for what he had pulled off. This is the stuff that film moguls are made of.

Anthony Havelock-Allan: Del had two backers who paid for the cost of the script. How it arose originally was that Del wanted to make a big film and find a big name. Having found the big name [Noël] he still had the backing of these two individuals who weren't nearly rich enough to make a film. Del had run out of money. He'd got so far, but didn't know where the next lot was coming from.

"I can keep things going for another few days," Del said, "then we're going to have to shut down. But there is one hope," he offered. "Sam Smith, president of British Lion, has promised to come to Denham on Monday. He will look at the material we have shot. If he likes it, he will persuade his company to support us."

We left Del's office dazed.

That weekend David worked long hours in the cutting room assembling the footage we had shot the first two weeks.

On Monday, Smith viewed over twenty minutes of screen time. "Well," he said as he drew breath and we held ours, "The Royal Navy and Noël Coward are good enough for me."

It was great news! British Lion guaranteed our distribution and the funds started flowing. Del, with a little help from us, had pulled it off. Noël never knew how close we were to catastrophe.

By choice, *In Which We Serve* was shot in black-and-white. Three strip Technicolor, the only system available at that time, was too vivid and would have ruined the sought-after documentary quality.

HMS *Torrin* hit by gunfire from a German cruiser and dive-bombed by Messerschmitt fighters begins to keel over. The crew is forced to abandon ship. Seconds later, our principal characters find themselves swimming towards one of the rubber rafts "Carley floats" thrown overboard by the crew—easy targets for the ever present bombers.

Tracking into them one by one, the camera picks out those with whom we are involved for their particular flashbacks. For this we used longer than normal "ripple dissolves" which fit the watery scene and gave a very strong sense of going back in time. Then the sound of gunfire returns the audience to the present and the desperate situation of the seamen clinging onto their lives around the float. We shot these sequences in a large studio tank, sixty feet square, and raised about four feet from the floor, wave machines gave the impression of being at sea. The surface of the water had to be covered with fuel oil, which was supposed to have escaped the sinking *Torrin*. Obviously we couldn't use crude oil, but we found an equally unpleasant synthetic substitute. For two weeks, our principals spent several hours a day in this tank covered in the stuff.

John Mills: It was absolutely ghastly working in the tank with all that goo. It stank and was full of muck, diesel oil, soot everything. The actors were shivering one morning waiting to slip into the tank. Noël came out of his dressing room. "What are you hanging about for?" he asked. "Come on, get in the water." He dived in. He surfaced, smothered in this stuff, and said, "Dysentery in every ripple."

By the end of the first day the cast, led by Noël, went on strike because the water under the inch thick gooey surface was too cold. "We are not going back into that tank until it is properly heated."

Fortunately it was Friday, thus allowing the plumbing department the weekend to get the temperature up to the requested eighty-seven degrees.

On Monday morning, Noël announced that, as the actors' "shop steward," he would test the waters. Once again he dived in . . . and was out again in seconds, yelling, "It's boiling! Do you think we're lobsters?"

The heating fellows had overdone the whole thing. Underneath the thick blanket of oil, the water had risen to a much higher temperature than anyone had realized. So now we had a two-hour delay while cold water brought the temperature down to a more actor-friendly level.

The effect of a series of machine-gun bullets hitting the water in rapid succession had to be created to simulate a German attack.

Jock Dymore, our chief electrician, who was a sturdy, gentle natured, cheerful fellow, had constructed a trellis-type contraption just beneath the waterline. Attached to it were about five hundred packets of explosive powder, which had to be kept dry until fired.

The studio storeman was more than surprised when Jock ordered ten gross of condoms to be delivered to our set. Filled, knotted, and wired into the crisscrosses of the trellis, each was electrically linked to a control panel beside the camera.

When everything was in place David called, "Action!" The camera rolled, the electrical contact slid into place and presto, instant machine-gun fire. A few seconds later hundreds of bits of condoms floated to the surface!

David and I were delighted, we got what we needed on the first take.

But with their faces blackened with slime, the actors were thoroughly disgusted. By the seventh day relations between cast and crew had seriously deteriorated to the extent that David and I couldn't go too near the edge of the tank for fear of being pulled in to share their misery. Noël was the ringleader!

It was getting difficult to film; the tension on set as thick as the goo. We asked Noël if we could have a little chat with him at the end of the day.

"By all means. If you think anything can be accomplished," he curtly replied.

That evening Tony, David, and I joined him in his dressing room.

"Well? What's the problem?" As if he didn't know.

Tony was the designated speaker.

"Noël, you are behaving very badly."

"Oh, in what way?"

"You are the producer of this film. You are the writer. You are one of the directors. And you are part of the management. It is not seemly for you to gang up with the actors against us."

Without a moment's hesitation, he replied, "When I am acting, I am an actor. The other actors are my friends, and you are the enemy."

Somehow we struggled through the next three days without too much trauma and finally said goodbye to the wretched tank forever.

Everyone at Denham had to do a stint of fire watching as part of the war effort. About twenty of us would spend the night at the studio prepared to deal with any incendiaries that might suddenly drop on us. The studio had fitted up a property shed as a kind of dormitory. But at this point in the war, night bombings were not a threat so evenings were mostly spent playing cards. Actors were normally exempt, but Bert Batchelor, the trade union shop steward and a devout Communist, disliked Noël, whom he considered an equally devout fascist. And he insisted that Father—as director, writer, and producer—should be required to fire watch just like everyone else.

Noël Coward: I was told I was down to fire watch on Saturday night. This looks like a frame-up on the part of the dear studio workers. They know perfectly well that for me this is the hardest week of the whole picture. Nevertheless, I intend to do it if I die in the attempt. I shall also look to see if the fire-watching organization is efficient and, if it is not, I shall report it.

On Saturday night, promptly at eight, Noël breezed in to join the electricians, carpenters, grips, and others, who were on duty that night. They were settling down to a poker session.

"What's going on here?" Noël interrupted, "Where are the fire hydrants?"

Everyone looked blank.

"The fire hydrants," he repeated, "Aren't we supposed to be fire watching?"

A few half-hearted replies.

"We have been given the responsibility of protecting this building against possible enemy incendiary bombs and you are playing cards! You will stop at once! We will inspect every hydrant in the studio. We will check all hoses, roll them out, make certain they're all in order and know how to handle them efficiently. Let's get started!" Noël kept them at it until the early hours of the morning.

He was never asked to fire watch again.

A few days later, we were filming a scene out of continuity in which the *Torrin* is shelled just before she capsizes. On this particular day Noël was not at the studio. Our special effects crew, an offshoot of the electrical department, was in charge of explosions.

Jock Dymore and his two assistants, Ronnie Wells and Syd, set up the explosions that were to hit the stern of the vessel. The plan was simple. Each effects man carried a large bottle of flash power, the kind used in those days to take flash photographs. Empty film tins were placed at strategic spots on the deck, hidden behind equipment. These were filled with powder and wired to a connector. When detonated, the result was a splendid and completely realistic explosion. If an actor got too close, it was Jock's responsibility to abort the effect—he was most careful about this.

Take one. Each explosion worked perfectly. But, as is so often the case, we decided to shoot one more. It might be even better. Jock and his men, flash powder bottles in hand, climbed onto the deck, which was about twenty feet off the ground and set about refilling the tins. What they—and we—didn't realize was that the tins were still white-hot from the previous take. As they began pouring the powder from their bottles into the tins there was a violent explosion, and the three men were blown into the air. They landed on the studio floor in flames.

David and I watched in disbelief from the rostrum twenty feet above the deck as electricians and carpenters rushed forward. The three men were screaming as blankets, grabbed by property men, were thrown over them. It was all over in seconds but the result was devastating.

I leaped down from the camera rostrum and knelt beside Jock. He was still conscious. "Never mind me," he said. "I'm all right . . . look after my boys."

That night I went to see him in hospital. He was cheerful because Ronnie Wells and Syd would survive although badly burned, particularly on the face and arms. Jock died later that night of multiple burns and shock.

I still remember every detail with horror. Since then, no one in the film world has been more careful with explosives and fire than Ronald Neame.

One of the last scenes to be shot involved a complicated piece of action with the Captain on the bridge of his perilously listing ship. Three enormous water tanks were built on the back lot with steep chutes aimed at the set. On cue a lever would be pulled releasing thousands of gallons of water, which would sweep the Captain overboard into an artificial sea.

The day before filming, Noël, David, and I started off to look at the set and to test the impact of the water. The plan was to use a stunt double—a professional, who knew how to protect himself—as we weren't about to risk another accident.

Noël wouldn't hear of it. "I'll do it myself," he said, "It will make it possible for you to come in close." We were extremely reluctant to go along with him, but he insisted, reminding us he was also the film's producer and codirector.

Even though the three of us were a safe distance from the water and the ship, Noël paled a little. David and I did too. The tanks were far larger than we had imagined. The bridge of the *Torrin* seemed insignificant by comparison.

The water was released, crashing down with such force that the whole set disintegrated. Had Noël been on the bridge, he could have been drowned or seriously injured. Afterwards, we went to Noël's dressing room for a recuperative tot of brandy.

The set was rebuilt; the force of the water pressure suitably reduced and we got the shot a few days later. I admired Noël's courage. He was visibly frightened, but, even after watching the disastrous test, he was determined to go ahead.

Twelve years earlier, the Duke and Duchess of York had visited the set of *Blackmail*. While we were filming *In Which We Serve*, I again had the pleasure of meeting them—now King George VI, and Her Majesty, Queen Elizabeth—along with the fifteen-year-old Princess Elizabeth and her younger sister Margaret Rose. Noël and a crew of genuine seaman ceremoniously piped them aboard the *Torrin*. The royal family was seated in gold chairs on a specially erected rostrum to watch Noël perform his final speech to his men.

Once interior filming was completed, all that remained was to get some footage of a real ship to intercut with the studio work. A small unit accompanied Tony, David, and me to the Firth of Clyde in Scotland, where a new destroyer was about to do its speed trials. It was bitterly cold and we weren't popular with crew when we insisted they wear white tropical uniforms—the *Torrin* was supposed to be in the Mediterranean. Meanwhile Guy Green was filming a destroyer in the South Atlantic.

Guy Green: By the time we got into the South Atlantic, I'd still not shot anything. Then we got word of Pearl Harbor, and also news that the *Prince of Wales* and the *Repulse* had been sunk. The captain of the ship we were on told us, "We have orders to put you down here. There's a naval base up the road." So there we were on a beach in West Africa. We got a lift from a captain of a sloop who was going back to England. While on this boat, we saw an old destroyer on its way back to Plymouth. I was rowed across to the ship. The captain was marvelous. He did everything I wanted, high-speed stuff and turns. It all turned out well. Everyone was pleased.

Weeks of editing followed. Father wrote a musical score which was not outstanding, but suitable. Sound effects were added and gradually the finished picture came together.

"The Beaver," still believing the film a disaster, wrote to Noël requesting a print for showing in his private theater. Noël responded by saying that ordinarily he didn't allow his films to be seen until the press show, but, of course, in the case of Lord Beaverbrook, he would gladly make an exception. Beaverbrook's secretary replied, "On second thought, Lord Beaverbrook finds he is too busy to see the film and, therefore, withdraws his request."

In Which We Serve premiered on September 27, 1942, at the Gaumont, Haymarket as a benefit for the Royal Naval Benevolent Fund. Lord and Lady Mountbatten attended, along with the King of Greece, tons of admirals, and well-known wartime figures. People were visibly affected by the story. All the survivors of the *Kelly* told us they thought the film showed remarkable accuracy.

Journalists from every newspaper were there—gossip columnists and critics. The *Daily Mail* the next morning ran the headline, "Best film of the war." The *Sunday Times* proclaimed it "the best war film ever made in either Britain or America."

Beaverbrook's papers had been ready to tear us to pieces, but both the *Daily Express* and the *Evening Standard* gave us rave reviews. Lord Beaverbrook after all was a big man. He showed it by heaping praise on a film he had tried to destroy.

Noël received well-deserved accolades—an Award for Service to Freedom, and the New York Film Critics Award. Besides being nominated for Best Picture and Best Original Screenplay, he also received a special award from the Academy of Motion Pictures Arts and Sciences, for outstanding production achievement. The film created tremendous good will for Britain abroad.

Norman Spencer: This was Dickie Attenborough's first film. He told me he was so excited to be in this great film. He came with his parents to the premiere. When the cast list rolled at the end, he was astonished to find that he wasn't listed! The next day he stormed into Tony Havelock-Allan with all the strength an eighteen-year-old could muster to ask about the omission. Tony told him, "I'm sorry, it's just a mistake." And to this day, his name is not listed.

We couldn't have been happier with the film's success. Recently married David and Kay came along with Beryl and me for an unruffled weekend in Brighton. We stayed at the Old Ship Hotel and unexpectedly Noël joined us. He was as relaxed as I'd ever seen him, and by the end of our brief holiday, we had all agreed to stay together and make *This Happy Breed*, based on another of Noël's plays.

Beryl and I had adjusted to the idea of never being parents, but quite by surprise she became pregnant during *In Which We Serve*. We hadn't said anything, because after two disappointments we didn't want to raise false hopes. Our improved financial position had made it possible for her to go to a well-known consultant in London, who assured us we would have a healthy baby this time—he would be our insurance policy. Beryl was due to give birth in December.

After the weekend in Brighton, Noël left for Oxford to rehearse a revival of *Present Laughter*. Tony, David, and I went to see him at the Mitre Hotel, where the rooms had names, instead of numbers: the Duke's Room, the Count's Room, the Emperor's Room. We were escorted to his suite, which was at the top of the stairs. There to welcome us was Father sitting propped up in an elaborate four-poster bed. "Did you notice the fabulous room they've given me, my dears?" We *had* noticed—the Queen's Room!

The four of us had lunch in the hotel restaurant. At a nearby table a group of men were discussing *In Which We Serve*. "It's utterly ludicrous," said one, "a man like that playing the captain of a destroyer." Our conversation dried up and we listened intently. Noël had to leave for rehearsals but as he passed their table, he stopped, faced them and said, "Personally, I thought I was *very good*."

He gave me a present several weeks later—a leatherbound copy of his book, *Present Indicative*. This gift is important to me, not only because of its contents, but because of the inscription inside:

> Please accept this, dear Ronnie, not merely as a souvenir
> of something that is past but as a talisman for the future.
> With my love and gratitude,
> Noël Coward
> "In Which We Serve"

· 8 ·

Cineguild

$\mathcal{B}$eryl worked for the Red Cross as a part-time nurse, but when she became pregnant, she had to drop out. The London specialist gave us every reason to be optimistic and when she made it past the eighth month, we felt all would be well. Meanwhile Derek had adjusted himself to a daily routine, no longer believing Hitler would march into London. A young man had moved in with him and he seemed content. Being gay in those days meant living with the closet door firmly shut—certainly our mother had no idea of his lifestyle. The artistic community has traditionally been more liberal about most things, including sexual preference, and consequently he spent much of his time in this society.

Beryl's mother was the only one still living with us. Her father had grown weaker and quietly succumbed to the effects of his stroke, and Curly's sister had moved back to London.

With a baby on the way, Beryl and I decided it was time to buy a house. We found Somerhill in Chalfont St. Peter, three miles from Denham; a two-story, white stucco house, with four bedrooms. We moved in, fixed up a room for my mother-in-law and, for the third time, organized a nursery. It was a happy interval for all of us as we decorated the house for Christmas and awaited the birth of our child.

We passed Rose Walk on to Beryl's pretty younger sister, Pat, who continued the rental, then purchased the house, living there with her husband and two sons for many years.

Kay and David, Mary and Johnnie Mills, and Tony and his wife, Valerie Hobson, were our neighbors, all of us living within a three-mile radius. Since gasoline was in short supply this was a godsend to friendship. Often we'd meet for dinner, either at one of our homes or at the Bull Hotel in Gerrards Cross—and we organized weekly poker games.

73

On Sundays, we would usually enjoy lunches together at the Greyhound, in Chalfont St. Peter. During the war, however, the menu in most restaurants was somewhat restricted. If we were given anything resembling butter, it was actually a small pat of margarine. Hard liquor was scarce—we made do with Algerian plonk and beer.

Throughout the war, when we dined at home, we ate mostly chicken and eggs, but I also remember having lots of Spam, baked, minced, or fried. Living in the countryside around many farms, made it easier to get fresh fruit and vegetables and Ivy sent care packages from America once a month, filled with tinned beef, tuna, peas, and beans.

Johnnie and Mary owned a lovely period cottage in Denham Village, which I would happily have swapped for ours. The Leans had a tiny place with a terrific garden. It was out of character, but David was green-fingered and knew his way around the countryside, recognizing birds, and understanding various changes in the season. He must have had the type of complexion that attracts insects because he would invariably come to the studio with his face covered in bug bites. The day before Christmas Eve it became evident Beryl was going to give birth at any moment and so I drove her to the prearranged nursing home close to Windsor Castle. Early the next morning I went up to London to look at locations for *This Happy Breed* and on my return, walking into an office at Denham, I was met with "Congratulations, Ronnie, it's a boy!"

Christopher Elwin Neame was born December 24, 1942. We'd considered calling him Noël, but figured "Noël Neame" didn't sound right. But, being a Christmas Eve baby, we decided upon the equally appropriate "Christopher."

There was a tiny church about five hundred yards up the road from Somerhill and although it was closed most of the time, we managed to arrange for a vicar to come from the village to perform the christening. As the church had no running water, I had to bring tap water from the house. The clergyman blessed it and instantly it was holy!

Noël insisted on being Christopher's godfather, he already had twenty godchildren, including Juliet Mills. At the service he held our new son. Cradling a baby didn't come naturally to him and I'd never seen him look quite so uncomfortable. His christening gift was a lovely silver plate inscribed; "Christopher Elwin Neame from Noël Coward. May 9th, 1943."

It was a wonderful day with everyone coming back for a party in our garden. John Bryan brought several bottles of Scotch for the occasion, although goodness knows where he got them, and Guy Green took the photographs. The only disappointment was that David and Kay had been quarreling and he had come alone.

One month after the christening, we were stunned to hear that actor Leslie Howard, who had kindly consented to do the narration for *In Which We Serve*, had been shot down over the Bay of Biscay as he was returning to England from a visit to Portugal. His accountant and friend, Alfred Chenhalls, who was the spitting image of Churchill, had accompanied him on what was allegedly a goodwill mission. It is believed that enemy agents gave the Germans an erroneous report leading them to believe Churchill was aboard. I will always treasure a writing desk from Leslie that still remains with my family.

Tony Havelock-Allan felt it was time we formed our own production company. Father didn't like the idea. He felt slightly threatened by this step of independence. However Tony was aware that David was becoming restless and might want to take on projects other than Noël Coward plays. With our own company we could still work with Noël while maintaining our freedom to make other films. Tony suggested the name Cineguild, which David and I thought excellent.

Anthony Havelock-Allan: We decided the sensible thing to do was to make our own deals because otherwise other people would make them for us, and we would get a smaller percentage. I came up with the name, simply because the biggest theater company in New York at the time was called the Theater Guild. I hoped it might please Noël to have a sort of reference to the theater.

Noël looked at the three of us and said, "What a stupid name!"

David and I wrote the screenplay of *This Happy Breed* with more independence than we had on *In Which We Serve*, because Noël was away in South Africa and Asia. Once we got to the stage where a scene seemed to be working, we'd go to our ground floor office and we'd try it out—David playing Robert Newton's part as the father and me the Celia Johnson role of the mother. Not exactly type casting! One day while we were blocking something out, we saw four studio carpenters looking at us through the window. They must have thought we were stark staring raving mad!

Even though I was the cameraman on the picture, I was also management. According to Tony's memory, the three of us each got eight percent of the net profits and took the salary of five thousand pounds per project.

Noël Coward: It was pleasant to be concerned with the picture but not trapped by it. I could never quite prevent a sinking of the heart every time I drove through the gates of Denham Studios. They recalled so many leaden and difficult days, but at least in these circumstances, with David and Ronnie doing all the actual work, I could say what I had to say and get out again before the atmosphere really defeated me.

Norman Spencer came with us and stayed. Always immaculately attired and precise in both appearance and manner, he was a very professional, well-spoken man, who liked his job. He was also a good observer of human nature with a tremendous sense of humor.

Cineguild became one of several companies that J. Arthur Rank put together under a banner known as Independent Producers, among them The Archers (Michael Powell and Emeric Pressburger) and Individual Pictures (Launder and Gilliat).

Arthur was an unpretentious man from the North of England, whose family had made a fortune as millers. His beliefs were deeply rooted in a religious background and he had originally come into the film industry to make movies reflecting a strong sense of morality.

Distributors weren't interested in them because quite frankly they were boring. In order to bypass the system, he formed the J. Arthur Rank Corporation and bought, outright, both the Gaumont-British and the Odeon film circuits, thus acquiring eight hundred cinemas.

Of course, he knew that in order to fill all these cinemas, he would have to provide them with feature films. A good ninety percent of these came from America, but they demanded high rental fees, so in self-defense, Arthur decided to make British films and was willing to spend as much money as needed to compete with Hollywood. Always greatly supportive of us young filmmakers, he trusted us enough to give us complete freedom to make whatever we chose, and cast films in any way we felt suitable.

What was produced over the next few years were some of the best films to come out of Britain. Unquestionably Rank and, to a lesser degree, Michael Balcon and Alexander Korda, were responsible for Britain's Golden Age.

When Arthur's accountant, John Davis, complained that we were spending too much money, Arthur would immediately say, "Don't discourage the boys, John. It's their job to make the films and ours to sell them."

This Happy Breed depicts the humor and resilience of average British people. The play's action takes place solely in the Gibbons's family home, where they have lived since the end of World War One. But since the plot was very much dialogue driven, we needed to open it up. The exteriors we devised involved the family in some of the great events of the period; Victory celebrations in 1918; the Wembley Exhibition of 1924; the General Strike in 1926 and the death of George V in 1936.

Kay Walsh plays Queenie, Ethel and Frank Gibbons's willful daughter. When we shot a scene with the characters dancing the Charleston, it was she who taught the extras how to do it. Johnnie Mills was Billy Mitchell, the boy next door.

The decision had been made to photograph it in color, but I wanted to use this in a different way. Up until now films had been too vibrant. In order to make Technicolor less glorious we exaggerated the age and shabbiness of everything; tidemarks round the bath, stains on the walls. With shades of gray and brown to "dirty down" the sets and costumes, I was able to light the picture so that everything looked drabber than normal.

The Technicolor people, concerned that their process would be degraded too much, insisted on having one of their quality control experts present during filming. Joan Bridge, originally hired by Natalie Kalmus, wife of the Technicolor inventor, received a screen credit "Technicolor Associate." One day I noticed her scraping off a piece of wallpaper from our living room set to take back to her laboratory. She was making certain it would be reproduced on screen correctly!

Celia Johnson was the only actress I ever knew who thought acting was of secondary importance to a private life. She was first and foremost a wife and mother and, in any event, preferred the stage to film. In fact, she wasn't really sure she even wanted to be in *This Happy Breed*. She didn't think the story was good. To her the studio was a most extraordinary place and we were the most peculiar people: "None of you has any interest in the war. The only thing that concerns you is if you can't get fifty horses when you want them without going to Ireland!"

We filmed for six days a week, always letting Celia go by 12:30 P.M. on Saturdays because she had a long rail journey home to Nettlebed—if she missed the afternoon train, she'd have to wait hours for the next.

On one of these days we were ready to begin rehearsing an emotional scene in which Queenie returns home after running away several months earlier with a man. Having her daughter back means everything to Ethel.

David, who had finally been given his due as sole director, asked Celia if she would rehearse quickly so we could plan camera positions and be ready for Monday morning.

She demurred, "It's the same every week and it's just not fair! You promised I would be away on time, and promises are meant to be kept!"

More pleading from David. Finally she agreed to go through the scene just once.

A few minutes later as she spoke her last line, there wasn't one member of the unit who hadn't got tears in his or her eyes, from the toughest electrician and carpenter to those of us around the camera.

Celia, looking at her watch said, "If I run, I can just make it!" And she ran, completely unaffected, not remotely aware that she had created a piece of magic!

Like the rest of us, she found it difficult working with Robert Newton. Before he was cast, Noël had forbidden him to drink while we were filming. Promising to go on the wagon during the ten weeks schedule, he had signed his contract with an extra restrictive clause. Any and every time he came onto the set drunk, he would forfeit five hundred pounds of his salary. He was only earning nine thousand pounds for the whole picture so he clearly had to be careful.

Bob was as good as gold until we neared the end of principal photography. I suppose he thought, "Well, there's only twelve days to go and even if I get sloshed every morning there'll still be some salary left." The next day he arrived drunk, but sobered up enough to be able to work from eleven o'clock onwards. His agent was informed and told he would have to pay the penalty.

From then on, until the film was finished, he forfeited three thousand five hundred pounds while we slipped three days behind schedule.

Anthony Havelock-Allan: We just had to take a chance with Newton because he was on the bottle. He was a very strange character. I'd known him well socially, before we used him. His father was a rather good painter, Algernon Newton. Bob was always eccentric, but an amiable drunk to begin with. Then as time went by, he became difficult. He would come into the studio so full of drink, not even aware that it was affecting him, and at first it didn't. He could act perfectly well until something tripped him, if he couldn't remember a line or something. Then we had to wait until he was sober. In Hollywood, I heard that he was caught naked up a lamppost!

Noël's play *Present Laughter* was closing a successful run at the Haymarket Theater and, as he usually did on such occasions, he hosted a party for a hundred and fifty guests. It started at 10:30 P.M. in both the Green Room and bar, which occupy two floors of this magnificent building. Tony, David, and I, and our wives were invited. Specifically Noël did not invite Robert Newton. He felt he had misbehaved and should be taught a sharp lesson.

A group of us were at the bar upstairs, while below the talented Joyce Grenfell was amusing other guests with her delightful monologues. Then from the doorway came the sound of a loud, indignant voice. "And why was I not invited to join this dazzling company?" roared the drunken Bob as he staggered into the room. I moved towards him, followed by David and Tony.

"For God's sake," I said grabbing his arm, "stay away from here, or you'll be in real trouble."

He shouted at me, "You!" Then he looked at David and Tony, "All of you!" he waved his arms, "Noël Coward's yes men! That's what you are, nothing but yes men! I want a drink, and I want to find out why I wasn't invited."

By the time he got to the bar, there was silence. Downstairs Joyce Grenfell was still entertaining and Noël was with her, as were most of the others, as yet unaware of what was happening.

Rolling his eyes around the room Newton spotted the large painting of John Buckstone—a long dead comic actor, who had also been the manager of the theater for twenty-five years during the last century, and been a favorite of Queen Victoria.

Weaving his way through the crowd towards the portrait, he fell to his knees and looking up at Buckstone, asked, "What would you have said if you were here tonight? If you could see the desecration of your great theater by this matinée idol and his decadent friends?"

We hauled him to his feet and again tried to persuade him to leave. Pushing us aside, he headed for the stairs and the sounds of piano music coming from beneath. Noël had written rude versions of most of his songs and he had just replaced Joyce at the piano to sing one of them when he spotted Bob coming over. Someone pulled him to the floor, but not before he had made an exaggerated bow to Father.

From his sitting position he began a slow handclap and shouted a variety of sarcastic remarks. We had to do something. David and I each grabbed a leg. Tony and another man his arms and we managed to carry him like a sack of potatoes to the stairs. Noël continued to play the piano and sing, pretending nothing unusual was happening. As we started up, Bob shouted, "I came here with a hat! I'm not leaving without my hat!" Someone found it and placed it on his tummy.

The police arrived. Quickly assessing the situation, they escorted Bob off the premises. The party returned to normal.

"We're all so Bohemian, aren't we?" was Noël's only comment.

After the party, when Beryl and I were walking up the Haymarket towards Piccadilly Circus, we saw a crowd around a doorway, and in the street was a police van, the kind with bars on the windows. Scuffling with the police, his shirt torn off, his trousers about to fall to the ground, was Bob. He was bustled into the van and driven away.

The next morning Robert Newton was not at the studio. We had to bail him out of Bow Street police station and he finally arrived at Denham around eleven-thirty. For the next few days we had to photograph him on one side of his face. The other had a piece of sticking plaster covering a nasty cut. The only remembrance Bob had was waking up in jail with a monumental hangover. In the end, Noël took pity on him—his penalty payment was waived.

Once the film was over, he joined the Navy and became an "able-bodied seaman." There was an unwritten law during the war that only officers could eat and drink in the best hotels and restaurants. Bob ignored this bit of British snobbery. Whenever he was on leave, he would drop into the Dorchester, the Savoy, or Claridges, get drunk at the bar, then stagger into the restaurant to see who was around.

One evening, he was standing unsteadily in the doorway of the Dorchester Grill when he spied his admiral seated with a group of senior officers at the far side of the room. He staggered towards them finishing up behind the important man and slapped him heartily on the back.

"Hello, Old Cock! How about buying me a drink?" Bob spent the next week peeling potatoes!

On another occasion, this time at the Savoy, he noticed Laurence Olivier and Vivien Leigh dining with Anthony Asquith, a prominent and much loved British director, nicknamed, "Puffin"—a man about whom one never heard a bad word. His list of credits would include *The Importance of Being Earnest* and *The Yellow Rolls-Royce*. He was sensitive and he was kind; he was also homosexual. Bob made his way over to "Puffin" and with an exaggerated bow, said, "Good evening, and how is the First Lady of the Screen tonight?"

Olivier, who knew Bob very well, grabbed him by the scruff of his neck, and frog marched him out of the restaurant, through the foyer and into the street. Olivier was such a strong and vibrant man that he accomplished by himself what it had taken four of us to do.

Cineguild's next project was another Coward play, *Blithe Spirit*. As was the case with *This Happy Breed*, most of the action takes place in one interior location, a living room. Tremendously successful on stage, running in both London and New York, it was a valuable property and American companies wanted to buy it. Noël wouldn't give it to anyone but us. This turned out to be a mistake because he was more possessive of this play than any of his others, and instructed David and me not to mess around with it.

Added to this David hadn't been enthusiastic from the outset, feeling he didn't have the requisite touch for light comedy. But the public had been saturated with propaganda films over the last few years and were longing for lighter fare.

The unlikely story centers on Charles Condomine, played by Rex Harrison, a middle-aged novelist, whose exciting days of youth have been exchanged for a more mundane life with his second wife Ruth (Constance Cummings). His deceased first wife, Elvira (Kay Hammond), comes back to haunt Charles by reminding him of their adventurous times together and, in so doing, disrupts his life and sanity.

Anthony Havelock-Allan: It's a wonderfully funny play and reads divinely still, but we had forty-eight minutes screen time in one room and that's too much. It's not film, it's television. But Noël didn't want us to open it up, not even as much as we did. It killed the thing. In addition, none of the workmen on the set thought Kay Hammond was nearly as attractive as the second wife, Constance Cummings. That was a mistake, plus the fact that Rex looked about twenty-six years old and the part was written for a man in his forties.

It was difficult photographing Rex. He was terribly vain and insisted on being shot only from the left side of his face. Also, he was insecure and didn't know if he was funny or not—I don't think David did either.

Margaret Rutherford was ideal as Madam Arcati, the eccentric medium, who tries to communicate with Elvira. She had played in the original stage production and was absolutely typecast. About four days before principal photography, she came to my office with the wardrobe lady, presumably to show me her idiosyncratic outfit for the opening sequence.

"It's wonderful. Where on earth did you get it?"

"What do you mean where did I get it?" she said indignantly. "These are my own clothes."

Noël presented me with yet another photographic challenge. As opposed to having a double-exposure ghost—one that would be transparent on screen—he wanted Elvira to be solid, as she had been on stage. In the theater, the effect was created by dressing Kay in gray chiffon and giving her a gray wig and gray makeup and her lips and fingertips were bright red. She was followed with a green spotlight, which created a ghostly gray-green aura. If she stepped out of her light for a moment, it didn't disrupt the reality of the play.

For a film we had to be more precise, ensuring the green never spilled onto other characters or objects as she moved around the set. I solved this problem by using two "brutes," fitted with green filters and shutters. Her movements were choreographed, so when she passed behind other people, an electrician would close the shutters on one lamp while another electrician opened those on the second. The process was made a little easier by David's decision to see her from Condomine's point of view only—when anyone else looked in her direction, she wasn't there.

The living room set had to reflect the affluence of the owners. To help with this, Tony had persuaded a London art gallery to loan us four valuable paintings by Christopher Wood for the walls.

He severely cautioned us, "For heaven's sake be careful. They're worth a fortune."

We assured him we would be, but David and I decided to play a joke on him, asking art director Percy Day to help us.

Percy was such an accomplished artist himself he could copy anyone's work. We asked him to reproduce one of Wood's paintings of yachts on the seashore. It didn't take him more than a couple of hours and when he'd finished we couldn't tell his apart from the original. Then we tipped over a brute and jammed it into the duplicate picture shredding its canvas. Norman Spencer called Tony insisting there'd been a terrible accident!

Anthony Havelock-Allan: I first thought, "Oh, crikey, what am I going to say to the gallery." Then I realized I was having my leg pulled. The paintings were insured, but if you ruin a picture, it doesn't matter how much it is covered for, it's a ruined work of art. And Christopher Wood's output was very small.

Noël had been abroad for most of the filming, but he was back in time to see the rough cut. After the screening David asked what he thought of it.

"You've just fucked up the best thing I've ever written."

Personally I thought the film was rather good and a lot of other people thought the same. It won an Academy Award nomination for Special Effects. The main effect was the ghost, Elvira, that I created on film. But the end title reads: "Special Effects by Thomas Howard." He got the Oscar!

·9·

Hollywood

*T*he Allies had clearly won and we would see the end of war in a matter of months, maybe weeks. Representing Germany's last gasp, the buzz bombs were replaced by V-2 rockets, which gave no warning of their approach. They were fired at angles to drop not only on London but the whole of the South of England. But being few and far between and in comparison to what Britain had already suffered, they did not seriously disrupt daily routine.

Arthur Rank, who presided over Independent Producers board meetings, announced that since war was drawing to a close, it was time for the Rank Organisation to concentrate on reequipping the studios. He felt that someone should go to Hollywood to see how this could best be achieved. To my surprise the board unanimously voted it should be me.

It was a tremendous opportunity and a great honor, but my excitement was tempered by the thought of leaving my family. Beryl was positive I should go, saying she and Christopher would be far safer in England than I would be in a ship crossing the Atlantic.

There was no question of flying; aircraft between Europe and New York were reserved for use by the armed forces and VIPs only. So arrangements were made for me to sail on the *Queen Elizabeth* from Scotland, with U-boats prowling the English Channel, liners departed from a safer haven. This meant I'd have to stay overnight in Glasgow. Using considerable influence, Rank managed to get me an accommodation at the Central Hotel in a large and comfortable room with twin beds.

Once settled, I found myself in the bar and in conversation with a highly decorated American colonel. Even at this stage in the war, I was hesitant to speak freely with strangers, but he appeared genuine enough and it transpired that he was leaving on the same ship.

Over a shared dinner, the colonel told me he had a bit of a problem. There was no room available in the hotel and he was going to have to spend the night on a sofa in the lounge. Gratefully he accepted the offer of one of my twin beds. The 83-ton *Queen Elizabeth* was nothing short of gargantuan. Years later, on boarding the same vessel in New York, actress Beatrice Lillie asked, "When does this place get to England?" There were two thousand passengers for our voyage and all available staterooms had been converted into dormitories.

There was a smattering of civilians aboard. However, the bulk of passengers, around eight hundred, were American wounded on their way home, plus a few hundred German prisoners of war headed for prison camps in North America.

My dormitory was three decks down and full. I grabbed the last bunk, deposited my luggage, and, as instructed, headed for the first class ballroom where we were to receive information about safety precautions. On the way there, what a bit of luck, I ran into the colonel and told him about my crowded quarters.

"No problem," he said. "Because of my rank, I've been given a dormitory entirely to myself. I would like to return your kindness of last night by giving you fifteen of my thirty bunks."

In case he changed his mind, I relocated immediately, afterwards proceeding to the ballroom, which was jam-packed with various sorts and sizes of people. We were instructed to maintain wartime procedures. Just by striking a match on deck, we could put the ship in jeopardy. In order to make it more difficult for the enemy, the *Elizabeth* zigzagged across the ocean.

Twice each day we had to go below so the German prisoners could be given exercise on deck. They were such a sad looking bunch of young men that one couldn't help feeling sorry for them. Surely, they hated the war as much as we did.

Shipboard life was like existing in a private domain, insulated for a short while from the problems of the real world. The voyage was easy, the weather good, and no U-boats were sighted. I began writing down my impressions of fellow passengers and crew and of their daily activities; my idea was to take a diary home.

Five days later I looked in awe at the skyscrapers of New York as they gradually appeared through the mist. Noël had told me what a wonderful moment this would be and he was right. Hundreds of American wounded crowded to the ship's rails to cheer the Statue of Liberty as we cruised slowly by. Among them were fifteen young soldiers who had been blinded in action. They stood at the rails and were made to feel the excitement of the moment, with vivid oral pictures drawn for them through the eyes of their friends.

The arrival of the *Queen Elizabeth*, and its sister ship the *Queen Mary*, was always an event and this was no exception. But knowing their American boys were returning home, every vessel in the Hudson Estuary welcomed us with their sirens.

On disembarkation the customs confiscated my diary on the grounds that it might supply useful information to the enemy. I wasn't quite sure what use my ramblings might mean to the Germans, but I handed it over, then looked for the colonel to say goodbye, but he was lost in the crowd.

Rank had arranged with United Artists to have me booked into the St. Regis Hotel. I took a taxi there and in less than half an hour I was installed in a luxury suite. There were very few English people in New York, as a result of currency restrictions among other things. The rarity of my British accent had an effect on the hotel staff, who afforded me every possible courtesy including advice on where to enjoy the best meal in Manhattan.

"Without doubt," I was told, "your first meal should be at '21' but unfortunately it is so popular you must book weeks in advance. Even if we phoned on your behalf, there's no way to get a reservation."

Encouraged by the affect my accent, I decided to telephone the *maitre d'hotel* myself. "I'm here from London for just twenty-four hours," I explained, "and before leaving my partner and friend, Nöel Coward, told me that if I didn't dine at '21' he would never forgive me. So I was wondering . . . ?"

It worked like a charm! Not only did I get a table, but one of the choicest. The meal was excellent. I hadn't enjoyed food like this since before the war, steak, baked potato dripping with real butter, and chocolate dessert with thick cream.

The contrast between war-torn Britain still in the midst of blackouts and Manhattan, brightly lit with spectacular buildings, glamorous restaurants, packed theaters, was almost too much to take in. There were lights and more lights wherever I turned. At home, we were short of matches. Here, matchbooks advertising one thing or another were placed everywhere.

The next morning I visited the United Artists' offices where Arthur Kelley was in charge. Arthur Rank was highly respected by them, owning as he did the two largest theater circuits in Britain and I was treated as a VIP.

Kelley said arrangements had been made for me to fly to Los Angeles over the weekend, but the trip had its complications. Air travel from coast to coast took eighteen hours with many stops along the way and, at each of these, one was liable to be bumped if a seat was required by somebody of military or government importance.

"But," he assured me, "United Artists has a method for overcoming this—tell the authorities you have an 'Orchid Pass.' Remember, an 'Orchid Pass.'"

As a special additional favor, Kelley reserved a few seats for the first week's run of the new musical *Oklahoma*, at the St. James Theater. He and some other Rank employees joined me. There is no way to describe this lively energetic spectacle. While we in England were saving pennies for groceries, America was hosting this lavish production, with vibrant performances of songs that are still popular today.

With assurances of an unhindered passage to Los Angeles, I phoned my mother in Glendale to tell her I'd be leaving New York early on the Friday morning and could join her for a late dinner that evening. Having not seen her or Curly for several years, I looked forward to our reunion.

At New York's Idlewild Airport at seven A.M., full of enthusiasm for the day ahead, I settled into my seat towards the front of the cabin of the aircraft—a Dakota, which could only carry thirty passengers.

We took-off on time for our first destination, Rochester, where we had a thirty minute stopover, those going on remaining aboard. Then up the aisle came an official checking tickets. I handed mine over. After a moment he said, "I'm sorry, Mr. Neame, but I'm going to have to take you off."

This was a bit of a setback, but I had my answer ready.

"I have an Orchid Pass."

"Even so, I'm going to have to take you off, sir. We have a U.S. officer in a hurry and he has priority."

"What about my baggage?" I asked testily.

"We'll take care of it."

Reluctantly, I rose to my feet and, with as much dignity as possible, left.

Five minutes later I was at the desk in the small airport terminal. There were no planes out so I was instructed to take a train to Chicago where I might have better luck. Again there was nothing available, and after waiting hours in Illinois as a standby passenger, a clerk beckoned. "You're in luck," My spirits rose. "There's a plane due here in thirty minutes but it will only get you as far as Kansas City." Unfortunately this was air travel during the war!

I arrived somewhere in the middle of the states the following morning bleary-eyed and approached yet another departure desk.

"No planes out today, probably not tomorrow," the clerk said.

"Is there a hotel somewhere nearby?"

"You won't find a room in Kansas. The city's bustin' at the seams."

A woman in a well-cut Army uniform heard us talking and offered me the room she had just vacated at the Gould Hotel. "The bed's not made up, but," she smiled, "if you don't mind sleeping in my sheets, I'm sure the hotel won't."

The night clerk at the Gould was most understanding explaining that once you have a room you can usually hang on to it. Completely worn out, I slipped into bed and in less than a minute was fast asleep.

Awake by about eleven, I phoned the airport. There were no planes leaving for Los Angeles for someone using an Orchid Pass with a British accent.

Next I called my mother to explain my predicament, and then simply waited for two days, reading and going to the movies.

When I could stand it no more, I accepted defeat and inquired about trains. It would be a three-day journey, but what I hadn't realized was that trains in those days had wonderful accommodations, spacious sleeping quarters, and dining rooms with white tablecloths and elegant cuisine. I should have traveled that way in the first place.

A few days later I was installed in an attractive room at the Beverly Wilshire Hotel and that evening had the long awaited dinner with my mother and Curly. Ivy was more radiant than she had been for years, relieved to shed the image her fame had created for her. In America she'd never been a celebrity, therefore no one could think of her as "the once famous Ivy Close." She looked sun-tanned and healthy. I longed for this happiness to continue.

Spyros Skouras, the boss of Twentieth Century Fox, was another great friend of Arthur Rank, with the Organisation distributing all Fox product in the UK. It was on their lot that I was to be based for my fact-finding mission.

The studio's respectful general manager, Lew Schreiber, provided me with an office in the new Writers' Block; the site is now occupied by one of the high-rise buildings of Century City. Lew asked if I needed a secretary. I said that would be helpful because I had to wire a weekly report back to Rank. Did I prefer a blonde or a brunette? Jokingly I said, "I like redheads." And would you believe it, the next morning there was a redhead sitting in the outer office sharpening pencils! She said she had a car, which I didn't, and offered to act as *chauffeuse* should I need one. I asked about all the pencils she was sharpening. She told me that Fox contract writers were expected to be in their offices by 9:00 A.M. and the pencils were to encourage them to get on with it.

An invitation to lunch in the executive dining room was extended to me—the idea being to meet Darryl F. Zanuck. He arrived late and sat at the long, oval table, presiding over sixteen of us. Here was the man who would one day change the direction of my career. He explained he had been putting the final touches to *Wilson*, the biography of the American president with Barbara McLean, the *doyenne* of film editors. The film went on to win five Oscars the next year, but even so, people stayed away in droves.

During the next six weeks I was to learn a great deal of valuable information, but my first job was to get to know people and to feel at home.

Escorted to one of the large stages, I was introduced to director Gregory Ratoff, a flamboyant Russian, who immediately adopted me. "You are welcome on my set whenever you wish." He then presented me to his cameraman, the great Leon Shamroy. Their current project was a musical, *Where Do We Go from Here?* with June Haver and Fred MacMurray.

I watched Shamroy at work. He was the most confident cameraman I have ever met. Whereas many mess about with the lights or adjust a flag or barn door on every take, Shamroy lit a scene, then walked away from it. Plus he was very fast. His chief electrician, the gaffer, almost as well trained as he was, did much of the background lighting.

Shamroy, who seemed to have more authority at Fox than virtually anyone else, became a friend and, in due course, helped me bring about a closer liaison between British and American cinematographers. Other cameramen I met were Joe Ruttenberg, Harry Stradling and Charles Rosher. They were a powerful group. Every day I spent a few hours on Ratoff's set, and gradually began to learn why Hollywood studios were so much more efficient than those in England—basically their films were shot in less time than ours.

I was impressed with the speed at which gaffers, grips and property men tackled the myriad chores. And, the working day itself was different. We stopped for the requisite twenty-minute tea break at 11:00 A.M., and again at 3:30 P.M. with the whole unit of about fifty people having refreshments at the same time. On an American set coffee flows all day long, consequently production is continuous. They also had the beneficial flexibility of when lunch could be taken, while our unions dictated it should be from exactly one to two o'clock. At Fox, if the next setup called for construction changes, the break could be called, at say 12:15 P.M. while the "heavy gang" went on through—thereby ensuring that when the unit returned, the alterations would be in place.

Finishing time in Britain was at 6:00 P.M. We might be given an extra fifteen minutes if we had already turned the camera on any given shot, but this brought about an absurd situation. The director often started shooting even though he wasn't ready, hoping that during the next frantic fifteen minutes he might get something printable. In Hollywood you could shoot as late as you liked without any restrictions except, of course, money. After 7:00, it became expensive—"Golden Hours." Thus far it had been impossible to convince our company executives that to pay the unit reasonable overtime was far cheaper than having to go back to that set or setup the following morning.

Also, whereas in London nine setups per day on a quality production were about all we could manage, in Hollywood fourteen or fifteen were the average. The cameramen were faster partially due to their superior equipment and to having such experienced gaffers.

A large scenery flat could be removed with ease by two men instead of the four we needed. Two levers were incorporated into their construction and, by raising these, wheels could be placed beneath thus allowing it to be repositioned rapidly.

In order to facilitate striking a set, some resourceful American had devised the double-headed nail. Once it was hammered in, it stopped halfway so that when it had to be removed, a crewmember simply flicked it out.

My agenda for the next few weeks included visits to Paramount, Warner Bros. and Universal-Fox remaining as my headquarters. Conscientiously I dictated lengthy memoranda to my red-haired secretary about all this.

I had always believed there should be more accord between British and American cameramen, including some sort of exchange system whereby if an American photographed a film in Britain, a British cameraman could do likewise in the States. Prior to the war several top talents had come to England, including Harry Straddling on *Pygmalion*, but it had never happened the other way round—the controlling union was opposed to any such reciprocity. They were polite and listened, nothing more. Senior members of the American Society of Cinematographers were all for such an arrangement, but their less confident majority was not. Several meetings at the society's headquarters led nowhere.

During these talks Charles Rosher and I became great friends, and, thanks to him, I visited MGM. Rosher, by then over sixty, had been Mary Pickford's cameraman. She wouldn't work with anyone else.

Currently Metro's lion was really roaring! Judy Garland was starring in *Under the Clock* directed by her husband, Vincente Minnelli. They were working on a big railway station set, and I spent a couple of hours watching, never imagining for a moment I would one day direct this wonderful actress.

On the *Mrs. Parkington* set, Greer Garson was starring in a role for which she would receive an Academy Award nomination. I was introduced to the other cast members: Walter Pidgeon, Agnes Moorehead, and Peter Lawford. And I chatted with cameraman Joe Ruttenberg, who took me to meet Greer. Having seen *Mrs. Miniver* during my stopover in Kansas, I was particularly impressed. She was welcoming and warm to a newly arrived fellow Brit, inviting me to a cocktail party early that evening.

The time in her Bel Air home passed so pleasantly that when I suddenly realized it was 7:00 P.M. I panicked. I was late for a dinner party. There are people who are always early, others who arrive on time, and those who are guaranteed to appear late. As for me, I'm such a punctual person, that I practically hyperventilate when I run behind schedule.

I made a dash to another part of Bel Air, hoping I hadn't missed dinner altogether. The guests were already seated at the table enjoying the first course when I got there. My sincere apologies made and my tardiness forgiven by the rotund host, Alfred Hitchcock, I slid into the one vacant chair. Hitch was still the same genius from those early days at Elstree, but now he had become an important Hollywood director, having been brought to America by David O. Selznick five years earlier.

Only after I had regained my composure did I realize I was sitting next to Ingrid Bergman, who was in the midst of recounting her experiences on *Gaslight*, which she had recently completed with George Cukor.

The next morning Charles Rosher phoned to ask what I was doing at the weekend.

"Dinner with my mother and stepfather on Sunday."

"Why don't you join me on Saturday and we'll take a drive to Malibu."

This would be my first visit to the California coast. "Gladly," I answered.

"I'll pick you up at ten."

He pulled up outside the Beverly Wilshire Hotel on the dot, a white haired man in a black convertible. In the car beside him was a gorgeous young blonde.

"Ronnie, I'd like you to meet a friend of mine, Audrey Totter."

"Good morning, Miss Totter," I responded, realizing absolutely why Hollywood was known as the glamour capital of the world.

I climbed into the back seat and we headed west, soon speeding through the irregular shadows cast by the palm trees along the Pacific Coast Highway. To our left the sun created dazzling images as it shimmered on the water and the warmth in the air, even in the middle of winter, was something new and special for me. We had lunch at a restaurant overlooking the ocean where we stayed to watch a pastel sunset.

Audrey explained to me how M-G-M groomed young, contract actors with the idea of finding potential stars, initially casting them in small parts. The year we met, she made her debut in *Main Street after Dark* and went on to become one of the best-known *femme fatales* in *film noir*.

Later that day, Charlie and I saw Audrey home to her apartment at the Chateau Marmont. As we said good night there was the smell of night blooming jasmine heavy in the air. To this day, when I am around this flowering vine, my memories go back to my first visit to Hollywood.

Audrey Totter: Charlie Rosher told me, "There's a young man here from England, and he'd like to see the town. Will you show it to him?" I liked Ronnie immediately. He was charming and we were all impressed by that British accent. Metro taught me how to drive and I had a sporty two-door Ford that I paid eight hundred dollars for. So we did all the things that tourists do, Grauman's Chinese, Sunset Blvd. I remember there seemed to be something bothering Ronnie, maybe it was the war; I don't know. But we did have some lovely times.

I had come to California to work, but in my wildest dreams I couldn't have anticipated a world so completely different. I enjoyed every minute of it, though I did so with the knowledge that while I basked in luxury and sunshine, my family was still enduring the deprivations brought about by war.

The lack of thought and kindness associated with studio publicity departments should come as no surprise. Someone at M-G-M notified the *Hollywood Reporter* that "Rank representative Ronald Neame and M-G-M player Audrey Totter have become an item."

In order to help Rank reequip his studio in England, one of my major objectives was to find out the availability, and the possibility of buying, Mitchell cameras, unequivocally the best movie camera in the world. The stumbling block came about because wartime currency restrictions meant we could only pay for them in pounds sterling, and the Mitchell people flatly refused to accept pounds.

That's as far as it went. But I did find out one important bit of information—Mitchell had never taken out patents in Europe!

After closing down my office at Fox and saying goodbye to my secretary, I prepared for the journey home. It was difficult leaving Charlie and Audrey and sad to say goodbye to Ivy and Curley. Surveying the comfort of my hotel room for the last time, I began packing my belongings, including some new clothes I'd got for Christopher and a bottle of scent for Beryl.

In a few hours I was boarding the *Super Chief*, headed for New York and a three-day stay at the St. Regis. On the first night, United Artists' Arthur Kelley took me to dinner at the Plaza with some of his associates. There I met Alexander "Sasha" Galperson, a warm hearted Russian. He was a Londoner in New York on business and, since our hotels were quite near, we shared a few more meals together, agreeing to keep in touch once we returned home.

Manhattan's skyscrapers receded into the distance as our convoy of thirty ships, moving at the pace of the slowest, set sail for a ten day voyage—ten days if our protective submarines and two destroyers kept the Germans at bay. My vessel was packed with returning women and children, who had been evacuated to Canada—a cargo of ill-mannered teenagers and screaming babies. With no gracious colonel to rescue me, I found myself berthed in an extremely noisy dormitory that presaged a less pleasant journey than on the way out. But my luck held.

Discovering my profession, an officer, who had a half-occupied, two-bunked cabin, asked me to organize a ship's concert. We struck a bargain.

Keeping to my end of it, I encouraged whatever talent there was aboard to join in. Mothers and children sang, read poetry, danced, and one played the harmonica. The performance was less than adequate, but, mercifully, I traveled in comfort.

Somewhere in mid-Atlantic an idea came to mind. Arthur Rank desperately wanted to make films that would break into the American market. When I left England I was a cameraman, but with my newfound knowledge I was beginning to feel confident enough to move forward. Why, I thought don't I ask "Uncle Arthur" (Rank's nickname) to let me produce a film? One that would please the American market.

Then, settling back for the duration, I contentedly looked forward to happy days with my family and to a new production with David and Tony, based on a one act by Noël, that we were to call *Brief Encounter*.

· 10 ·

Expectations

$\mathcal{K}$nowledge gained in America proved useful in England. As a result of my trip, many laborsaving devices were adopted and negotiations with unions helped bring about a more practical working day.

The unresolved problem remained our desperate shortage of up-to-date cameras. Rank owned four old Mitchells—six new ones were needed. I explained to Arthur the impossibility of obtaining the Mitchell because of the company's unfeasible demands. Then, in an attempt to help the situation, I informed him about the lack of patents. "Perhaps we could make our own version."

Arthur thought this was an excellent idea. With the help of the camera department, I learned of a precision engineering company in the Midlands. After a preliminary meeting with the managing director of Newall Engineering, we handed over one of our old Mitchells for inspection.

A few days later, he called us to report he was quite confident that it could be duplicated, however "tooling up" would be expensive and only worthwhile if the order was for fifty.

Fifty cameras! The whole thing had become impossible! I went back to Arthur and once again this remarkable man displayed his determination.

"Ronnie, we need cameras. If we have to order fifty then that's what we'll do!"

The Newall was not as good as the Mitchell, but it was a reasonable substitute and in the end it paid off. Several companies purchased cameras from Rank, and those Newalls were put to good use in England for many years. Understandably, the Mitchell Camera Company was not too happy. Ronald Neame was on their shit list!

During my meeting with Uncle Arthur, I did not forget my decision to become a producer. I explained my ambition and he couldn't have been

93

more cooperative. "Tell me what you want to make. Let me have an approximate cost and bring me a good film." Truthfully it was as simple as that!

I asked David if he would consider me as his producer. He wondered if it was such a good idea for me to drop the camera, although he accepted I'd be a supportive partner and provided we found the right subject, he said he'd be happy to go along with me. I knew I would be on slightly shaky ground. David got on tremendously well with his cameramen, but as a rule he had a more problematic relationship with producers.

He suggested Charles Dickens' *Great Expectations,* a stage version of which he'd recently seen at Rudolf Steiner Hall. It was adapted and directed by Alec Guinness, the young actor who also played Herbert Pocket. Martita Hunt was the eccentric Miss Havisham. David and I read the book twice before we finally decided it was the right subject.

I told Arthur what we had in mind and he immediately green-lighted the project with Tony as our executive producer. Noël was not happy; he didn't want us involved in a new film while still working on another of his. By way of emphasizing his position, he cautioned us against making a period piece. "What do you know about old costumes? Stay with the contemporary." Rightly he had sensed we were stepping away from him.

While I was in America, David and Tony had started scripting *Brief Encounter* and I'd joined them on my return. With his collaboration, we transformed Noël's somewhat static, one act play into an effective shooting script. There was no question of trying to find box office names, simply we wanted actors who would be right for the parts. Celia Johnson was our first and only choice for the role of Laura Jesson and Trevor Howard, then little known, was our preference for Dr. Alec Harvey.

Noël Coward: The remainder of 1944, although eventful for the world, was not particularly eventful for me beyond the fact that I adapted *Still Life* into a film script, rechristened it *Brief Encounter* and persuaded David and Ronnie to put it into production. This, after some argument, they agreed to do, which was lucky from all points of view, for it turned out to be a very good picture.

The story is about a married woman with two children, who, by chance, meets a married doctor in a railway cafeteria. Despite their best efforts not to do so, they fall in love. The film begins at its conclusion, Laura sitting with Dr. Harvey at a table. They are saying goodbye, a sense of duty sending them back to their respective spouses. They only have a few more minutes together when a woman Laura knows sits at their table and starts chattering loudly about things that don't matter. Her words become a blur, as we focus in on the unhappiness of the two parting lovers.

Because of David's choice of telling the story through flashback, we decided to have a narration spoken by Laura. Used correctly this device can give another dimension such as providing necessary information that cannot be achieved by visuals or dialogue; and it can add depth to a character. Unfortunately, so many narrations are written after the event to get a film out of trouble. This is wrong. It must be built into the overall construction.

Early in the film, Laura is at home seated near the fire while her husband does the crossword. Moving in closer, we hear her thoughts as she looks over to him. "Fred—dear Fred, there's so much I want to say to you. You're the only one in the world with enough wisdom and gentleness to understand. If only it were somebody else's story and not mine. As it is, you're the only one in the world that I can never tell."

So begins the story of her accidental meeting with Dr. Harvey and their subsequent relationship. The narration, as we used it, gets the audience interest upfront and holds it throughout the film.

Another scene has Laura in a public phone box telling a lie to Fred about why she will be home late. Putting the phone down, she exits the booth. Her voice over: "It's awfully easy to lie to someone when you know you're trusted implicitly, so very easy and so very degrading."

It was the first time Cineguild had to divide itself into two parts—the shooting of *Brief Encounter* and the preparation of *Great Expectations*. For the latter, we engaged the successful playwright, Clemence Dane, to create the screenplay. She wanted to write the first draft without our input and we agreed because we felt *Brief Encounter* should have our full attention for the next few weeks.

The Carnforth, Lancashire, railway station was chosen as the main location, the perfect small provincial setting. This film confirmed David's love affair with trains. From then on almost every film he made had to have a train sequence.

On May 4, 1945, filming was disrupted by a jubilant cast and crew cheering the BBC announcement of Germany's surrender to the Allies. Four days later Churchill officially declared the end of war in Europe. Johnnie and Mary Mills, Beryl and I went to London for a celebration dinner at Les Ambassadeurs in Mayfair. Afterwards we walked to Hyde Park Corner and down the Mall to Buckingham Palace where we joined the cheering crowds at the gates.

Suddenly a catastrophic period of all our lives had come to an end and the future looked bright and beckoning.

Several sequences were completed in Carnforth, however most of the film was shot at Denham, with exteriors at Beaconsfield and Regent's Park.

Two scenes remain held in my memory, partly because, to quote Noël, I was the "little darling," who wrote them and partly because they gave me my first opportunity to create dialogue single-handedly. The first occurs between Celia and her children in the bedroom. The second takes place after Trevor falls into the lake at Regent's Park while he and Celia are sitting in the boatman's hut by the fire.

Tony, David, and I received joint screenplay credit for *Brief Encounter*. Each of us was presented with Academy Award nominations.

It had been a mistake to leave the script for *Great Expectations* in the hands of Clemence Dane.

"It's no bloody good," said David.

"So what are we going to do about it?"

Never thinking ourselves writers as such, we had, nonetheless, learned how to adapt other people's stories quite efficiently. We decided to have a crack at it ourselves and so, taking three weeks away from the studio, staying with our wives in the Ferry Boat Inn at Fowey, we started getting on with it. While Kay and Beryl enjoyed the summer sunshine, David and I were determined not to return to London until we had a completed script.

Dickens' material, his dialogue, his characters and his fantastic situations, are wonderfully appropriate for film and the experience promised to be highly enjoyable.

The first thing to be considered was how to turn this sprawling novel into a movie running just two hours without spoiling the whole.

We began by underlining all those sections that would make good film and were quite ruthless in cutting any of those excellent characters if they did not advance the story, thereby doing full justice to the ones we kept. Several Dickens' movies have failed because screenwriters have tried to retain too many within a limited space.

In creating a one-line continuity, a rule we made for ourselves proved invaluable. Each scene had to be entertaining, increase the development of the characters involved, and advance the story. Now and again we had to settle for two of the three, but not often.

Gradually, it expanded into a full-length screenplay with dialogue taken largely from the book. Dickens had read his stories in public, so he'd made certain his words could be spoken. The first draft was completed in less than three weeks, although a lot more work still had to be done back in London. There we'd have the benefit of Tony's contributions.

John Mills: I think the script for *Great Expectations* was a lesson on how to cut down an enormous novel into a size that didn't lose any of its quality. Ronnie and David shacked up in a hotel and came out with a marvelous bloody script. You couldn't fault it.

Looking back, it amazes me how quickly we put together two films. While David was shooting *Brief Encounter*, I was in preparation for *Great Expectations* with designer John Bryan.

Although we had seen each other often, John and I hadn't been able to do a movie together since *Major Barbara*, prevented by his contractual obligations to Gaumont-British. Typically his sets were planned for both composition and lighting. He was considered expensive because he was a perfectionist. He drove construction workers round the bend, making adjustments right up to the last moment, and, while everyone else's nerves were on edge, he always remained cool.

Having been a cameraman for many years, it was easy for me, in association with John, to present David with the ideal conditions for him to come up with a visually exceptional film.

In England then (as today), we had some of the best character actors in the world. This time ours included Bernard Miles as Joe Gargery, Finlay Currie as Magwitch, the convict, and Francis L. Sullivan as lawyer Jaggers, as well as Ivor Barnard, Freda Jackson, Hay Petrie, O. B. Clarence, and Torin Thatcher.

Sixteen-year-old Jean Simmons played young Estella and Tony's wife Valerie Hobson, the grown-up Estella. Tony hadn't asked for her to be cast, Valerie just seemed right. Martita Hunt joined us in her original stage role of Miss Havisham. Our chum John Mills was Pip in adulthood.

John Mills: I think it was David who rang me because I had done *In Which We Serve* with him, Ronnie, and Tony. He said, "I've got a part I would love you to play. I don't know how you'll feel about it because it's not easy. It's a sort of 'coat hanger' role, where a lot of marvelous characters hang all over you." I asked, "It wouldn't be Mr. Pip would it?" He said, "That's what it is!"

Johnnie is a stylish, handsome man, who keeps fit by swimming every day and never eating meat. We used to call him "Nob"—I'm not sure I ever knew why—it's just a name that stuck. From a young age, inseparable from his wife Mary, he is the most devoted husband I've ever met, and she the most devoted wife. As a novelist in her own right, Mary wrote some wonderful stories, my favorite being *Whistle Down the Wind*. Besides her other talents, she managed Johnnie's career, ran their home, and raised three beautiful children. Their two daughters are actresses Juliet and Hayley.

Nob is an actor laddie and proud of it. His main ambition growing up was to be a performer. Warm, easy to read, and extrovert, he is sprightly with sparkling eyes expressing charm, as well as mischief.

One day he gave our crew an outrageous performance, stating with authority that if you ate a tin of baked beans and a few hours later held a match to your backside, your fart would ignite. Nobody believed this, but literally with great flare, he proved his point!

Finding the right boy to play Pip as a child became a headache—no one suitable came to light. Then I had an idea. We made a short film of John Mills looking into the camera and asking the people of England if they knew someone who might play him as a little boy. This was screened in seven hundred Rank theaters during each program. Letters and photographs poured in from all over the country. One of the hopefuls even turned out to be a girl in disguise. The whole thing became too much to handle, so it was decided to deal only with kids from the south, a polite but brief note to the others thanked them for their interest.

After many sessions with the casting department, the choice was narrowed down to six. We screen-tested the finalists and eventually picked thirteen-year-old Anthony Wager. He was the son of a plumber living in Mill Hill, which, conveniently, was only about ten minutes away from the studios. I had a long talk with his parents, counseling them that to take an adolescent out of his or her own environment and exposing them to the heady, often artificial life of filmmaking is not necessarily for the best. Ultimately Anthony was determined to become an actor, and his parents approved. The only problem with him, beside the fact that he was hopelessly in love with Jean, was that he was growing so fast and in danger of being taller than his adult counterpart, Johnnie!

During a short leave from the navy, Alec Guinness did a screen test for us in a little room in North London. It was immediately apparent he should recreate his stage role as Herbert Pocket, but there was a difficulty—how to get his leave extended? Several times he phoned to see if I could arrange a way for him to participate only to be told I was doing my best. Eventually, having gone from one ministry to another and back again, I was able to secure extended leave for him for the duration of the production.

Great Expectations turned out to be the first of six pictures I was to make with Alec, two as producer and four as director. He was a private person, almost to the point of self-effacement, yet he had great determination and meticulously knew exactly what would be right for a part he was playing. For many years we periodically spent time together, on set or simply as friends. He has stayed in my home. Many evenings Beryl and I have dined in his Petersfield home with him and his wife Merula. We often lunched together and talked for hours on end, though I have to admit I did most of the talking. Yet, with all that, I still wonder if I really knew him. His retiring nature became a quest for anonymity that perhaps went so far as to have a reverse affect—in a way drawing attention to himself by the very fact.

Many actors, although playing varied roles, always seem to finish up being themselves. Not Alec. He was like a chameleon. When he portrayed a character, he gradually became that character and in every film or play in which he appeared, he was always someone completely different. Once he told me it all started from the feet, the way a person walked.

When the screenplay was completed, as was our practice, we held a meeting with the unit to read through it and give them a chance to raise questions about any aspect of the production. In the past David had always asked me to handle this, believing I was better at speaking in front of people than him. Just before the start, he took me aside and said; "I think I'd like to read it this time, Ronnie, if you don't mind."

"By all means."

After the meeting, he added, "I'm sorry, but you were in grave danger of taking over."

In my new role as producer, he felt I might overstep the mark!

In theory, once a film starts shooting, the producer has completed his job until post-production. That is if everything goes according to plan. It seldom does and the producer has to sort it out. In the case of *Great Expectations*, it was the cameraman who gave us the problem. Bob Krasker was highly experienced, but he and David weren't working well together.

This pleasant Australian had photographed *Brief Encounter* without incident. However that was a sensitive film, which needed a gentle appearance on the screen. *Great Expectations* called for a harder edge, more dramatic lighting, and Bob couldn't seem to achieve this affect. My suggestion to David was that Krasker should resign and Guy Green hired in his place.

"When can you arrange it?" he asked.

Steeling myself to terminate the employment of an important member of the unit, I asked Bob to come to my office that same evening.

He was obviously upset when he learned of our decision. I told him how genuinely sorry I was, adding, "You're too talented for this to affect your career." And it was true. Carol Reed grabbed him up almost immediately to photograph *Odd Man Out*.

Probably the most famous scene in the picture is the churchyard scene, which occurs early in the story. Actually, it was shot in the studio. At dusk, young Pip is putting flowers on his mother's grave and in the background, John Bryan's trees look like giant, hovering figures reaching out to the boy.

Guy Green: Everybody admired John's work. He had this ability to build sets in perspective, which saved a lot of space in the studio. In reality, the church was a model. But it looks quite real. In terms of the whole thing being a trick, you believe it, but it restricts you a bit as you can't go too far forward with the camera.

Pip is scared and starts to head for home. Suddenly, while he is running from the grave, the convict confronts him. There were two alternative ways to play the moment—the first with suspense, the second as a surprise. In other words should the audience be made aware of the frightening Magwitch crouching behind the gravestones, about to pounce on the boy? Suspense. Or, do we not introduce him suddenly—*BANG!* This would be surprise. We opted for the latter and created such a frightening moment that to this day audiences still jump out of their seat.

Another early scene is with young Estella and young Pip in Miss Havisham's creepy house.

Jean Simmons: Anthony Wager and I had to go up some dark stairs, with me holding the candle. We had to do it many times for David. It was late at night, I remember, and I was so tired. I let the candle just kind of hang down and it caught my pinafore on fire. Everybody stood aghast, but Anthony came and tore it off me and put it out. This boy was the one who saved me. Everyone else just stood around. Some years later, in 1989, I had the guts to come back and play Miss Havisham. It was crazy, but I thought, "Why not?"

The most difficult scene to prepare was the one in which grown-up Pip pulls away the tablecloth in the Satis House dining room in an effort to save Miss Havisham from the fire. He and Miss Havisham have had a final confrontation in which she tells him she had deliberately encouraged Estella to abandon him. At the end of their argument, he storms out of the room. Halfway down the stairs, he hears her screaming. He rushes back upstairs. A log has fallen from the fireplace and set her clothes alight. In a desperate, but unsuccessful attempt to save her, he pulls off the tablecloth, laden with its contents, and throws the material over her. It was a skillful collaboration between set designer, lighting cameraman, and director.

The laying of the table was a work of art, the moldy wedding cake, the cobwebs, the candlesticks, and the rotting fabric. David created the complex camera movement to emphasize the rapidity of the action. It was a tremendously effective shot, but extremely complicated to shoot.

John Mills: It took five hours to set the room with the table, the cob-webs, the mice, everything. And just before we started, Ronnie came on the set. He said to David and me, "If you can get this in one take, it would be great." "Right, but why?" I asked. He replied, "Because it will take another five hours to set the bloody thing up again!" And we did it in one. It was sheer luck!

Once the studio sequences had been completed, we filmed on the Thames Estuary. Dickens writes about "the cold, shivering marshes," and on them we built Joe Gargery's house and the Inn from which Pip and Herbert Pocket try to smuggle the convict out of the country.

In keeping with the ever-present misty atmosphere conjured up by the author, smoke from canisters, the kind thrown overboard from destroyers to camouflage ships, was allowed to drift low across those marshes. Positioned about three hundred yards away from the camera, we counted on the wind to spread the effect widely, too widely, as it happened. After only a few min-utes we heard the sound of foghorns from ships blindly trying to feel their way down the Estuary. Understandably, complaints from the coastguards were soon heard.

Filming on the River Medway, part of the main estuary, we quickly re-alized was no easy matter with the ongoing process of getting on and off boats. As luck would have it, we found a small island that was about a half mile across—a sandbank with a ruined fort. Norman Spencer obtained a landing craft and boat crew for the remainder of the shooting period, and, early each morning, we'd set sail from our base in Rochester loaded with the unit and cast, extras, equipment, and myriad miscellaneous items. Had it not been for our island and big floating truck, we could never have filmed on that wonderful location.

Norman Spencer: When we were shooting there, Ronnie bought himself a new Bentley. We were driving along a long straight road. Ronnie was so chuffed, he said, "Norman you take the wheel. Go ahead, open it up." I was going very fast when a police car appeared. Ronnie dissolved into fits of laughter. "Norman, you bloody well got caught." The policeman asked me, "Is this your car?" Ronnie said, "No it's mine." "Could you see the speed from where you were sitting, sir?" "Yes," replied Ronnie. "Well, I'm afraid we'll have to book you too." You should have seen his face drop.

Brief Encounter was now ready for public previewing, complete with a musical score decided on by Noël. Fitting like a glove, Rachmaninov's Second

Piano Concerto was played by the gifted Eileen Joyce, the wife of agent Christopher Mann!

David and I were still on location. For the sake of convenience, we opted to hold the first screening nearby in Rochester, but we learned too late that it was situated near Chatham Docks—therefore providing an audience of mainly sailors, dockers, and their womenfolk. Under usual circumstances, they might be the kindest people in the world, but in this instance we had a tough group, completely wrong for a sensitive film.

About five minutes into the screening, a woman in the front row started to chuckle. Laughter is contagious and several people around her joined in. A few minutes later, during a love scene, the hysterics grew worse. And then it became a running joke. Led by the lady, the audience caught on and waited for her cue. They sent the film up as if it were the funniest comedy of the year. Shuffling through the comments cards, David and I were convinced we had a disaster on our hands. One summed up the audience reaction—a "Mister Chad" figure holding a sign that read, "Wot tripe!"

Tony soothed our anxiety by telling us he would arrange another screening and when the film reached a more appropriate public, the accolades were resounding. *Brief Encounter* became legendary and even today is considered an all-time classic.

Although Cineguild's association with Noël had been a great success, this was our last film together. It was David's decision, and, despite Noël's earlier sarcasm and objections about our ambitions, he was tremendously gracious. I remained close friends with him for the remainder of his life.

We had to come to terms with *Great Expectations'* ending. Dickens obviously had his own problems with it as he wrote two. One has Pip and Estella accidentally meeting, then parting forever. The other has the two of them returning to Miss Havisham's house. Pip takes Estella's hand, seeing "no shadow of another parting." In our opinion, neither of these worked for the film.

It was Kay Walsh who came up with the solution. She wrote the final scene, and earned herself a well-deserved credit. Pip saves Estella from being ensnared in the same life as Miss Havisham.

> Pip: I have come back to let in the sunlight! (Pip goes to the windows and rips down the draperies) Look, Estella, look. Nothing but dust and decay. I've never ceased to love you even when there seemed no hope for my love. You are a part of my existence, part of myself. Estella, come with me out into the sunlight. (He takes her hand and they run from the house, they pause in the garden, and look back towards the decaying building, then continue through the gate into the sunshine.)

Great Expectations exceeded our expectations.

The collective Independent Producers grew in stature in the industry, (Cineguild was by now an important entity) and the monthly board meetings continued, during which Rank's accountant, John Davis, was given twenty minutes to present his financial report. He would come in with his big book filled with numbers and proceed to tell us we were spending too much. Semibald with a high forehead, fastidiously clean-cut, John was strictly a numbers man, only interested in the bottom line. He disliked films and everyone associated with them and it would be absolutely true to say vice versa.

Arthur realized he made a certain amount of sense, though not the kind we wanted to hear, and therefore suggested he become a board member. All our companies rejected him. So Arthur made an alternative suggestion: George Archibald (later Lord Archibald) as managing director. He was a good chairman, but the poor man had a terrible time controlling us.

By the end of *Great Expectations*, David's marriage to Kay was over. There had been foreshadows, many fights and separations. What I gathered was that David felt his career made too many demands on him and he'd decided it was best to live alone. A few days later, he sent someone to collect his belongings, and then moved into the Athenaeum Court. Kay also moved from Denham to London, renting a flat from Eric and Louise Ambler.

Knowing David and working closely with him for over six years, I understood the subtle changes that were taking place between us. He didn't like producers because they occasionally had authority over him and, maybe, because he felt them intrusive. Those close to him were the people he who would spend the whole day with—the cameraman, the script girl, and editor.

Outsiders coming onto the set were automatically suspicious. One could almost hear him thinking, "What does he want?" So although we were still tremendously good chums in our off hours, I was now the person to say, "Do you think we can get off this set tonight?" Or, "David, if you expect the rest of the unit to be here at 8:30 A.M., you should also be on time!" I would have much-preferred saying, "It doesn't matter when you arrive," and "Don't worry if it takes another week to complete a scene." That, though, is not what is expected of a producer.

I was not comfortable being stuck in an office instead of helping more creatively on the floor. I began to accept I didn't like this role.

With my mother, Ivy Close.
Baby brother Derek on the
left.

Stuart Elwin Neame, my father,
nicknamed "Senny."

Derek grown up lived mostly in France.

Front row:
proud father,
Curly Batson,
David Lean.

Center:
Beryl and
Christopher.

Back row:
(from left to right)
Valerie Hobson,
Noël Coward,
my mother.

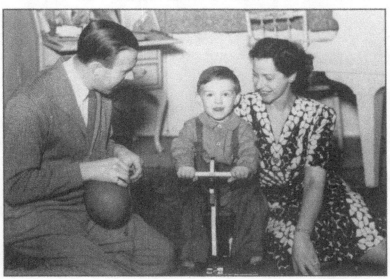

Beryl and I celebrating Christopher's birthday on wheels.

George Formby with three of his five leading ladies: Phyllis Calvert (left). Kay Walsh (center). Googie Withers (right). *Courtesy Ealing Studios.*

A Young Man's Fancy with Griffith Jones and Anna Lee. *Courtesy Ealing Studios.*

In Which We Serve with Noël Coward as Captain D., wearing good friend Lord Mountbatten's cap.

A young cameraman with co-director David Lean.

Alec Guinness and John Mills in *Great Expectations,* acting together for the first time.

David and I on set with young Pip (Anthony Wager).

Top left:
Cinematographer
Ossie Morris.

Top Right:
Golden Salamander
with Anouk Aimée
and Trevor Howard.

Center:
Explaining William
Friese-Greene's
invention to the
Queen Mother
on the set of *The
Magic Box*.

The Magic Box
with Laurence
Olivier as Police
Constable 94B.

Alec Guinness, Glynis Johns, and Petula Clark in *The Card*.

Gregory Peck and his fans in *The Million Pound Note*.

The Horse's Mouth: me with cigar, John Bryan, Michael Gough, and Alec Guinness.

John Bratby creating Gulley Jimson's paintings.

Tunes of Glory with John Mills and Alec Guinness, two impeccable actors.

· 11 ·

The Academy

"It is time we formed a British Film Academy," producer Alexander Korda announced, in his thick Hungarian accent. Everyone in the room thought it was an excellent idea pledging to do whatever they could to make it a reality.

Korda was a witty, intelligent, larger than life character known for his altruism, particularly in helping Jewish refugees who had escaped Germany. He was also known for his extravagance. That evening he had asked about thirty filmmakers to join him for dinner at one of London's premier hotels, Claridges, where he maintained a permanent suite. Among those present were Michael Balcon, Carol Reed, Frank Launder, Sidney Gilliat, Michael Powell, Emeric Pressburger, David Lean, and me. Tony was in Rome.

Michael Balcon agreed to oversee the preliminary steps, in effect becoming the first Chairman in 1946.

Weeks later, he asked fourteen of us, (Tony, David, and I arrived together) to meet him at the Hyde Park Hotel where each of us was duly appointed as a director of the newly formed academy. Our intention was to create a smaller version of the American Academy of Motion Picture Arts and Sciences, which had been in existence since 1927.

Throughout the following year, we became organized while trying to keep our heads above water financially—quite honestly, no individual was willing to put in much money of his own. Members, of course, contributed, but revenue from such a small group was inconsequential. Eventually, Arthur Rank stepped in to help and Lord Louis Mountbatten became a benefactor. Membership requirements were rigid for this elite group. Television wasn't considered important enough to be considered.

As a result of our determination the BFA became a reality with Tony Havelock-Allan becoming Chairman for the second term. David attended all board meetings and contributed enormously.

Initially we didn't favor the idea of giving annual awards, as in Hollywood, feeling it would lower the tone. This, though, was unrealistic, and we had to relent; limited awards would be an excellent way in which to call attention to our films and to enhance our industry's reputation.

Balcon had persuaded sculptor Henry Moore to design a statue. He, in fact, made five. The idea was to select the best film of the year, which could have been made anywhere in the world, and hand the award to the picture's producing company for one year only.

Carol Reed's *Odd Man Out* was released the same year as *Great Expectations*. As recorded, it is the first film the BFA selected as Best Picture.

My turn came at the end of Tony's. I was elected the third Chairman. All the while the BFA was becoming increasingly more recognized—albeit still a makeshift organization—and the idea of an award's ceremony was taking shape.

During the first weeks of my chairmanship, Uncle Arthur generously loaned us the Odeon, Leicester Square, one of the biggest theaters in London, for an hour between screenings. There, the audience, who had paid to see the feature films, received the added bonus of attending our affair.

John Bryan designed a set, consisting of several pedestals and a few back panels, which had to be erected quickly between screenings, and one of Henry Moore's statues was placed on a pedestal in the center.

The 1948 ceremony reflected the fact that the American Academy had honored several films from our country. Surrounding the two feet high Henry Moore were five Oscars kindly carried back from America by Jean Simmons. Hollywood complimented Cineguild by giving three of them to *Great Expectations*—a well-deserved Oscar to John Bryan for set design, Wilfred Shingleton for set decoration, and Guy Green for his black-and-white cinematography. And David Lean received a nomination for Best Director. He, Tony, and I also received an Academy Award nomination for Best Screenplay.

The fourth and fifth Oscars on display were for *Black Narcissus*. These Oscars had been distributed by the Academy of Motion Pictures Arts and Sciences on March 20, 1948 and they arrived in England soon afterwards.

Jean Simmons and Lord Mountbatten were on stage with me to announce the Oscar winners. Lord Louis participated as a personal favor to us and because he was an enormous fan of British films. The event was running well over the hour and so, as soon as I could, I called for the curtain to be closed. As it was being drawn, Lord Louis said, "Wait a minute, Ronnie, I want to say a few more words." Hastily, I signaled for the curtain to be reopened. He then gave a warm speech confirming his support for what we were all doing.

The Oscars were not handed out that evening they were merely displayed. But after he struck the set, John Bryan collected his and a group of us escorted him to Les Ambassadeurs where we enjoyed a celebratory dinner with his Oscar placed in the center of our table.

The Odeon presentation was the BFA's first official ceremony and the first time the Henry Moore was exhibited publicly. It's a shame our event seems to have been omitted from history because that was when Lord Louis was the most active in giving us his help. I am grateful to Jean for her confirmation.

Jean Simmons: At eighteen years old, I was naive and hadn't been in the industry very long. I remember accepting the awards in Hollywood, wearing a black, off the shoulder dress, and afterwards rushing around with my autograph book. The Oscars came back with me, but I was chaperoned like crazy. Then back in England I recall being on the stage at the Odeon Leicester Square. Lord Mountbatten was also there and Ronnie Neame, but the exact ceremony is a vague memory.

Also while chairman, the next year my colleagues and I welcomed to London one of the great moguls of American movies.

"An Evening with Sam Goldwyn" was arranged at a theater in the Wardour Street area. He'd brought with him a print of his latest picture, which had not been seen by anyone, saying he would be very glad if it could be screened exclusively for our members so they could give their views. It was a testament to the growing integrity of our Academy that someone with his stature would ask our opinion.

The lights were dimmed and we settled back in our seats. . . .

Within five minutes I could tell it was not going well, the restlessness of the audience confirming it. When people are enjoying a film, unless it is a comedy, you can almost hear the silence. When they are not is when the coughing starts. The story was simple and overly sentimental—a poor young boy is determined to give his mother a beautiful funeral. Sentimentality can be all right, but not when it becomes mawkish, and such was the case in this instance. The movie received sparse applause. And my mouth dried as I escorted Mr Goldwyn onto the stage.

"Who would like to open the discussion?" I enquired.

From back of the theater came a voice, "Why on earth, Mr. Goldwyn, did you make this film?"

I expected Goldwyn to storm out of the theater, but he listened attentively to the rest of the inevitable criticisms, which caused me increasing embarrassment, and addressed them honestly and without resentment. Before leaving, he said, "Thank you all very much for your comments, I greatly re-spect them."

To my knowledge, he never released the picture in England!

Through the years, the BFA grew and prospered. Somewhat reluctantly, we had to admit television was becoming important and its members must be included. At that point the name was changed to the Society of Film and Tele-vision Arts, later to the British Academy of Film and Television Arts. We now give so many awards that in 1997 the decision was made which separated the presentations into two evenings, one for film, and the other for television.

In 1996 I was happy to be invited to an evening celebrating BAFTA's fiftieth anniversary in the presence of Her Majesty the Queen.

Only two of the founder chairmen survive—Tony Havelock-Allan and me.

· 12 ·

Take My Life

$\mathcal{I}$t had been a mistake to try to mold myself into someone who sits behind a desk with budgets and schedules. I disliked being a producer more by the day. Going back to being a cameraman was an alternative, but I felt this would be a retrograde step.

Tony understood how I felt and did something I will always remember with gratitude. He handed me a script, *Take My Life*, a Hitchcock-type thriller, written by novelist Winston Graham. "Why don't you consider directing it and I'll produce?"

As a partner within Cineguild, it was easy for me to make this exciting transition, though it had to be with the agreement of David, my other partner, and Arthur Rank.

The story is about an opera singer, Philippa Shelley, who is searching for proof that her husband is innocent of murdering his former girlfriend. In an attempt to cover-up a family quarrel, they have both given conflicting stories to the police about the night of the crime, resulting in the husband's arrest. The mystery is solved by a significant piece of music played by the killer (a composer) that only he could have known.

Since I had been a cameraman, part of the job was relatively simple. I knew about lenses and setups and how to plan the shooting of the various sequences, but dealing on a one-to-one basis with actors would be a new experience.

Tony and I cast the Norwegian actress Greta Gynt (onetime girlfriend of Filippo Del Giudice), a popular leading lady in the forties and Hugh Williams as her husband. Rosalie Crutchley played the murdered woman and Francis L. Sullivan, our portly Jaggers from *Great Expectations* was the prosecutor.

Three others familiar with Dickens joined us: John Bryan was the set designer, with his decorator, Wilfred Shingleton, and Guy Green, the cameraman.

Guy had a wonderful eye and the quiet patience to handle my occasional temperament. One of the things I liked about him was his wife Rita. More than once I teased him by saying if he hadn't married her and if I wasn't already married, I might have stepped forward. She was blonde, pretty, and tremendous fun, a complement to Guy in every way.

Rita was pregnant at this time, but they were becoming slightly worried because she was overdue. Naturally I told him about the specialist Beryl and I had gone to see in London. Having lost two children ourselves, perhaps I was being overprotective. He assured me they had a good doctor, and I'm certain he was right, so no more was said. However, even with the best care, sometimes life strikes a blow—Rita and the baby died in childbirth.

Ossie Morris was Guy's camera operator and he too was about to suffer a tragedy. His wife Connie had just given birth to a daughter, named Diana. He was having lunch with us one Sunday when the phone rang. Beryl answered it. After she hung up, she came back out to the garden and told Os he must go at once to the hospital. What she hadn't said was that a nurse had told her Diana was dead.

Ossie had recently been released from the Air Force, decorated with several medals for distinguished service. He is an extremely modest man, who never talks about his exceptional achievements during the war—he was in fact a war hero. After he'd completed his mandatory thirty bombing raids over Germany, he went on to fly VIPs across the world. Handling a bomber is, in some ways, similar to operating a camera. The latter isn't dangerous, but it requires steadiness and precision.

Ossie Morris: The Air Force didn't want to release me. They said I was too experienced. Ronnie got me out and Chris Challis out of the Navy. I had been very depressed about it and told Ronnie how I felt. He pulled strings somewhere. I don't know how he did it. There were four camera operators who started together at Pinewood in 1946: Challis, Ernie Steward, Skeets Kelly, and myself. Skeets had been a prisoner of war, but he'd been released by then.

The film came in on schedule and on budget without difficulty. There were some excellent and suspenseful moments, but I was somewhat disappointed with the overall pacing. I explained my problem to David, who said he'd take a look at it. By switching the order slightly and tightening up certain areas, he yet again demonstrated what a unique skill he had. It was a generous gesture on his part.

Take My Life—the first of twenty-five films I directed—received excellent reviews. "An exciting story made infinitely more plausible by the smooth narrative style of the director." It has to be admitted, critics tend to look kindly on first-time directors! Since then I've learned to handle bad reviews along with the good.

Anthony Havelock-Allan: My only criticism was that we had good stage actors who acted a bit too "stagey." Ronnie was obviously going to be a very good director, and it was this that was partly to blame for the differences between the three of us. David wasn't happy about it. He also didn't approve when I wanted to go off on my own to make *Blanche Fury*.

As my production was concluding, David decided to make *Oliver Twist*. He chose to stay with Dickens because he was attracted to the author's larger than life characters and the story's visual potential.

A dinner meeting to discuss the future of Cineguild was held at the White Tower. This venue had become a kind of club for film people just like the Ivy (Noël's favorite restaurant) was a club for theater people. Joining the three of us was a colleague, Stanley Haynes, who had worked on *One of Our Aircraft Is Missing* and had been the production manager on *Major Barbara*. He was an intelligent young man with a good-sized ego and an eye to the main chance.

It was decided to implement a new format for the company. As I was involved in the final postproduction stages of my film, Stanley would join us to work with David on the screenplay of *Oliver Twist*—it being understood that I'd make myself available to produce. Most filmmakers, having once started to direct, seldom want to do anything else, and I was no different. But I felt I owed this to David for the help he had given me in the cutting rooms.

Additionally it was agreed we could produce or direct independently of one another, but would all work as part of Cineguild and therefore under the Rank banner. We each felt happy with this arrangement.

As soon as word of the production got out, Alec Guinness contacted us expressing his desire to play Fagin. Quite out of the realm of possibility. He was much too young to portray the villainous old miser.

"Just give me a screen test," he implored, "and you'll see."

We did.

He worked with makeup artist Stuart Freeborn and together they created a face based on the drawings by George Cruikshank from the original edition of Dickens' novel. The result was magical. What a fantastic persona this man had created.

Alec Guinness: At first, I don't think Ronnie was keen on my playing the role, always having the impression he wanted someone older. The word

"Jew" was carefully obliterated from the script. And silly ideas were suggested. "Oh, couldn't he have a little snub nose?" This was absolutely ridiculous. I wouldn't have been able to play Fagin with another makeup. I did my best to do it in the way Dickens had pictured the character. Ronnie and David got a little scared of those sorts of things, and, in fact, it did cause some problems.

Casting young Oliver was simple. My childhood friend from Golders Green, Jack Davies, now an established screenwriter and critic, had a young son, John Howard Davies, who he thought would be perfect in the part. He was a fragile-looking, pale boy with curly blond hair and the most enormous, expressive eyes. But he was only eight years old, which could have presented legal difficulties. Youngsters under twelve were not allowed to participate in filmmaking, nevertheless we slightly ignored the rules because we had the approval of his parents. His mother, Dorothy, was with him the entire time and we hired a tutor to give him daily lessons. With the stricter regulations of today we wouldn't get away with it.

Oliver is caught in the grasp of two villains, Fagin and Bill Sikes. Casting Bob Newton in the latter role was a difficult decision. His acting abilities were never in question, but his alcoholism was!

One of the subsidiaries of the Rank Organisation was the Rank Charm School, an acting academy for teenagers. For the part of a young girl who feeds oysters to the Artful Dodger, they suggested a young woman who was gorgeous—and to say shapely is too small a word. I knew in two seconds Diana Mary Fluck was our Charlotte. Later she wisely changed her name to Diana Dors.

Anthony Newley, aged fourteen, was the Artful Dodger. And another exceptional contribution came from Kay Walsh as Nancy Sikes—although parted from David (who was by then living with someone else), she was still one of our regulars.

Nancy's murder was a particularly compelling sequence with Bill Sikes' bull terrier as the focal point. Nancy has freed Oliver. Sikes finds out and bludgeons her to death. We don't see the violence, we hear it. What we do see is the dog scratching at the door urgently trying to escape the madman's fury.

In order to get this gentle dog to seem desperate, a property man opened the door before the shot, letting the terrier see a stuffed cat. As action was called the door was shut and the property man made meowing sounds off screen. At which point the trainer released his animal who flew at the door, clawing his way towards his inanimate adversary.

Later, rather than sooner, the predictions about Bob Newton came to fruition. Many exteriors had already been shot on the back lot at Pinewood

in bitterly cold weather, and the moment had arrived for David to film Bill
Sikes' death. The villain, holding Oliver as a hostage on the roof of an East
End London house, falls and inadvertently manages to hang himself from the
chimneystack.

Guy Green: Bob, who had had "a couple" was up there with young
John Howard Davies. David was worried, "I'm afraid he's going to fall." So
we attached a rope to his belt and fed it through the tiles of the roof as a
safety wire in case he stumbled.

Fortunately he didn't, but there was still one more night to do on the
sequence. The next morning, he phoned and said he was ill and we'd have
to manage without him. On the previous night he'd been fine—other than
inebriated—so what had so rapidly happened? Then I suddenly remembered. Bob was anxious to leave England for a holiday.

"I don't believe you're ill," I told him, "but ill or not, you've got to
come to the studio at once where our doctor will examine you." He arrived
within the hour. His personal doctor had told him he was suffering from
pleurisy as a result of the extreme cold on the lot and another night of the
same might easily cause pneumonia.

Our doctor concurred. "On no account should this man go out in the
cold night air."

I let Bob go home and had the unpleasant task of informing David he'd
have to use a stunt double.

Twelve hours later, I received a telegram: Hope you had a good night's
work—stop—Off to France—stop—See you in two weeks—stop—Bob.

Robert Newton was clever enough to fool two doctors and the rest of
us, but he was finally hoist with his own petard. None of us ever hired him
again!

Normally it is the director who supervises music recording, but David
was in America when this was done. Therefore, as producer, I took over.

The composer was Arnold Bax, famous for being Master of the King's
Musick. Although he had written for the concert stage, it was his first time
composing for a movie. There was a scene in which we needed thirty-seven
seconds of music. When we rehearsed it, his section ran forty-five. I pointed
out the discrepancy. "Can't alter the music," he huffed. "You'll have to alter
the film." Needless to say, that didn't happen.

Another sequence, in fact the first in the film, takes place during a storm
as Oliver's mother, who is in labor, struggles towards a workhouse. A cutaway
to briars, with their spikes bending in the howling wind, visually emphasizes

her torturous pains and the music had to underscore her agony as well. But when we started this section it wasn't there.

I crossed over to Arnold, "What about the briar sound?"

A short pause. Then, "It completely slipped my mind."

Muir Mathieson, our conductor, had also forgotten.

"I need that music."

"Now? You want me to do it now?"

"Of course, now!" I replied. "We can't afford to call an orchestra of seventy-five again tomorrow!"

Grudgingly, he went with Muir over to the podium. I watched him as he jotted down some dots and squiggles.

"Try that," he said.

Muir handed it to a copyist and shortly the pages were given out to half-a-dozen musicians.

"All right," Muir said, tapping his baton and raising his arms for a downbeat. Out came this incredible musical pain. Arnold had created an extraordinary sound, which lasts only a few seconds of screen time. On command, he'd thought it up in an instant.

Nowadays, conductors of film music depend on a "click track" to maintain exact timing. Muir relied on an old-fashioned alarm clock with a sweep second hand, which allowed him to let the music flow, instead of being rigidly controlled. Miraculously he always finished the section bang on the cut.

As a matter of principle, he refused to conduct unless a British composer had written the score. Staunchly he supported musicians such as William Walton, Ralph Vaughan Williams, Malcolm Arnold, and William Alwyn. Many of us feel Muir was overlooked and should have been knighted as a champion of British music. He had my admiration and I am indebted to him for his work on eleven films with which I was associated.

American distribution for *Oliver Twist* was of special interest as we hoped it might gather the same accolades as *Great Expectations*. Rank's representative applied for the necessary Production Code Seal from the Motion Picture Association of America. However, immediately there was an objection to the portrayal of Fagin. In previews, several American Jewish organizations had condemned the character.

The New York film critics and Board of Rabbis complained to the extent that the opening, scheduled at Radio City Music Hall, was postponed. The film was accused of being anti-Semitic. We felt this was ridiculous! Dickens' created these two villains—the intelligent, shrewd, witty Jewish Fagin, and the blustering bully, gentile Bill Sikes. We should have been accused of being anti-gentile as well!

We sincerely meant no disrespect, but in retrospect, it was naïve of us to select *Oliver Twist* as a project for Cineguild considering the events that had recently engulfed the world.

It wasn't until years later that the film was finally released in the US. John Davis, who'd been furious with us for damaging Rank's chances to break into the American market, collaborated with distributors Eagle-Lion by allowing them to cutout the so-called, "offensive material"—which meant diminishing Alec's performance.

In spite of controversy abroad, the film was selected as the Royal Première in 1948. Queen Mary was in attendance, and kindly came to the assistance of young John Howard Davies when photographers shoved him back into the crowds. Taking him aside, she arranged her own pictures with him.

Passionate Friends

$\mathcal{B}$eryl and I sold our house in Chalfont St. Peter and purchased Mount Fidget, in Fulmer, only a mile from Pinewood Studios. This was the first time we had ever really splashed out. The house, which had four acres of cultivated garden and eight acres of woodland, was originally the stables of a grand manor.

Among those who joined us on Sunday afternoons were John and Janie Bryan, Johnnie and Mary Mills (who had sold their home in Denham and bought a house within a few hundred yards of ours), also Beryl's sister Pat and her family. Other regulars were Tony, Valerie, and Rex Harrison and his wife Lili Palmer.

Before we moved from Chalfont St. Peter, we adopted "Pots," a near Labrador, an enormous galloping animal that knocked things over with its big tail. As Christopher grew older, this wonderful character became his playmate. He was a bright dog and knew instinctively that it was his job to awaken Christopher in the morning and in the evening make sure he went to bed on time. Each weekday Pots walked with him the half a mile to and from the bus stop making certain Christopher got to school and back.

My mother and Curly came to stay with us from California. She seemed very proud of what I had achieved in life and getting to know her grandson also gave her a great deal of genuine happiness. One of the bright spots of the visit was when Curly, a highly proficient horseman, taught Christopher how to ride.

Around this time I met Eric Ambler. A household name as a novelist, he'd already seen several of his books filmed successfully, including *The Mask of Dimitrios* and *Journey into Fear*. While he continued to write a novel every other year, he also wrote scripts based on the work of other authors.

Eric's manners and vocabulary were impeccable and his conversation animated and bright—invariably he could turn an ordinary event that had happened to him into a fascinating anecdote.

We began discussing the possibility of making a film together, which frankly did not interest David or Stanley, who were too busy trying to find a subject of their own.

In my search for suitable material, from among the many books and plays I read, I found one that had promise, a love story written by H. G. Wells, called *The Passionate Friends*. It was a period piece, but could have happened at any time, and Eric felt he could easily bring it up-to-date.

Before starting any project, I had to get the okay from the Rank Organisation. Arthur liked the idea and, surprisingly, so did John Davies. They gave us the green light.

I got together with Eric every two or three days, at his lovely Regency house in Pelham Crescent, to discuss the development of the script. Then I'd leave him to write a sequence. When we next met he would often open the conversation with, "Try this for size," as he handed me several pages. Always believing it a good idea for a writer to hear his words, I would read the scene aloud.

Everything progressed well, and within seven weeks we had a first draft we felt we could show with confidence.

Eric, who had also become the film's producer, Beryl, and I went to check some possible locations in Italy, staying at the Villa d'Este where we thought we might use one of their terraces. Our suite had a luxurious sitting room with two bedrooms and a private patio overlooking Lake Como.

Although very expensive, the hotel rooms were paid for by Rank's overseas partners, leaving us to be responsible for any other costs. Because of postwar restrictions, we were only allowed to take fifty pounds each out of England and, even with the smuggled extra five-pound notes, hidden in my socks, we hardly had enough to pay our way.

In an attempt to economize, we walked down to the local village for bottles of beer and cheap brandy that we brought back to our suite surreptitiously in order to avoid paying corkage. A dozen or so empty bottles had been accumulated by the end of our enjoyable stay and had to be disposed of in an equally clandestine manner. While the wealthier guests were relishing a sumptuous dinner on the terrace below, and the orchestra was playing soft romantic music, we took the bottles from where they'd been hidden in a wardrobe, and one by one, tossed them into the lake.

It was a lovely, sunny day when we awoke on the last morning and took a final look at the magnificent view. What we saw caused us considerable consternation—the evidence of our deceit. Bobbing up and down in the water, directly adjacent to the terrace, were all our bottles. We pretended not to notice them.

Unfortunately, the terrace at the Villa d'Este was not as photogenic as we had hoped. It was on the shady side of the lake and would not allow us the sunny lighting the scene needed.

Back in England the casting got underway. Ann Todd was our choice for Mary, the heroine; she'd recently starred in *The Seventh Veil* and was a hot property. You can imagine our pleasure when almost immediately she responded, "I think it's a beautiful script and I would love to play in your film."

As her former lover, Steve, we thought of Marius Goring who had been such an asset as the murderer in *Take My Life*. He reacted with equal enthusiasm.

There was one other part of great importance, the older husband. We knew who we wanted, but were not too confident about getting him. Nevertheless a script went to Hollywood for Claude Rains to read. He was a fine actor who had starred on Broadway several times, and known to be very particular about what parts he would accept.

Eric and I were stunned by his quick response. The cable read: Would be delighted to join you—stop—When do you want me over there—stop—Regards Claude Rains.

Guy Green was to be the cameraman with Ossie Morris as his operator. And John Bryan was soon getting sets underway on two stages at Pinewood. Everything had fallen into place so smoothly it was quite remarkable.

David and Stanley, who had not yet found a subject for themselves, were surprised and a little irritated at the speed with which we had gotten things together. Could the tail be starting to wag the dog? they must have wondered. One day Stanley, perhaps a bit too casually, asked if he and David might read our script. Eric and I, still full of confidence, were more than pleased at their interest and delivered one to each.

It's important here to remember that Cineguild was linked to several other producing companies through Independent Producers, Ltd. So as there would be no conflict of interests, the board met once a month to discuss our various projects and therefore, out of courtesy, we sent a script to the chairman, George Archibald.

Writing what follows is painful to me. I would be happy if I could skip the whole horrendous episode. But unfortunately there have been so many conflicting versions of what was about to happen that I would like to put the record straight.

Two days after he'd received the script, Stanley Haynes telephoned from London.

"David and I have read your script."

"Oh good," I replied.

"Not so good. We both think that you and Eric are in trouble."

I couldn't believe it. Ann Todd, Marius Goring, Claude Rains—not to mention key members of the crew—had all been tremendously enthusiastic. How could this be?

"You mean you don't like it?"

"I'm afraid not. We should all get together immediately and discuss it." A short pause, then, "After all, it is a Cineguild production."

He booked the private room for that evening at the White Tower, which we sometimes used when holding important meetings. He asked George Archibald to join us. Eric and I drove to London together, unsure quite what had hit us, but certain it was something pretty heavy.

I don't know if the following chain of events was precipitated by David or Stanley, or both of them. All I do know is, it was the moment that began the downward turn of our friendship and of Cineguild. And I was heading into a storm, which would almost destroy me.

Already there, David, Stanley, and George were conferring with each other when Eric and I arrived. We ordered drinks. Scotches, large ones.

Stanley told us he would act as chairman and began immediately with, "Let's talk about *The Passionate Friends*. David and I think you have a very bad script and, if you go into production with it, you'll finish up with a very bad picture."

Eric went pale, but said nothing. I looked towards David. After all, Stanley Haynes represented just one opinion. He could be wrong. It was David who was the oracle. If David Lean thought a script was bad, it was bad.

"I agree with Stanley," he said. "It won't work as it is."

George didn't comment, but clearly he was very much influenced by their opinion. Here we were with sets being built, contracts with stars being exchanged, Claude Rains preparing to leave from America for England, a lot of money already spent and a script that was supposedly "no good."

The evening was a nightmare. Throughout my life, although I'm not very good at handling small problems, when something really catastrophic happens I can usually rise to the occasion. This was *the occasion*.

Stanley suggested a solution. I would continue preproduction, postponing principal photography for three weeks, while he and David, together with Eric, wrote a new screenplay, based on the book, at the same time taking into account their objections. This, claimed David, was a most generous gesture on Stanley's part. And Stanley complimented me on being so lucky as to have David's input.

Eric had been quiet throughout the evening, which was unusual. Under ordinary circumstances, he talked quite a lot. After the others had left I asked, "What do you really think?"

He was completely shattered, but said, "I'm afraid they're right."

I believe it was Dickens who wrote: "There is nothing easier than to destroy a man's confidence in himself. Nothing easier. And it is the work of the devil."

In retrospect, we should have suggested a meeting the next morning when we could have read the script together and dealt with the objections in a sensible way. It was an error to have given in so easily. Neither David nor Stanley ever gave us specifics. Were there sequences that needed attention? A scene that was on the slow side? A character who required more development?

Using the words "very bad" about a screenplay by someone as able as Eric Ambler was completely unjust.

The following day I phoned Arthur Rank to tell him David was helping with rewrites he thought essential. Although the delay would be costly, I asked if we could put the shooting date back. Uncle Arthur answered, "Do what you think is best Ronnie. I have confidence in you."

I continued preproduction, taking over Eric's producing responsibilities while he was working full-time on the script.

I told Ann Todd what had happened. At first she was upset. She had really liked the original script, but when told that David Lean would be one of those rewriting, she happily accepted the situation. Marius Goring was also cooperative. Claude Rains wasn't due to arrive until the second week of shooting, so for the moment, I said nothing to him.

Some ten days later, the first pages arrived. It was the same basic plot, but everything else was completely different. The storyline is about a married woman who, while waiting for her older husband to join her on holiday, runs into her former boyfriend. As was the case in *Brief Encounter*, she is torn between her sense of obligation and her heart.

Eric Ambler: You have to consider David and Stanley were in psychoanalysis. During our discussions they were going to their sessions every day. David didn't want a writer to work with him. He wanted an amanuensis like Stanley. He tried to work his analyst's observations into the film. It was painful to watch him trying to write even a step outline. He would stick out his tongue, frowning with intense concentration. Really he had physical difficulty. During *Passionate Friends* I resolved never again to produce. And knew I'd never make another picture with David Lean.

When I phoned David and Stanley in London, they told me to relax, that everything was going well, "Eric was coming through with good stuff."

Some of the sets, already constructed at great expense, were no longer needed for the new version. Instead, others, not budgeted, would have to be built. The extraordinary thing is that not once did any of my partners come to the studio. Had they done so, something might have been salvaged from the wreckage of the original sets. Conversely, I was never invited to a script conference.

The preparation of a motion picture is an exact science based entirely on the screenplay. Schedules, actors, contracts, wardrobe, sets, studio space, locations, and myriad other items are dependent upon it. And I didn't have one. Filming finally commenced with about forty pages of a story that, good or bad, bore practically no resemblance to the one we'd started with. We shot for a couple of days and then Ann started to play up out of an insecurity born of not knowing where her character was headed.

Guy Green: Ann Todd had a condescending trick. Instead of simply accepting Ronnie's direction, she'd ask, "Should I do it this way? Or should I do it that way?" She robbed Ronnie of his confidence. He found himself in an untenable situation.

Apart from my close friendship with John Bryan and the support of my wife, I was a lost soul. Guy and Ossie were also supportive, but they didn't know everything that was happening behind the scenes. There was no way I could have succeeded and by the end of the fourth day, it is no exaggeration to say I was contemplating suicide.

Stanley phoned saying that he, David, and Eric would like to see the rushes. Would I please have them sent to London. I did as requested.

The next day, he phoned again, "Ronnie, we must see you after shooting this evening and we would like you to come up to London. Let's say seven-thirty."

My mind is a blank as to where we met. I know I didn't have anything to eat. Every other detail is perfectly clear. My three colleagues decided the rushes fell far short of expectations and were unacceptable and something had to be done quickly. I didn't try to defend myself—there was no point.

"What do you suggest?"

"We've worked out a plan," said Stanley. "We will shut down production until the script is finished. Then we'll start up again with David as director. Eric will bow out as producer, taking only writing credit. And although, strictly speaking, I am David's producer, I will step away from this one and leave it with you."

Stanley then issued his *coup de grâce*, "You won't find it easy to direct again, will you?"

I was stunned. He was right. I would never direct again. I also knew David and I would never work together again.

Anthony Havelock-Allan: Throughout the dispute at the beginning of production, I was on Ronnie's side because Stanley was trying to undermine the whole process for his own benefit, and that's not a professional thing to do.

That Saturday, I went to see Uncle Arthur at his home in Reigate, and explained that not only had David felt it necessary to take over the writing, but was now taking over as director. Arthur could have been highly critical of me, thinking I'd let him down, but he wasn't. Our long friendship had been based on the premise that I had his complete trust and he knew I tried to live up to it and would never willingly let him down.

On Monday, my stomach in knots, I gave a speech to the full unit of forty. "I've spoken to my friend David Lean and he's going to take over the picture. I will be producing. And I can assure you of one thing, it's going to be a bloody marvelous production."

Now everyone knew what had happened, except Claude Rains.

His first words to me when I met him at the airport a few days later were, "I'm so glad to meet my director."

I hope I didn't shuffle my feet as I broke the news to him. For his part, he couldn't have been more gracious and understanding.

David then decided Marius was not right for the part of the former lover and that Trevor Howard was more suitable. Another change was made.

A happy release from the tension came when John Bryan and I took off for three days to Lake Annecy in central France where we hoped to find a location more suitable than the Villa d'Este. There was certainly an ideal sloping bank down to the water, but no hotel. John's genius moved into gear. Getting hold of a large sheet of glass (six feet by four feet), we positioned it between the lake and us. Then he painted his conception of the hotel and terrace on the surface of the glass, including tables with umbrellas and chairs. We took a photograph and on our return to England, showed it to David. "This is your terrace," we said. He was delighted.

When the unit arrived in France, it ran into the worst summer in years. Nothing but gray skies and rain.

Another location was situated on the slopes of Mont Blanc near Chamonix—more gray skies and rain there! The production fell behind schedule.

To make matters more complicated, David and Ann Todd began an affair, spending most of their time in David's suite, not minding about the weather, completely wrapped up in each other.

I thought he must have lost his mind. It was so unlike him to neglect his work. Film was everything to him. But apparently not so on this production. I received reports back in London from Norman Spencer saying that instead of being on the set when the sun came out, David was in a speedboat tooling around the lake with Ann. And Trevor, ever the gentleman, was becoming impatient. More than once, he gently reminded David, he was also part of the movie.

Rumors trickled down to Ann's husband, writer Nigel Tangye (who later divorced her), and once they reached the press, reporters and photographers started hounding David and Ann.

When the film was in postproduction, Tony and I agreed it was time to leave Cineguild. I'm sorry we all split up, but I don't think it could have worked out any other way. We'd reached a point where the contributions we could make didn't add up to what David wanted. He needed to go off in his own gifted direction. Also, after *Passionate Friends* (released in the U.S. as *One Woman's Story*), our relationship could never be the same.

He and Stanley wanted to buy Tony's and my shares in the company, but we decided to keep them with the proviso that if they were still working together after eighteen months, we would give them to them.

Anthony Havelock-Allan: I didn't like Stanley Haynes. I don't think anybody did. He certainly didn't stay around for long. As far as I know he didn't create anything except havoc. He was one of those people who was an automatic wrecker. Not stupid by any means, but his principal idea was always to insinuate himself into a situation and to do so in such a way that it always offended people. When I saw *Passionate Friends*, I thought it wasn't bad, but not all that good. I don't think David taking over added anything at all.

Just as Stanley Haynes had risen to power within Cineguild, John Davis had risen to power within Rank. The board of directors was told by the bank that the overdraft must be reduced by three million pounds over the next twelve months or they would be forced to put an end to the whole organization.

The bank also required John Davis to take full control. Arthur Rank stepped down. And Davis reduced the debt at the expense of those of us who were dedicated to film. The Golden Years were over!

Alexander Korda, Rank's biggest competitor, took advantage of this turn of events and immediately made offers to many now ex-Rank people, who might be useful to him, including David. Through Cineguild, he and Stanley worked together for Korda on *Madeleine*, starring his new wife, Ann Todd. Subsequently he asked David to direct *The Sound Barrier*. When it was suggested that Stanley Haynes should be the producer, Korda said, "I do not need a producer. I am the producer."

Stanley felt that he and David were partners and, without him, David should have refused the project. David didn't see it like that and walked away from Cineguild. Our company never made another film.

For four or five years, Stanley tried to put something together on his own, but each attempt failed. Finally, he committed suicide. Much later I heard he'd sent Kay Walsh a letter blaming his imminent death on David Lean.

· 14 ·

Crashing on Regardless

$\mathcal{M}$y hopes of a directing career ended with *The Passionate Friends*. At the next monthly meeting of Independent Producers I presented my position, explaining why I was dropping out of this arena. My colleagues attacked me for considering such a thought. They were adamant that it would be weak and stupid to allow one setback—albeit a big one—to put an end to my ambitions. I am particularly grateful to Frank Launder, Sidney Gilliat, Michael Powell, Emeric Pressburger, and Max Setton for helping me fight my way back.

John Mills: When *Passionate Friends* was taken away from Ronnie, I think a lesser man would have gone to the wall. It was such a shock to him, to his pride. And he survived it. People within the industry understood and were marvelous. They rallied round and supported him realizing that, even though his friend was a brilliant filmmaker, David Lean had done a bad thing. It's not a film he'll be remembered for.

Sasha Galperson, the convivial Russian gentleman I had met in New York, and I had continued our friendship. He'd heard about my circumstances and, determined to help me move forward, suggested we might do something together—he as producer with me directing. It transpired that he had a project in mind, *The Golden Salamander*, a novel by Victor Canning. It wasn't an important film, but if I was going to try my hand again, I wanted to do something sooner rather than later. I explained the idea to John Bryan, who, ever loyal, said he'd join me as set designer. This gave me the final piece of encouragement needed, and so, to use one of John's favorite expressions, I decided to "crash on regardless."

The center of the skullduggery in Canning's novel is a small town on the coast of North Africa about fifty miles west of Tunis. Going off on a recce, John and I flew to Tunis, then drove to a nasty little town named Tabarka. We arrived at night in pouring rain—never did a place look so unlikely for filmmaking.

However, the next morning the sun came out and everything appeared very differently, houses were silhouetted against a billowy-clouded sky. Beautiful, yet it wasn't right for the entire production.

Two days later we found Nabul, a dirty, unattractive place, but visually correct. We also picked Carthage, Ain Draham, and Tunis. Looking at these locations with John, *The Golden Salamander* began to come alive. A week later I was back in London working on the screenplay with Victor, and two months after that we were ready for casting.

The principal character in *The Golden Salamander* is an eighteen-year-old French girl. Acting on a tip-off, Sasha and I went to Paris, met and immediately hired the adorable Anouk Aimée, who had then appeared in only one film. She's a lovely actress with inner qualities perceivable by the camera. I believe she would have become an international star had she been able to speak better English.

Noël, also in Paris at the time, invited me to his flat and then on to his production of *Present Laughter* in French. I must have been the only one in the audience who understood what he was saying—he spoke the same British schoolboy version of the language as I did. Opposite him was Nadia Grey, a young, though well established, Rumanian actress, who could speak half a dozen languages fluently. For a brief moment, I considered using her instead of Anouk, but, in the end, the French girl's innocent quality was correct for our story.

It was with a certain amount of trepidation that I approached Trevor Howard to play the lead part. After the débâcle of *Passionate Friends*, I feared he might have lost faith in me. Gratefully this was not the case.

When Sasha and I met to discuss progress, I assured him we had found and secured the necessary locations, and then, jokingly mentioned, "It would be lovely to have my own car over there." He took me at my word and shipped my new black Triumph to Tunisia.

Many Arabs believe we come into this world three times and gain insight with each. A "third-lifer" exudes a wisdom that has nothing to do with culture, education, or class. He can be a peasant from a remote village in China, or a Bedouin sitting in the doorway of his mud hut in Africa. If you talk to him, even through an interpreter, you will soon recognize how many times he has been here. Without doubt, I'm a "first-lifer"—Noël a second—and Sasha Galperson, a definite third. He had that aura—if, unknown to each other, he and I were to enter a restaurant at the same time, he would get the best table while I'd get the one nearest the kitchen. Charming and with great presence, Sasha was a big man in every sense—yet gentle.

He stayed with us for the entire location period and, even in the extreme heat we experienced, he always wore a jacket and panama hat. Not that he was on the set all the time, he came if I needed him. Otherwise he was taking care of finances or doing some public relations chore with the local people.

Canning's plot deals with gunrunning. Anna (Anouk) and her brother, Max (Jacques Sernas), operate a small hotel and bar in Tabarka. David Redfern (Trevor Howard), while en route to the town, comes across a stranded truck loaded with guns. Because the vehicle is blocking the road, he has to get out of his car and walk three miles in pouring rain. When he reaches the hotel, he tells the patrons what he has seen. Rankl (Herbert Lom) is the villain who not only kills Anna's brother for knowing too much, but decides to kill David Redfern as well. Miles Malleson plays Douvet, the local gendarme.

Agno (Wilfrid Hyde White) assumed to be the bad guy is the resident piano player at the local motel. One of the catchy songs he performs is "Clopin Clopant," which we decided to use as the theme of the movie. The drama concludes with a surprise move—Wilfred steps forward to save Trevor.

By now I felt Ossie Morris was skilled enough to become a lighting cameraman and asked him if he'd like to do the film. He accepted, wondering if he was ready for the responsibility. "I was a cameraman," I reminded him. "I'll be behind you." He went on to become one of the best directors of photography in the industry, with an Oscar and many other honors to prove it, including an OBE (Officer of the Order of the British Empire).

Ossie is the kindest man I've ever had the pleasure of working with. He always seems to put other people's preferences before his own. There were occasions during the production when he thought he'd let me down, but the truth is I couldn't have managed without him. Beneath his soft-spoken, conscientious exterior lays an observant, highly logical and precise mind.

Ossie Morris: When Ronnie gave me *The Golden Salamander*, I thought, "I've got to do something that won't look like a chap's first film." Since it was a French story, I decided to copy that style of photography and got some special French filters. I also wanted to use the Mexican style on the exteriors with the very heavily corrected sky to give it a bit of class and quality as against the ordinary run-of-the-mill stuff. Johnnie Bryan called Ronnie from London. He said, "I've seen the rushes, Trevor doesn't seem to have any lips." On this picture, if anyone told Ronnie there was a problem, he'd collapse in a heap on the ground. It's hard to believe. He said, "Os, what have you done? What filter did you use?" I told him a 23A, a red one." "Take that bloody filter off and put on a number 16." From then on he insisted on seeing hand tests. I've got all the prints to this day.

An opening sequence takes place in a village square, it's market day and the area is jammed with Arab vendors. Of course they had to behave completely naturally as they went around selling their wares, but this was impossible once they'd spotted the camera.

Assistant director, Geoffrey Lambert, had recruited some Arabic-speaking French residents and used them to explain to the motley crowd what was required. Once everything was organized, I called "Action" through a loud hailer, but instead of getting on with their business as requested, they started fighting—they must have seen too many action films. It was absolute pandemonium until we finally made them understand.

All in all, it wasn't one of the easiest of places to shoot. Jim Hydes, the makeup artist, was kept busy in the hot weather, forever patching up streaked faces. And sand was an ongoing problem as it got into everything, including the camera, scratches on the negative were not unusual even though the assistant endlessly cleaned the gate.

Location fever is a common phrase in the business. Creative natures, insecurities, long periods away from home—those of us in the film world tend to stray. Trevor and Anouk began a relationship. So long as they both showed up and did their work, this was an advantage from my point of view. Their liaison is often apparent on the screen, which in this case, helped the story. Fortunately, Trevor's marriage to actress Helen Cherry remained intact until his death.

Freddie Francis was Ossie's operator, but before filming in North Africa was completed, he decided to leave and go back to England. Quitting in the middle of production is unacceptable and I recall saying to him, "It's unprofessional. If you do this, you and I will never work together again."

Freddie Francis: Micky Powell rang and asked if I'd do his next film, *Gone to Earth* with Jennifer Jones. It was very naughty of me, but I left Ronnie. We shouted at each other. He told me I was doing the wrong thing. He was right, but I was so besotted with Micky. Ronnie and I finished on bad terms and didn't meet again for years. When we did, he was charming to me, as if the incident had never happened. But he was true to his word. I never did work for him again. Today I consider him a dear friend; he is a founder member of the British Society of Cinematographers. His services to our industry have been even greater than his many wonderful film credits. During the war, together with Anthony Havelock-Allan, David Lean, and Noël Coward, the four of them elevated the British film industry to a new and higher level.

Ever since the formation of Cineguild we had used the same proficient costume designer, Maggie Furse, whose creations on both *Great Expectations* and *Oliver Twist* were exceptional. The requirements for *The Golden Salamander* were less demanding and Maggie's particular talents would have been overkill, so we engaged her pretty assistant Liz Hennings. Liz was a princess, the daughter of the King and Queen of a group of islands in the Pacific.

There were some areas in Tunis that were visually spectacular. On our day off, Liz and I took a drive to the seashore. I talked to the hotel manager who prepared a superior picnic lunch. We drove my specially imported car up into the hills that overlooked a truly blue Mediterranean. There we spotted a small-unmade road that we hoped might lead down to the beach. It took a good twenty minutes to negotiate the rocks, boulders, and potholes; then suddenly, after a particularly bumpy two minutes down an escarpment, we emerged onto a flat sandy area within yards of the sea. There in front of us was what I can only describe as a picture book miniature Blue Lagoon. It was enchanting, made even more so by the fact that no other task was demanded except to listen to the sound of the sea lapping against the rocks. Walking down to the water's edge, we laid out the picnic, feasting on *fois gras*, smoked salmon, cracked crab, and *Montrachet*. It wasn't until the sun was low on the horizon that once again we negotiated that boulder-strewn road and reluctantly came back to earth.

We were fortunate to have Cornel Lucas as our stills cameraman—an important photographer within the Rank Organisation (they were planning to build him a portrait studio of his own at Pinewood). When he joined us on location, he was the last man you'd expect to get into any kind of trouble, but he did.

Cornel Lucas: I had to do some pictures of Miles Malleson, who played a policeman, and I said, "Instead of shooting you on set, why don't we go and find a police station and photograph your character in his true environment." He and I and my assistant Gavin found one five miles away. There was a man on guard with a gun and a sergeant with him. They both left us alone in the room, while they went off to see if they could get us permission to photograph. I started opening files and putting documents on the table, getting into things I shouldn't have. I said to Gavin, "Now's our opportunity." As I was putting my equipment away, the sergeant caught us. We were placed under arrest and the police department called a strike on the picture. With all the policemen off the set, Ronnie was unable to shoot for the rest of the day. Later he asked me, "How could you do this?" I said I was sorry, but we got some very good pictures.

Bob McNaught was our production manager, a fun-loving Scot. We had worked together before, and I used to call him our "mean man." Every film has to have one, the person who watches the pennies closely and who strives to keep on budget. However, he must also be wise and be prepared to adjust the price of the items in that budget, either up or down to suit the problems of the moment.

Sometimes Bob went a little too far. When we were looking for locations, we often stopped at a local restaurant for lunch. There were usually about eight of us on these recces. After lunch one day, he inquired, "Ronnie are you planning to come back here again?"

"No."

"Then I won't leave a tip."

For another scene between Anouk and Trevor we needed a very large fish squirming on the end of a line so violently that it nearly pulls the two actors into the water. Bob found us such a fish, but before the scene started, it had died. He tried with two more with the same result.

I was far too tough on him about this and he walked off the set. Not long after, one of the unit truck drivers returned from a trip to town announcing, "I've just seen Bob walking towards Tunis."

Feeling he had failed, he had gotten himself into such a state that he'd set out on foot for a hundred mile trek! I drove down the road and found him and apologized for my irritability. Eventually a fish was caught and lived long enough for us to complete the scene.

It's interesting how location units tend to split up into cliques. Makeup artists and hairdressers become chummy; the camera crew becomes a little group, the electricians and prop men another. But everyone becomes a family with the director tending to be a father figure. In the case of Sasha he became a favorite uncle.

Having so many friends on this production was not only pleasurable but helped me regain confidence. *The Passionate Friends* began to fade into the background.

The Golden Salamander was intended to be a modest first production with Sasha and we were both convinced we'd make many more together. In him, I had found a new partner. But three months before we had started shooting, he had undergone a serious operation for stomach cancer and a few weeks after completing principal photography, he became gravely ill again, returning to hospital in London. I visited him every day, giving him news of editing and keeping him up-to-date generally.

He was an intelligent man, who must have realized his condition was terminal, yet he spoke with enthusiasm about the future. I asked his doctor about this.

"How can Sasha not know the real situation?"

He explained that a defensive shutter comes down. Part of his brain knew death was imminent; the other remained optimistic. Just as the music recording sessions were finished, I was told Sasha had died.

I miss that lovely man, my friend, the "third-lifer." In the ordinary way the last credit on the screen goes to the director, but on *The Golden Salamander*, I gave him the acknowledgement. It was a personal way of showing my respect.

The film reviews were encouraging—one British critic stated, "Neame's Lizard is a Wizard."

The Golden Salamander was the last film under the old Rank banner. After postproduction, I left my splendid office at Pinewood and rented a small one in Hanover Square, London.

John Davis was in the process of reducing Rank's three million pound overdraft. He shut down all film production, which in itself meant immediate and substantial savings of hard cash. First came the dumping of studio and production personnel, followed by closing a number of the less successful theaters and selling the real estate on which they stood. Some he turned into bingo halls within a year. These transactions, coupled with other savings, made it possible for him to satisfy the bank. The Rank Organisation was allowed to stay in business.

I know now that what happened was inevitable and clearly John Davis was the right person for the job. I think we had become too complacent and overconfident. We thought Uncle Arthur would go on laying his golden eggs forever. Despite the optimistic promises from his various overseas partners, our films did not do well outside the United Kingdom. American film audiences didn't want British films.

Ironically, a few years later, because of the enormous demand for American television product, they were heavily distributed in this market. The door Arthur Rank had spent millions trying to unlock opened by itself.

· *15* ·

The Magic Box

$\mathcal{R}$oy and John Boulting were identical twins, so much so that it was impossible to tell them apart, except one wore glasses. In order to fool people they'd switch glasses brother to brother, deriving a great deal of fun out of deliberately confusing everyone.

As a producer-writer-director team, they always worked together, so I was surprised one day when John—I could only assume it was John because he said so—came to my modest office and asked if I would produce a film he was about to direct.

"What about Roy?"

"Roy's working on something else called *High Treason*," he replied, "the picture I want to make has to go into production immediately so as to be ready in time for the 1951 Festival of Britain."

It was to be based on a biography, *Close-Up of an Inventor* by Ray Allister, the life of the man whom we British claim to be the unheralded inventor of the moving picture with his magic box—William Friese-Greene. Especially as there was as yet no screenplay, Boulting felt I could be helpful since I'd worked for a long time with his son and still knew the family whose cooperation would surely be needed.

There were, in fact, many stories about William Friese-Greene that had remained in my memory and could be of interest. Friese (Claude) once told me about the desperate straits in which his father often found himself and the equally desperate measures he took to counter these situations. For instance, when his sons went to school by train, he instructed them to wait until it slowed to a crawl as it approached the station and then quickly jump off, run across the fields, thereby avoiding the fare!

Although working on *The Magic Box* held little financial reward, as it was to be an altruistic contribution from the British film industry to the Festival, I

131

accepted the offer. The Scottish head of Associated British Picture Corporation at Elstree, Robert Clark, advanced us both five thousand pounds to keep us going and each week he deducted a portion of that from our pay. Starting work at once, we were given tremendous support from all branches of our industry.

Despite the horror of *Passionate Friends*, I had remained close to Eric Ambler, and John and I felt with his experience he would be our first choice to write the screenplay. Eric, bless him, put aside an uncompleted novel and quickly got going.

There were three main actors in the film to whom we would pay the minimum union rate—the impeccable Robert Donat with his melodious voice as Friese-Greene—Maria Schell as his first wife—and Margaret Johnston as his long-suffering second wife.

Beyond that, the plan was to cast as many stars in cameo roles as possible. It fell to Eric to write characters that would, hopefully, be attractive to important actors. Most were enthusiastic and cooperative in the knowledge that the film was to form part of an important national festival.

We particularly wanted Laurence Olivier. "And needed him to work for practically nothing," I told his agent Laurence Evans, "25 guineas a day."

We handed over the script with the offer of any cameo Larry might like to play. His response was that he rather liked the idea of Police Constable 94B. It was clever of him—the scene he chose was pivotal to the story and was actually the most important in the film.

Friese-Greene has been working through the night in his laboratory and has just completed processing the very first motion picture footage, which he'd photographed earlier that day in Hyde Park. Terribly excited by his achievement, he runs out of his house to tell someone, forgetting it is three in the morning. The only person in the street is a policeman on his beat.

"Come and see! I've something to show you! Something I've done. You must come and see!"

Constable 94B becomes suspicious. "Something you've done?"

He reluctantly follows an excited Friese-Greene into the house and up the stairs to his workshop "Where is it? What you've done?"

Friese-Greene turns out the lights. By now the officer is sure he has a madman on his hands. Suddenly the illuminated wall comes alive. Inadvertently, the policeman becomes the sole audience for the first moving pictures.

When Larry signed, the trade papers ran the story, "Olivier Joins Cast of *Magic Box*." From then on everything and everyone fell into place. Agents started calling us to ask why their most important clients weren't in the film.

By the time the campaign finished we had fifty of the best names in British cinema including Richard Attenborough, Marius Goring, Glynis Johns, Bernard Miles, Michael Redgrave, Margaret Rutherford, Sybil Thorndike, Peter Ustinov, Kay Walsh, and Googie Withers. Predictably, there was only actor who turned us down—Alec Guinness.

Many of my friends participated in this production; director of photography Jack Cardiff; production manager Bob McNaught, John Bryan, and Muir Matheson was our musical director.

Jack Cardiff: I think it was Ronnie who wanted me. It was a high prestige picture and an honor to be invited. Everybody wanted to be on it. They asked the unit to accept either half salary or less than their full salary. But there was not a family feeling on *The Magic Box* because the actors would only be there for a day or two, and then be gone, and we'd be on to someone else.

Queen Elizabeth, later the Queen Mother, visited the set with her daughter Princess Margaret and I had the pleasure of showing them a model of the first motion picture camera.

Donat brought warmth and heart to his portrayal. But he had carried a heavy burden throughout his life. Chronic asthma. He'd be fine between assignments but the moment he started work, attacks of this wretched disease would lay him low. We installed ozone machines on the set to help keep the air clean though they were of little use. It was heartbreaking to see him struggling to breath.

A poignant moment came during the shooting of a scene he had with Michael Redgrave. Boulting rehearsed them and called for a take. Donat fluffed his lines, and each time he tried again, he struggled more for breath. Redgrave approached Boulting with a suggestion. "I might alleviate Robert's anxiety if I start fluffing my lines as well." It worked. The more Redgrave stumbled, the more Robert Donat helped him—and himself.

The last scene in which the broken and poverty-stricken inventor appeals for unity at a public meeting, before collapsing and dying, is both moving and prophetic. Robert Donat himself died much too young at the age of 53.

The Magic Box was delivered just in time to be screened at the Festival on September 18, 1951 and received good notices.

Afterwards John Boulting presented John Bryan and me with a parting gift each, a long cardboard box. Inside were beautiful long-stemmed flowers. Beneath them was a shiny, black Winchester rifle! We were both baffled by the present. Was it his sense of humor or did he want us to shoot one another?

· 16 ·

The Card

*J*ohn Davis, realizing he would have to make a few films to protect Rank theaters from being completely dominated by Hollywood product, engaged an American gentleman with the rather grand name of Earl St. John to take charge of production. One day Earl asked me to lunch and suggested I might like my old offices back at Pinewood. This was an unexpected opportunity, fitting in well with plans I'd already put in motion.

While working on *The Magic Box* I had taken a look around the extensive library at Elstree in the knowledge that there were many properties the studio had purchased over the years, but never produced. *The Card*, a novel by Arnold Bennett, is a comedy about the son of a washerwoman who cons his way into becoming mayor of the town. With the right actor playing Denry Machin, it would be a great project.

Robert Clark sold me a six-month option and I immediately turned again to Eric Ambler. He loved the book and said he'd be happy to write the script. So while I was still working with Boulting, I began preproduction on my next film.

I had a chat with John Bryan.

"How would you like to become a producer?" I inquired.

"Very much," was his response.

As it transpires this was one of the smartest suggestions I ever made in my life. Although often working independently, we became a producer-director team that lasted many successful years. I owe so much to John. His brilliance as a designer and, as it turned out, his ability as a producer did more to help me than anything else in my career.

Predictably, Eric came up with a first-rate script, one in which we both had sufficient faith not to seek other peoples' opinions! A few weeks later John and I were happily back at Pinewood with a newly formed production

134

company—and, once more, fully funded by Rank. It was exhilarating to find I could get just about every member of my old crew back again—including Ossie Morris and Bob McNaught.

The story describes Denry, the Card, as "the cheekiest man in town" and there was only one actor for him—Alec Guinness! Alec said "Yes."

Denry has four ladies in his life: his mother (Veronica Turleigh); a washerwoman, who always manages to outsmart him; his gold-digging girlfriend (Glynis Johns), who tries and almost manages to outcon him; the gentle, pretty young girl who adores him (Petula Clark); and the Countess of Chell (Valerie Hobson), the lady who helps him become rich.

Working with Valerie was like working with family. Through Tony Havelock-Allan, I'd gotten to know her quite well, a great lady, full of charm, and kindness and never temperamental. She and Tony made the ideal, real-life romantic couple, often repeating their vows in the same church where they married.

The Card went into production in 1952, shooting first in the studio with the location work left until the end of the schedule. This was in an area of central England known as the Five Towns—Longton, Fenton, Hanley, Burslem, and Tunstall, which in 1910 combined into Stoke-on-Trent.

They were dedicated to the manufacture of pottery—Wedgwood, Doulton, and Spode and therefore were collectively known as "The Potteries." The Five Towns local slang name was "The Smoke," justifiably so because, until the early 1940s, hundreds of enormous factory chimneys belched out dirty black soot that spread out across the countryside.

By the time we arrived, the Five Towns had been cleared of pollution but, since the film was a period piece, we needed the smoke back! On cue, twelve property men with large smoke canisters and walkie-talkies filled every chimney in sight with our disgusting, black, sulphur-smelling special effects. The locals thought we were crazy and perhaps we were, but we made the Five Towns look exactly as they did in 1905.

Some people in one's life seem destined to reappear continually. Such is the case for me with Glynis Johns. I had photographed her when she was fourteen and her costar Roddy McDowall was only eight. It was a "quota quickie" called *Murder in the Family* directed by an American—fierce-tempered, heart-of-gold, Al Parker.

Now I was directing her in *The Card*, and although we haven't been associated since then professionally, we have remained good friends over the sixty or so years that have leapt by. There was, however, an episode that occurred during the first week of production that momentarily strained our relationship.

Denry is a rent collector and Ruth Earp a dancing teacher, who, when he arrives at her house, is at the piano teaching nonexistent students. She doesn't have the money to pay the rent and tries to avoid the subject by flirting with him, at the same time giving him a detailed sob story.

The bulk of the scene—a long one with well over three minutes of dialogue—takes place in her parlor with both of them sitting on a sofa. I didn't want the scene to become static, so suggested to Glynis that on a certain line she should get up and go over to the mantelpiece to fetch a small box she will give to Alec.

Glynis asked, "Why can't the box be here on the table beside the sofa? Then I won't have to get up."

"Because I need the movement."

She and Alec decided to gang up.

"I'm quite comfortable here," she said. "I'd rather remain seated. Are you comfortable, Alec?"

"I'm quite comfortable," he answered.

There were a few seconds of heavy silence.

I reiterated the reason.

She was not pleased, but we chose a line and began to rehearse. She rose, but, because she was irritated, she got up abruptly, causing the camera to jolt in order to keep her in frame.

"Glynis, when you rise would you remember the camera is following you and get up a little more smoothly."

She got even more irritated. "I don't know what you mean. I always get up like this. How else would I get up?"

Now it was my turn to be irritated. "You know as well as I do how to get up to suit the camera, but since you seem to have forgotten, I will show you."

I took her place on the sofa, rose just as quickly as she had, but knowing the camera was following me, I moved smoothly, thereby removing the unfortunate jolt.

We continued to rehearse, but you could have cut the atmosphere with a knife. Alec said nothing, but I knew whose side he was on, and it wasn't mine.

We broke early for lunch in the hope that after we'd eaten, things would settle down. Alas, not so. During coffee, someone presented me with an envelope. Inside was a handwritten note:

Dear Ronnie,

If you think you can get a good performance out of me by insulting me in front of the entire unit, you are making a big mistake.

Glynis

I knew I had to do something, but what? I went to see Alec in his dressing room and asked him to be a little supportive of what I knew to be correct for the scene. He said, "I didn't know I hadn't been supportive."

Then over to see Glynis, telling her how much I wanted us to work together in harmony, and that if I'd insulted her it was certainly not intended. When we all met again on the set, it was as though nothing had happened. She rose from the chair perfectly and for the rest of the film there was no problem. The thing is, after half a century, she still thinks I was wrong.

Glynis Johns: I had not thought about the incident until Ronnie mentioned it again. It had been something that stayed in his mind. I don't think he was as comfortable directing me, as a female, as he was with Alec. Maybe he was over-protective about his directorial strengths. It was still early in his career. Maybe I was "Miss Know-It-All," who was covering up a scream of nerves, making certain no one was going to stop my talent coming through. It caused the wrong atmosphere between us. He was hurt. So was I. But it certainly was just one small incident quickly healed. And it has never affected our lifetime of mutual affection.

Through the years I have learned sometimes painfully, that actors have to test the strength of their director. I'm not certain whether it's out of a sense of insecurity or out of a need to challenge authority. To maintain control, a director must on occasion assert that authority. He must be certain about what he wants, but he must also be flexible and receptive to anything that will improve a scene. The tricky part is where to draw the line between being receptive and being weak. In *The Card*, there is a perfect example of being receptive.

Denry returns home with a hatbox filled with golden sovereigns to give to his mother. Obviously I had planned the way the scene would be shot and explained to Alec a suggested routine.

He said, "Ronnie, I thought I'd rather like to play this scene lying on the floor underneath that table over there."

I knew he was too bright not to have a good reason for what he was saying but how on earth could he possibly be lying on the floor?

"It's very simple," he said somewhat patronizingly. "I bring the hatbox to my mother and put it on her lap. When she opens it and sees all that money she screams, accidentally tipping the box over and spilling the coins. Instead of talking to her standing up, I will crawl around the floor retrieving the money."

I realized immediately this would take the weight off the lines as well as give us some unusual setups. Quite brilliant! In that instance I was extremely flexible and changed what I'd already mapped out.

Now a well-known singer and actress, Petula Clark was then still very young. While on location in "The Potteries," she had a birthday and the unit arranged a party for her. Just as she was about to cut the cake, she burst into tears.

"What on earth's the matter, Pet?" I asked.

"I'm getting so old!" she sobbed with aching heart. "I'm eighteen!"

Petula Clark: Ronnie got a lot out of a performer by being gentle. He is one of the kindest people I have ever met. Alec was shy, and when we had to kiss each other, I don't think the earth moved for either of us. I remember J. Arthur Rank visiting the set, a very tall, very severe looking man. I was slightly terrified of him, but not of Ronnie.

William Alwyn's score was absolutely fitting and unusually arranged for the opening titles, a jaunty tune whistled. I was the whistler, my first and only time as a musician.

When the finished picture was delivered, the public relations department contacted Guinness, the famous brewers. Together they arranged an advertising campaign executed by their art department, an enormous poster of Alec in his Denry Machin costume, boater hat, bow tie, and striped jacket. These were placed all around the country with the tag line: "Guinness is good for you in *The Card*."

This was my first directorial attempt at comedy, the most difficult kind of filmmaking. With a play, things can be tried out on an audience out of town and, if necessary, changes can be made in advance of the official opening night. A film is a finished article before an audience sees it.

The first public showing of *The Card* was at the Rank Odeon in Hammersmith. John Bryan and I were so nervous we couldn't pluck up the courage to go into the theater. Instead, we went to a pub across the road and fortified ourselves. Then we faced the ordeal.

As we walked into the foyer we heard laughter—as we climbed the stairs to the circle we heard more laughter—as we found our seats we were engulfed in a lovely, warm blanket of laughter. The audience was thoroughly enjoying itself. To everyone else it was laughter—to John and me it was a symphony orchestra. Clearly we had a success.

Exactly forty years after the première, I received an invitation from the British Film Institute to introduce my film at a special screening for the London Film Festival. And everyone still alive, who had been associated with the production, was invited to come along to the National Film Theater. Since Alec rarely attended any sort of public gathering, I was amazed when he accepted. One condition, he didn't wish to be introduced to the audience—just be there incognito, to see the picture and quietly to say hello to colleagues.

Usually when I speak at these occasions, I am relaxed, but not so that evening. I gave a short, somewhat inadequate speech. Perhaps I was anxious in case the film did not hold up. Perhaps I was too aware that Alec was in the audience. For whatever reason, I was visibly nervous. My voice and hands trembled.

The British Film Institute had an excellent print. The film went well. And judging by the audience response, it did hold up. After the screening, I received the ultimate compliment. Concealed under a hat, Alec slid up to me and smiled.

Alec Guinness: I hadn't seen *The Card* for years and years. At the time it was made I thought, "Oh, it's all right." But seeing it some years later in London I thought, "It's a jolly nice film, full of life and liveliness and very well directed."

In 1952, at the age of forty, with John and Ossie's help, and my family by my side, I felt I had finally arrived.

· 17 ·

The Million Pound Note

"*You* don't have to have money to be a success, you merely have to appear to have money," says one elderly gentleman to his brother.

"Nonsense," replies the latter, "you've got to have the money or you have nothing."

They decide to put it to the test and make a wager on the outcome.

This was the premise of the Mark Twain short story John Bryan and I made next. And riding high on the success of *The Card*, we remained with the Rank Organisation at Pinewood.

While attending a board meeting of the British Film Academy I was introduced to our future screenwriter, Jill Craigie. She was one of a handful of female film directors in England—her credits, in the documentary field, included the well-received *Out of Chaos*, *The Way We Live*, and *Blue Scar*.

Jill's husband, Michael Foot, was leader of England's Labour Party in the early 1980s. He was an extraordinary mixture, able to stand up in the House of Commons and argue in debate like a demagogue in flames, and yet on a personal basis retiring, a modest academic who liked nothing better than delving into books.

Their home in St. John's Wood was filled with tomes and works of art, some of which Jill had gathered from artists she had filmed. Rightly she was rather proud of this collection—in particular the original drawings for the stained glass windows of the rebuilt Coventry Cathedral by John Piper. A strikingly attractive woman, she had great energy over political matters although was not as left wing as her husband.

When we met for a coffee some time after the Academy meeting Jill told me she wanted to write features and voiced an interest in our project. We decided to let her have a go.

In the story, the elderly brothers go to the Bank of England and withdraw an extremely rare million pound note. Then standing on the front balcony of their home in London's Belgrave Square, they randomly pick the scruffiest looking man on the street—an American seaman called Henry Adams, who, temporarily down on his luck, is stranded in London. They invite him in and tell him their proposition—if he returns the contents of their envelope intact after one month he will be handsomely rewarded. A period piece taking place in the early 1900s, the whole thing relied on this one idea and consequently needed expansion.

Jill's forte, as it fortunately turned out, was inventing characters and devising situations. Opening up takes more creativity than trimming down a sprawling Dickens-like novel and requires a great deal of imagination. Her input gave *The Million Pound Note* an extra spark and added the all-important conflict to the situation.

During the Golden Years we didn't care about star names, we cast those we thought would play the part the best, but in order to strengthen box-office returns the film world had to change. To this end, John Davis would only sanction a project if a name was involved and if the celebrity was American all the better.

John Bryan and I thought Gregory Peck would be great as our millionaire, even though we didn't reckon we could possibly get him. Here was an actor at the height of his career, having recently starred in *Captain Horatio Hornblower* and *Roman Holiday*.

His agent told us Peck was in France. He agreed to read the script, and, to our delight, liked it, so we immediately flew to Paris and joined him for lunch in the Bois de Boulogne.

It was soon apparent that Greg was a gentle man, thoughtful and attentive—someone who thinks about his reply before he speaks. He'd heard about us and our work with Cineguild and by the end of the meal he'd agreed to accept the film. We realized this might have had something to do with his desire to remain in Europe since recently he had become involved with a French journalist, Veronique Passani, who, before long, became his wife.

But we still had to find a way to afford an actor of his stature.

John Davis approached Arthur Krim at United Artists in New York, and persuaded him to meet Peck's salary in exchange for the American distribution rights—a helpful gesture.

Once we had signed Greg, we assembled a fine supporting cast: Ronald Squire and Wilfrid Hyde-White, as the two brothers; A. E. Matthews as the roguish Duke of Frognell and the wonderful Reginald Beckwith as the mute weightlifter *cum* valet created entirely by Jill. The only difficulty we had was finding the right leading actress. In the end, we settled on Jane Griffiths as Portia.

"Mean Man" Bob McNaught became associate producer, while another producer was old chum E. M. Smedley-Aston, "Smed" from the Elstree days. Maggie Furse was again costume designer and Clive Donner was the editor.

Clive is spry, artistic, easy to work with, and has a good sense of style and humor. He is often outspoken and since he felt exactly as I did about many things, there was a good frame of reference for our friendship. Perhaps somewhat eccentric, his flat in London is directly across from a bird sanctuary and he is an avid bird-watcher.

Each film made me more aware of John Bryan as an ally and as a producer. Some producers are frustrated directors, looking over the shoulder of the man doing the job. John made it apparent all he wanted—apart from trying to keep reasonably on schedule—was to supply me with what was needed to make the best possible film. Today when you see the title produced and directed by the same person, there is almost always a strong line producer in the background, rarely getting fair recognition.

Before filming, Jill and I went through the script with Greg who made a few suggestions he felt would help his character. We agreed he should play the part straight, never reaching for laughs, allowing the situations to carry the humor.

One of the early scenes, shot in Belgrave Square, sees Henry Adams sitting on a doorstep opening the envelope he has been given by the brothers. Suddenly the wind snatches the enclosed million pound note away. Adams chases after it, but every time he nearly catches it, the note flutters on.

John choreographed this scene, climbing aboard the camera truck and clutching a fishing rod with the note attached to an ultra fine, invisible line. His hand movements as well as a natural breeze controlled it as it darted this way and that out of Greg's grasp.

Eventually recapturing it, Henry decides the first thing he'll do is have a good meal. He goes into a nearby restaurant where the manager, seeing how badly dressed he is, reluctantly shows him to an inferior table. Once satiated, he apologizes by saying he only has a large bill that he doubts the restaurant can change. With sarcasm he is told the establishment can deal with any size of currency. Handing over the million pound note, he watches the manager's eyes grow gigantic as his whole manner completely changes. His new customer is told not to worry about payment—he's welcome back with his friends anytime. He practically embraces Henry as he escorts him to the door.

The theme repeats.

Henry, deciding he should look more presentable, enters a Savile Row tailor's shop but is immediately snubbed by the chief salesman, who hands him over to a junior assistant. This young man, played by Bryan Forbes, starts to take measurements. Henry informs him that he only has a rather large note with which to pay. The assistant says, "What makes you think we can't change a large one?" Adams hands over the million pounds. At which point it seemed right to have some fun improvising the young tailor's reaction.

Bryan Forbes: Ronnie wanted everybody to do something different, asking each actor to have a spontaneous reaction to the sight of a million pound note. He asked me, " What can you do?" I said, "How about if I burst into tears?" He said, "Fine, let's try it."

We were fortunate enough to have Cornie Lucas again as our stillsman. Given our experience on *Golden Salamander*, I made him promise that for the duration of the production, he would stay out of jail.

Cornel Lucas: Gregory has a heart of gold. I had a propman who used to bring him his morning tea and years later when my mate was in King George's hospital with cancer, I was moved to hear that Peck had gone to visit him after so many years. The million pound note they used in the film is still in my possession. So if my bank manager ever says, "I'm afraid you're overdrawn, I can present it to him and say, "Cash it!" That'll shock him.

I. E. "Matty" Matthews was eighty-three years old and dressed in clothes that had been bespoke decades before. I'd put my foot in it with Margaret Rutherford during *Blithe Spirit*, asking her where she had found her wonderfully peculiar clothes. Matty responded in his turn to this second gaff with, "From my own wardrobe, dear boy."

He was as bright as a button right up to eleven A.M. After that, he went blank not knowing what film he was in, what character he was playing, or anything else about the production. It was as if a switch had been turned off. To accommodate him, I would schedule his scenes for first thing in the morning. What motivated these old characters, I don't know, but they never failed in their brightness of personality. Ronald Squire, cast as Oliver Montpelier, told me one day, "When I wake up each morning, I read the obituaries in the *Times*. If I'm not there, I know I have to go to work."

Predictably, the film has a happy ending. Not only does Henry Adams return to the brothers with their note intact, but also he has a pretty girl on his arm, and his pockets are full of his own money made on the stock exchange. "Does he have money or does he just seem to have money?" The two elderly brothers are left wondering.

Once filming was completed I contacted Christopher Mann and told him my aspirations were to remain a director and that I wanted him to be my agent—reminding him that any future contract would be sealed with a handshake! He was to remain my agent throughout much of my career.

The instant we were back together he told me he'd spoken with his partners at the William Morris Agency in Hollywood and MGM was interested in talking to me about a Spencer Tracy project.

I called John Bryan and told him about the possibility of an offer. We were tentatively developing another movie with Greg entitled *The Purple Plain*—however if I agreed to the MGM picture that would mean I couldn't stay on with him. We'd always spoken about the possibility of working independently before forming our partnership, but on the understanding that we'd try to make films together. John unselfishly encouraged me to go ahead.

Arrangements were made for me to attend press screenings of *The Million Pound Note* in New York when en route to Hollywood. And once again, I sailed on the *Queen Elizabeth*. The change in her appearance was extraordinary; no longer did she house troops and German prisoners of war, she was restored to her former beauty and opulence—including the provision of huge tins of caviar.

Michael Wilding, who had played one of the many officers in *In Which We Serve*, was aboard with his new wife, Elizabeth Taylor, and during the voyage we became a friendly threesome—she was due for sessions with Richard Brooks about her next film, *The Last Time I Saw Paris*. At our farewell on the fifth day, we promised each other we would meet again in Los Angeles. Turning towards the skyline of Manhattan, I marveled at the scenery as I approached it for the second time.

Immediately on arrival in Los Angeles I contacted my mother and Curly who were by then living happily in a small apartment on Doheny Drive—it was closer to the people they knew, easier to walk to a market, and it was situated in Beverly Hills. I rented an apartment nearby, just north of the Sunset Strip, and then reported to MGM to discuss the Spencer Tracy film, *Digby's Highland Fling*, scheduled for location filming in Scotland the following year, 1954. British writer John Dighton had been hired to rework the story, but it was immediately clear that there were insurmountable problems. Even so, he continued to try and make it work.

Passing time while I waited, I often met with Elizabeth and Michael. "Get your ass up here, Ronnie!" was her invariable invitation.

They had found a house she absolutely loved. It was newly built and had any number of the latest gadgets. The thing that most impressed the three of us was the intercom in every room. We had never seen the like. Just as children with a new toy, we went to different rooms pressed the buttons and talked to each other about nothing.

MGM arranged for me to have lunch with Spencer Tracy at Romanoff's. I found him down-to-earth, personable, and honest. He gave me a warning, though. "MGM is a tricky studio. It's a dangerous machine. The executives think nothing of mowing people down. The person who'll help you deal with them is Kate Hepburn. She's in London and I'll ask her to speak with you."

Once back home, I met with her at Claridge's. She is a brutally frank, incredibly articulate, and vehement lady. She spoke against the studio system generally, and MGM specifically. Her advice on how to survive amongst their hierarchy was simply, "Stay away from them!"

Daily Variety ran an item that *Digby* had been "put back" to the next year, a Hollywood euphemism for "cancelled."

· 18 ·

The Man Who Never Was

$\mathcal{B}$ecause of his marriage to Darryl F. Zanuck's daughter, Susan Marie, producer André Hakim had become powerful within Fox. Nicknamed "Laughing Boy" for his great sense of fun, he was considered the nicest of all his brothers, who were also in the film business.

I had been back at Mount Fidget for a week when André contacted me about a wartime story he had obtained, entitled *The Man Who Never Was* by Ewen Montagu.

With John still tied up on the second Gregory Peck picture, we engaged art director John Hawkesworth, a sandy-haired, cheerful man with a distinguished war record, as designer. Prior to hostilities he had studied painting in Paris with Picasso and started out working in films under designer Vincent Korda, as had John Bryan. Much later he was to go on to enjoy a successful career in television producing memorable series such as *Upstairs, Downstairs*.

The Man Who Never Was is based on one of the greatest deceptions planned against the enemy during the war. Montagu, a British naval intelligence reservist, devised an idea code named "Operation Mincemeat." If he could absolutely convince the Germans that the anticipated Allied invasion of Europe would begin in Sardinia rather than Sicily (the obvious route), they would deploy their defending troops to the wrong location.

To achieve this, false information would have to fall into German hands by way of a "messenger"—a Royal Marines officer drowned at sea. Montagu and his team, needed to find the suitable body of a young man. According to pathologist Sir Bernard Spilsbury, such a person had to have died from double pneumonia, the water in his lungs abetting the theory that he'd drowned at sea after an apparent air crash.

146

Montagu also had to create false documents that would serve as undeniable proof to the German High Command. These papers would be placed in an attaché case chained to the wrist of the corpse.

The decision was made to jettison the body from a submarine off Southern Spain and currents were studied to establish exactly where it would be guaranteed to float ashore. Despite professed neutrality, British Intelligence knew that the Spaniards would pass the information on to German agents.

Friend and fellow Savile Club member, Nigel Balchin, best known for *Mine Own Executioner* and *The Small Back Room*, was hired as scriptwriter.

Montagu's book, a nonfiction narrative, was on the Official Secrets List and technically could not be used to make a film, so, as a back up, we found a novel that had been written earlier, by Duff Cooper, Viscount Norwich, entitled *Operation Heartbreak*. Right up to the wire, we were waiting for government approval to use the authentic Montagu version. Finally, we received the green light.

Darryl Zanuck was financing the film and insisted that Clifton Webb, who was under contract to Fox and a name known to the American audiences, be cast in the lead. Certainly he could bring the proper arrogance and impeccable British accent to the role of Montagu—few people were aware that he was an American born in Indiana.

When Clifton arrived in London, I met him at the Savoy Grill. He was smartly dressed, his notable facial hair impeccably groomed. I wanted us to get to know each other, but first had the unpleasant task of informing him that his character in the film, as a naval officer, was not permitted to have a moustache.

He was very polite and soft-spoken in his firm reply: "I can't play any part without my moustache. It stays or I go back to the states."

We contacted the Royal Navy to see if they allowed any exceptions in this area of physical attire. It turned out that an officer could have a moustache if he also wore a beard. Clifton was immediately informed and, with this crisis over, cast and crew resumed preproduction!

We had already chosen an actor to play an Irish spy when a well-known agent, Dennis Van Thal, phoned. "I've just seen a test that Alexander Korda made of a young actor. You've got to see it; he's perfect for your spy."

Out of courtesy I screened the footage and he was right. We had to get him.

The other actor was paid off and Stephen Boyd cast in his place—it was his first film. Evidently, we weren't the only ones to recognize his talent, because at the end of production, Zanuck took him to Hollywood where he starred in *Ben-Hur.*

Ossie Morris accompanied me to Huelva in the South of Spain to finalize locations. There we went to see the actual gravesite of the "man who never was," who had been interred with all the ceremony accorded to a British officer. The headstone is marked with the fictitious name "Major William Martin."

We also met the managing director of Rio Tinto Mines, which had a copper mining operation in the area and he showed us an account book in which there is a record of a wreath purchased by the company out of respect for "Major Martin." Montagu and his group had created a completely believable deception.

Because a great many of the real characters who had participated in "Operation Mincemeat" were still alive, permission had to be obtained to portray them on film.

Panic set in when, four days before we were due to start, a letter was received from General Sir Archibald Nye, currently High Commissioner for the UK in Canada. "Under no circumstances," he wrote, "are you to portray me in your film."

We were in desperate trouble. Nye's part, to be played by Geoffrey Keen, wasn't large, but it was pivotal—cutting it would destroy the story.

Within hours I was heading towards Ottawa. On arrival the following morning, I immediately phoned Nye's office.

"You may remember," I began, "we were hoping you would allow us to show you in our film."

"I made it quite clear in my letter. I don't want any part of it."

"Yes, I understand, but I've flown all the way from London for the specific purpose of talking with you."

"You flew from London to talk to me?" He couldn't disguise his surprise. "Where are you now?"

"I'm in a hotel about fifteen minutes away."

"Well, since you came all the way here, I'll see you, but that won't change my mind about being in your film." He then invited me to join him for lunch at his home. "I'll phone my wife and tell her to expect you."

I arrived at noon.

The general's wife offered me a sherry, then asked, "What brings you to see my husband so urgently?"

I explained my predicament while we awaited the General's arrival.

"He's always like this," she confided. "I'll find a way to help you."

When he walked in, we shook hands, and Mrs. Nye quickly spirited him off to another room. During lunch, he leaned over to me and said, "You'd better have a talk with me later."

Drinking coffee in his sitting room, he gave me the specific problems he had with the script: "You see that's not the way it happened. Your screenplay has me saying things I would never have said."

Before I boarded the plane for my return trip, the General had signed an agreement allowing us to use him provided the script matched his requirements for accuracy.

We went into production.

The opening credits start with the body of the young officer washed up on a sandy stretch of Spanish beach, the gentle waves lapping around him, then comes a voice-over of an anonymous poem found by Nigel Balchin:

> Last night I dreamed a deadly dream,
> Beyond the Isle of Skye;
> I saw a dead man win a fight,
> And I think that man was I.

After the titles, the camera pans across London, zooming slowly into the Houses of Parliament. We climbed to the top of Big Ben to film that. The clock was being cleaned and repaired so scaffolding had been erected. Our camera and small crew stood on a platform right at the pinnacle of the famous landmark where there is a lightning conductor, which I grabbed hold of and shook. King Kong excluded, not many can say they stood at the top of a prominent building waving a lightning rod.

Over this scene the voice of Churchill was needed, so an unknown actor, who apparently did a wonderful impersonation of the great man, was hired. Because I was busy with other aspects of the production, Bob McNaught directed the recording session. I would have made time to do it myself if I'd known the young man would soon become known to all—Peter Sellers.

The film was made in CinemaScope, a large screen system that Zanuck hoped would revolutionize the industry. The picture was wider, allowing more visual information. On the conventional shaped screen if you wanted four people in frame you had to move back with the camera or use a wide-angle lens. But with CinemaScope you could get four people in picture and still keep in close.

Clive Donner: When wide screen came along, from Ronnie's point of view, it was rather emancipating. It had to do with the fact that David Lean hadn't been there before and hadn't laid down the way to do it. In a funny kind of way, this new technique emerged that was clean of David and it made Ronnie his own man.

One of the early scenes stands out in my mind because of its strong impact. Montagu has found a body that fitted the requirements of the fictitious Major Martin. He immediately arranges to meet with the dead man's father in the hospital room to get permission to use his son as the decoy.

Standing on either side of the corpse, Montagu has to explain to the father (Moultrie Kensall) that for reasons of security he may never be permitted to know what British Intelligence will do with it. He also makes it clear that the young man's name will never be revealed. The only thing his grieving father can know is that he will be doing a great thing for England.

The man reminds Montagu that his son was a proud Scotsman and asks, "Can you assure me, Commander Montagu, that as an officer and a gentleman, his body will be treated decently?" Montagu gives his word and the father sadly leaves the room having said goodbye to his boy.

In the first two-thirds of the film we adhered strictly to Montague's story, enhancing situations only when absolutely necessary for dramatic emphasis. But in the last part we added a fictional situation. Nigel's script made the Germans more intelligent than they actually were!

An Irish spy (Stephen Boyd) is sent to London by the Nazis to check on the validity of Major Martin. He sets a trap in such a way whereby if Montagu and his colleagues learn he is in cahoots with the enemy, they will arrest him. At the last moment, Montagu realizes the ploy and calls off the arrest. The spy radios back to his German operatives: "Martin genuine."

Clifton Webb had a wonderful sense of humor. He arrived on the set with a strong walk, and apart from once, was always ready, hitting his mark meticulously every time. When he relaxed, a lot of his conversation revolved around his mother, Maybelle.

Ossie Morris: Arthur Ibbetson, my operator would ask Clifton, "How was Maybelle last night?" "Oh, don't talk about mother. You'll never guess what's happened. She's been at the gin again. I'd locked it up. I promise you I hid the key. Mother found it. I don't know what I'm going to do with her." None of us ever saw her. For all we know she could have been a *Psycho* Mrs. Bates-type character. But Clifton was very fond of her.

On the day we were to travel to Huelva, Clifton stated emphatically, "I will not eat or drink anything Spanish." To accommodate him, we had an enormous crate of provisions sent over from Fortnum and Mason. The local customs officials asked why we had brought them into their country, condescendingly explaining, "We have food and water in Spain."

For lunch the caterers prepared a wonderful meal, featuring Andalusian specialties, while Clifton's hamper was set up for his private picnic. He watched the rest of us feast as he carefully removed the wrappings of his tinned repast.

The next day the entire unit was ready for filming except for Clifton. He'd come down with "touristas." And when Clifton didn't feel well it was as if he was dying. If one asked, "How are you?" "Oh," he'd respond, "Not so well, I only slept seven hours." Although his weak stomach proved an inconvenience, it didn't keep him from filming for long—and didn't alter his conviction to forgo Spanish food for the remainder of the ten days we were there.

Another of the film's most moving scenes takes place at the end beside the grave of the Unknown Soldier. Ewen Montagu, who has been decorated for his part in the deception, places his own medal on the young Scotsman's grave.

Over the years, there has been speculation about who the real William Martin was. I can't know for certain, but I don't think any of the names identified are correct. True to his promise to the father, Montagu never revealed that information.

The Man Who Never Was had an excellent script and it received good reviews and I still find the story compelling. To celebrate the completion of the film, Noël Coward gave a lavish party filled with celebrities at his apartment in Gerald Road. Towards the end of the evening there was a hilarious moment—he and Clifton danced together.

It was fortunate meeting Hakim and Darryl Zanuck again. Through them I met Darryl's son, Richard Zanuck, who would eventually ask me to make more movies for Twentieth Century Fox.

In a seventy-year career I have been "let go" or walked off three pictures. *The Passionate Friends* was the first and most painful because it involved a close friend. The second was about to happen with MGM, a studio Tracy and Hepburn had warned me against. The third would be years down the line on a Darryl Zanuck film appropriately entitled *Hello-Goodbye*.

MGM presented me with a remake of the 1934 Garbo film, *The Painted Veil*, by Somerset Maugham, now renamed, *The Seventh Sin*. Wanting desperately to make a movie in Hollywood, I ignored my own advice— never start with a bad script. Karl Tunberg had written it, with promises of improvement before production.

After a recce to Hong Kong, Beryl and I rented a house on Miller Drive in Beverly Hills. Once at the studio, I quickly learned there was friction in the executive quarters at MGM. L. B. Mayer had gone and Dore Schary was now the executive in charge, but his days were numbered. No matter. I was not involved in any studio politics and simply continued my preparations for the film.

During his school break, Christopher flew out from England and Beryl and I took him to the typical tourist attractions, enjoying watching him swim at the beach and sunbathe in Palm Springs. We had a traditional Christmas dinner in La Quinta with Ivy and Curley—our first family holiday since I was a young man. We had tried to get Derek to fly over to join us, but he still didn't like the idea of traveling to America. It was a bittersweet time. Ivy seemed to be restless. One minute she would be cheerful, the next she would be unhappy, and even though Curly seemed fit, he was coughing more than usual as a result of his heavy smoking.

After the break I returned to the mounting and chronic difficulties at MGM. Margaret Booth, head of the editing department, began watching my dailies before I was allowed to see them. At some point I was informed that the characters were "flat." The front office representatives put it more bluntly, saying they wanted "bigger" performances. I tried to explain that actors could only speak dialogue that is reflected in the script. Yet, in an attempt to placate them, I promised to do my best.

The situation did not improve. About ten days into shooting, Christopher Mann's counterpart, Bert Allenberg of William Morris, asked me to stop by his office on my way home. He spoke in Hollywood euphemisms, but the subtext was: "If you don't step aside they'll fire you."

He resigned on my behalf that evening. I was established enough to know I would direct pictures again in England, but no one comes to direct a first film in Hollywood, quits under pressure, and expects to work there again.

I was terribly depressed as Beryl and I and an unusually silent Christopher sat down to dinner.

The phone rang. Beryl answered and told me, "A Mr. Cukor would like to speak to you."

Cukor was working at MGM filming *Les Girls* with Gene Kelly and had achieved such stature that he was probably the only director on the lot who didn't have to kowtow to the executives.

"Ronnie I'm phoning because I imagine you're feeling pretty miserable this evening."

"That is an understatement, Mr. Cukor."

"I want to tell you what happened to you today won't make any difference to your career. I promise."

I listened skeptically.

"I speak with authority, so please believe me. I was the director who was taken off *Gone with the Wind*. And," he stated with all modesty, "I'm still working."

I told him how much I genuinely appreciated his call.

"I felt you might need some cheering up."

I was to meet George many times after that and always told him how much he had boosted me in that down period.

The film was taken over by Vincente Minnelli, who didn't want his name on it. Neither did I, but *The Seventh Sin* was released listing me as director!

· 19 ·

Windom's Way

I'd kept in touch with John Bryan while I was in California, but before I could tell him what had happened, he'd already read the trades, "Neame Bows Out of *Sin*."

He asked me to return to London as there was a film "in the works" called *Windom's Way* to be made for Rank. He didn't have to ask twice. Beryl, Chris, and I were on the next plane home.

I'd been back only a few days when John Davis called asking John and I to meet him at the Savoy Grill. When he finally arrived, almost an hour late, he turned to me saying; "And how is our American friend? I suppose you only eat big steaks these days."

We ordered our food and were conversing pleasantly enough when he brought up the past and how Cineguild had sided against him by refusing to vote him onto the board of Independent Producers. He said we had been a big mistake and went on and on praising himself on how he'd single-handedly saved Rank from bankruptcy.

"Any minute now," I said a bit flippantly, "there's going to be a bloody great halo appearing over your head."

"That's enough," he snapped. He got up and walked out, leaving us two looking at each other and holding the bill.

I was sorry if I'd sabotaged our production. It was foolish. For a day or two we didn't know whether we had a film or not. But fortunately Davis allowed preparations to continue at Pinewood and not one of us mentioned the episode again.

Clive Donner: John Davis was an unpleasant man, very sinister. One year at the Rank Christmas party for senior staff at the Dorchester, he made the most pathetic speech. "I don't understand why none of you accept me

154

as a filmmaker." We didn't because he didn't understand what film was about or that what he was doing was destroying everything we were striving for. He was a rigid man and heartily disliked.

Carl Foreman had written a first draft based on the James Ramsey Ullman novel and we brought in Jill Craigie to help. In the end I think we put together a reasonably good screenplay.

Peter Finch was signed as the doctor who has left his wife and civilization to work in a remote Indonesian island where rebels are challenging the government. Mary Ure was cast as his estranged wife, returning to him at the crucial moment. Michael Horden and Robert Flemyng rounded out our ensemble.

Chris Challis was the cameraman, a handsome tall fellow with bushy, curly hair. His wonderfully clear diction marks him out amongst others and he has a buoyant personality with plenty of drive as well as great powers of endurance and energy.

John Bryan didn't come with us on location. Instead he got the studio and lot sets ready at Pinewood. He acted as art director as well as producer, but he needed assistance because there were so many sets involved on two locations. John Hawkesworth, who had proven himself with his first-rate work on *The Man Who Never Was*, was now expressing a desire to become an associate producer and, as such, learned his new responsibilities quickly and competently.

John Hawkesworth: We couldn't possibly afford to go to the Far East for the locations, so it had to be Europe. I had been to Corsica, and suggested we look there. With Ronnie's enthusiastic cooperation it worked. It was a complicated film to make and he guided me all the way. I learned a huge amount from him that was to help my career. Perhaps the most useful lesson—never accept second best.

The cast and crew arrived in Corsica and settled into a hotel that was pretty sparse, with tatty rooms and a restaurant that had seen better days. There was one bright spot, however. The owner told us that when the Germans had occupied the island they'd lived there, but he had managed to conceal his wine cellar from them by placing a carpet over the trapdoor entrance. He said we could have anything we wanted at prewar prices, but couldn't guarantee if all the wine was still good. Each evening, we'd open one and taste it. Some bottles were vinegar, some were gifts from God.

The rebel camp set we had created in the mountains was terribly inaccessible, entailing a long walk from the nearest road. Added to which was the challenge of shooting there for ten days with an actor, Grégoire Aslan, who was afraid of heights.

All in all, Corsica was quite a difficult location—hot and uncomfortable—but, towards the end, John Hawkesworth put together a party for the unit, creating a wonderful atmosphere in the restaurant by placing candles in Chianti bottles, turning a dingy environment into a romantic setting. He even hired some local musicians for the occasion and soon everyone was singing and dancing. Peter Finch's girlfriend, Yo Turner, and I enjoyed a waltz together.

Later that evening, I could hear the two quarrelling in the room next along the corridor. Their door slammed. Then there was a frantic knock at mine. I didn't answer it, but, as we had no locks, I heard it squeak open and in the shaft of light saw Yo. I pretended to be sleeping and the door closed again quietly.

At 5:30 A.M. there was more banging at my door. This time it was "Finchy." "Where is she?"

"Not here," I assured him. He didn't believe me and started searching the room, looking in the wardrobe, under the bed, and in the bathroom. Eventually he apologized and left.

In truth, the finished film may have had too many messages for people to stay interested—it was neither a hit, nor a disgrace.

A few days after completing *Windom's Way* I went to Jamaica and it was there on the sad day of January 23, 1956, that I heard Alexander Korda had died. He had done a great deal for the British film industry and had helped several humanitarian causes.

Ossie Morris, Bob McNaught, and I were scouting the Caribbean for a picture André Hakim wanted to produce called *Sea Wife and Biscuit*, to star Richard Burton and Joan Collins.

Flying around the island was magnificent, looking down at tropical vegetation against a turquoise sea. Ossie had chartered the plane and he was our pilot. He thought this frightened me, but as with a camera, I had more confidence in him than anyone else.

Noël had a beautiful property on Jamaica he called "Look Out," where he often escaped for relaxation and to entertain royalty. Ossie flew us over there unannounced, but we found it empty, save for some fellow enjoying the sunshine.

The work completed after a few days, we decided to go for a swim on a deserted part of the island. I went out further than my two friends, venturing beyond the breakers. By the time I realized I'd gone too far, I was caught in a cross current. I tried to make for the shore, but couldn't gain any headway. Panicking, I realized I was going down. It's true life does streak before you. There was my family, moments within my career, various angles of my car. I looked at the sky for what I imaged would be the last time but then let reason take over. No use in fighting the current, I let it take control. When it deposited me ashore, I was a good two hundred yards away from Os and Bob—stretched out, tanned and relaxed, completely unaware of the near fatal drama.

Because of various delays, Bob took over *Sea Wife* as director. It was not successful, and my having done it wouldn't have made the slightest difference. Bob did an excellent job on this first of three films he would direct. I haven't seen it in years, but I'm told one of the reasons it didn't work is that the public couldn't accept glamorous Joan Collins as a nun.

· 20 ·

Alec Guinness

"*I*'ll show you how to understand a painting," says the reprobate artist Gulley Jimson to his on-off lady friend Coker. "Don't look at it. Feel it with your eyes. Feel the shapes in the flat, like patterns. Then feel it in the round. Feel all the flaws and sharp edges, the lights and the shades, the cools and the warms. Now feel the chair, the bathtub, the woman. Not any old tub or woman. But the tub of tubs and the woman of women." Coker remains contemptuous of his work, thinking it nothing but obscene.

Some years before, Claude Rains had handed me *The Horse's Mouth* by Joyce Cary believing the character of Gulley was absolutely right for *him*. I remember struggling to read it and couldn't get more than halfway through. So when Alec Guinness enthusiastically suggested it over the phone, I groaned silently.

"Try again," said Alec in a voice obviously intended to point out the error of my judgment. "Maybe you'll think differently."

He was a creative genius and therefore I treated his request very seriously and persevered. This time I found the story completely engrossing and brilliant.

But when I phoned him I said truthfully, "I honestly still don't see a film in it."

"There *is* a film, I assure you," he persisted. "Would you mind if I had a go at writing a screenplay?"

He obviously had in mind exactly how he would play Gulley and I knew him well enough to feel confident he'd not offer to write something unless certain he could do it well. So, in order to protect the film rights, I took out a six-month option for a minimal sum from Cary's literary agent and Alec commenced work on the adaptation at his home in Petersfield.

Christopher came home from The King's School for the summer of 1957 and we all piled into my latest car, a silver Jaguar Mark IX, and headed south for a holiday on the Continent. We stopped in Madrid and Seville and then on across the border into Portugal staying at a lovely pousada near Faro. Pousadas are the Portuguese equivalent of Spain's paradors—efficient and clean, bed and breakfast establishments.

While we were driving, Chris leaned over the front seat and said, "Daddy, we are good friends, aren't we?"

"Yes, of course, we are. Why do you ask?"

"Well, I'm fifteen and it feels a little funny to say, 'Daddy this and Daddy that.' Would you mind very much if I called you Ronnie?"

I was somewhat startled, but, after a brief hesitation, replied "No, if that's what you'd like to do."

As if to clarify his feelings, he added, "Of course, I would always respect you and when I'm speaking about you, I will refer to you as my father."

At first he overused the privilege. It was "Ronnie," with every breath. But then it became more comfortable and, forty-three years later, it would seem odd for him to call me anything else. It has, in fact, become a family tradition continued by my grandchildren and great-grandchildren.

There was an urgent message waiting for us when we got back home. Curly's coughing had turned out to be lung cancer and he had died in only a few short weeks. It was a terrible shock.

My mother didn't want to stay on in California without him and therefore some of her friends helped her make arrangements for a return to England. And Beryl and I started organizing everything from our end. For a while Ivy stayed with us in Fulmer, but she wanted to be in London, so we arranged a room for her at the Onslow Court Hotel, in Kensington.

The Horse's Mouth is a character study of a talented, eccentric artist, who is not only difficult, conniving, uncouth, and thoroughly disreputable, but he is also severely criticized by those who think he's not any good. Despite the detractors, he maintains his personal vision throughout the story, lording it over all from his dilapidated houseboat moored on the Thames at Chelsea.

One of Gulley's quirks, which Alec brilliantly exploited in the screenplay, is his love of working on a large canvas, the larger the better; walls are of particular interest to him. But whatever the size of the painting, he continually modifies and changes it and, even when he has completed the work, he isn't satisfied with the final effect. "It's not what I meant," he says, "not the vision I had. Why doesn't it fit like it does in the mind?"

John Bryan and I went to Petersfield many times to give our input, mostly on the technical end. There Alec would read to us from his manuscript—he wrote everything in longhand, including all the letters I received from him over many years. Within another few weeks we had a completed screenplay. Alec, with his tenacity and uncanny understanding of content, had been able to shape this complex, rambling conglomeration of characters and episodes into a coherent whole.

I went to visit Joyce Cary at his home in Oxford. He was bedridden with terminal bone cancer and almost completely immobilized, but he had an ingenious contraption set up by his bed that enabled him to maneuver a pencil and continue writing, despite his infirmity. He knew he was dying and I was humbled by his courage.

He asked me a favor. "Will you use my son, Tristram, to write the music? It would be wonderful for his career and he is a fine composer."

I willingly agreed, feeling safe in doing so as a few years earlier Tristram had written the score for *The Ladykillers*, a film starring Alec.

Joyce died not long after.

We contacted Tristram, gave him the screenplay and explained what we had in mind—something jaunty and cocky—mentioning that from the start we'd imagined it to be along the lines of Sergei Prokofiev's *Lieutenant Kijé*, which had the right tone for the story. He said he understood.

Financing an offbeat film such as *Horse's Mouth* could be a challenge, even with Alec Guinness attached. In this case, however, there were circumstances that worked in our favor. Two years earlier, in 1955, Alexander Korda had signed Alec to a three-picture deal in conjunction with a partner of his, Robert Dowling. With Korda's death, only one of the three films had been produced.

Dowling was a powerful figure on the board of directors of United Artists, having at one time helped them out of a financial predicament. He spoke with UA's Arthur Krim, whom I knew from earlier Rank days and through his association with *The Million Pound Note*.

Krim agreed to provide finance, although he couldn't imagine a film from the story any more than I had originally. With a tricky subject and no Hollywood star, I doubt if he would have given the project a second glance had it not been for his obligation to Dowling.

Needing someone to oversee our administrative affairs, Albert Fennell became part of the executive team. A quiet, even-tempered man, he was a constant smoker, who, not surprisingly, suffered mercilessly from ulcers. Although perhaps less erudite than Tony Havelock-Allan, he was equally supportive. It was Albert who came up with the name Knightsbridge Productions—John Bryan's and my new company.

While he was busy making the necessary arrangements for studio and office rental—this time at Shepperton—John and I turned our attention to finding an artist who could put on canvas and walls the unconventional works of Gulley Jimson. We wanted a talented and outré contemporary painter. The eminent art historian, Sir Kenneth Clark, told us, "There is only one man alive today who can give you what you want, and that's John Bratby."

Bratby began his career at Kingston Art School and continued at the Royal College of Art. His "kitchen sink" style reflected the less pristine side of life, dusty furniture, people without makeup, warts and all. In the 1950s he was one of the most important artists in Britain.

He didn't paint with a brush. He squeezed large dollops of paint straight from the tube onto the canvas and then used a palette knife to shape the thick oils. Because of this technique his pictures had natural depth which, when lit from a three-quarter angle, created images of a strength and intensity that could never have been achieved with brush-strokes.

His unorthodox reputation was enhanced by the manner in which he met his wife. Evidently he advertised in *The Matrimonial Times*, a London marriage journal. From the responses he received, he chose three and wrote to the ladies arranging an appointment. He instructed each one of them to be at South Kensington Underground Station at 11:00 A.M. on three consecutive Saturdays. He would, he said, be wearing a pink carnation for identification.

On the first two Saturdays, he was at the station. But he didn't like the looks of the ladies so he didn't wear his flower. On the third Saturday, he saw the woman he wanted, put the carnation in his lapel, and shortly afterwards married Jean Cooke.

John Bryan made the initial contact with Bratby, visiting him and his wife in their East London home. He returned to our office with a description of the couple's living conditions.

"It's just awful, Ronnie," he said. "There are bedclothes strewn all over the floor and unwashed pans and dishes scattered everywhere, but," he added enthusiastically, " John Bratby is our man."

Jean Cooke: Alec Guinness came to visit us. He absorbed everything that John did while he was painting. He watched his little pieces of business. I remember John had a great big rag, and he wiped his hands on it. Alec remarked it was all lovely, visual stuff that he could use for Gulley. When I went to see the film, I said to myself, "Yeah, he saw John do this, and he saw John do that."

Concerned from the start that Bratby would not adhere to a schedule, we erected some scenery flats on one of the sound stages to form a square room, thus making him a studio. In this way John Bryan could supervise him more closely, making certain he kept to our deadline. The makeshift setup gave Bratby some privacy even though it was open at the top, and anyone in the gantries could look down into it and watch the artist at work.

He cost us a small fortune in paint because once he'd squeezed a tube he would never use it again. He smoked incessantly so ashes and cigarette stubs were mixed and mashed onto the paint-encrusted floor.

One of the pictures required for the film was *Adam and Eve*.

"Very well, but," he explained emphatically, "I have to copy from life. Can't do it any other way."

Unfortunately he had a *reputation* with his female models, so to find someone prepared to sit for him in the nude was unlikely.

"Well, in that case, I can't paint an Eve for you."

"What if we get a girl and put a bra on her?"

"Then I'd have to paint the bra, wouldn't I?"

A girl was eventually found who would pose as Eve and during these sessions a good many electricians spent much of their time peering over the gantry railings!

We signed Kay Walsh as Coker. Beryl and I had kept in touch with her after her parting from David Lean, and Alec, who first met her on the set of *Great Expectations*, had remained a friend.

Kay is unconventional and outspoken, outrageous in an entertaining way. She can be bitchy when she feels like it and, once talking, takes over the room. Frilly clothing is not her style; pullovers and slacks are more to her liking.

Veronica Turleigh, Denry's washerwoman mother in *The Card*, was cast as Lady Beeder and Robert Coote played her husband. Ernest Thesiger joined us as Gulley's benefactor, Hickson. As Captain Jones, we cast Reggie Beckwith. The role of Sarah Monday, Gulley's former wife was given to music hall trouper, Renée Houston. And we found newcomer Mike Morgan as Nosey, the stuttering young artist who idolizes Gulley.

Ossie was in great demand working for John Huston, Carol Reed, and David Selznick. I would miss him, but understood he was very popular. As I'd promoted him from operator to lighting cameraman on *The Golden Salamander*, I figured why not do the same with Arthur Ibbetson? Arthur expressed similar doubts about his readiness.

"You're ready Arthur," I assured him. "Don't worry. I'll help you." This was to be the first of four films we would make together—he became a first rate cameraman.

Arthur was a chirpy sort of chappie who called everyone "guv" and he got on with everyone because of his ability to tease. He was a short, somewhat rotund fellow with a face like an egg, but he had unusually long eyelashes that actresses picked up on—any cheek from him was always silenced by their reference to his eyes. He had a wonderfully dry sense of humor, fascinating to everyone he encountered—a Yorkshireman through and through.

Altogether we assembled a top-notch cast and crew, including Colin Brewer as my assistant director. A quick learner, with a fast mind, he understood the procedures and mechanics of production. Col took a great weight off my shoulders and became a staunch ally, indispensable for years to come. It was a joy to walk on the set every morning and see so many friendly faces on both sides of the camera.

We hired Arthur Rank's niece, Anne V. Coates, as our editor. Jolly, chatty, and extremely competent, she is an attractive, hearty person, the sort who can work all day and still have enough energy left to enjoy the evening. Anne taught me women often make better editors than men. They have more patience. She worked on my next film as well, after which I could no longer afford her.

Anne V. Coates: Clive Donner was offered the film but couldn't take it so he put my name forward to Ronnie. I had a meeting with him and John Bryan, and I was so excited when they took me on. Also pretty scared. They were dubious about employing a woman. They especially said they'd never employ a married woman. I had been married secretly and worked for three months to prove that my work was exactly the same—married or single. One day, I said something to John, Albert, and Ronnie about being married. Their faces were a study. Just as I was leaving the office, Ronnie said, "Next you'll tell us you're pregnant." I said, "Yes, I am." Although they didn't pay me very much, they gave me a bonus at the end, saying, "We like your work, and think we underpaid you."

Alec decided that Gulley should have a distinctive voice, and the one he assumed was gruff and gravelly, perfectly defining his attitude towards people. His hair was unkempt and he created a walk that was slightly off kilter, giving the impression that his legs were beginning to let him down.

He always lived the parts he played, physically as well as psychologically. His wife, Merula, said, "Ronnie, you have no idea how glad I'll be when you finish shooting this film. I've had enough of living with Gulley Jimson. Alec has become so dirty, he won't even clean his nails."

The first week of shooting went well for all concerned, except for Alec. At the end of the third day he was not his cheerful self. By the end of the fifth day he was really depressed. When, on the sixth day, he didn't join us for lunch, I realized something was wrong. I asked John if he knew what was upsetting him. He was as mystified as I was. On the evening of the seventh day I knocked on his dressing room door.

"Alec, this is Ronnie. May I come in?"

His reply was testy. " Please do."

He politely asked me to sit down.

"Alec, what's the matter?"

A little tight-lipped, "Is there something the matter?"

"There must be. You've been miserable ever since we started shooting, and every day it gets worse. What's wrong?"

Still on the cold side, "Do you really want to know?"

"That's why I'm here."

"Then I'll tell you. I wrote the screenplay of this film, didn't I?"

"Yes."

"And I'm playing the leading part?"

"Yes."

"Well, Ronnie, not once since we started has anyone said to me 'That's good, Alec, or that really works, Alec, or well done, Alec.'"

I was stunned. "Is that what's wrong? Don't you understand we think you're wonderful? We're just trying to live up to you."

"Couldn't someone have said so? May I tell you something that may help you to understand actors?"

"Please," I replied, "God knows I can do with it."

What he said next could be useful for anyone wanting to work with actors:

"All so-called normal human beings go through a period when they want to act. This is usually between the ages of ten and fourteen. Little boys play cowboys and Indians; little girls dress up in their mother's clothes, putting on lipstick. As they mature into adults, ordinary people grow out of this adolescent phase and become doctors or accountants or bankers. But the actor, in the part of his mind that still wants to act, remains no older than fourteen. So, Ronnie, that's how you must treat me. I need to be praised. I need to be patted on the back. I need to be told I'm good! And the more you encourage me, the better I will perform for you." As an afterthought he said, "And just sometimes, I need to be smacked."

Actors differ in how they prepare for a role and also how they warm up to a scene. Alec was at his best around take two or three. Renée Houston was the opposite. She improved with every extra take. This was a problem for me. Alec had been perfect, but I had to do more in order to bring her up to his level. Occasionally I'd cajole her by saying, "If you're not careful, I'll print take one. Then what'll you do?"

It took several takes to complete the sequence where Gulley chases Sarah into her bedroom. They had gone to a pub together spending money on beer that should have been saved for Sarah's husband's supper. She promises to give Gulley back a painting he did of her years earlier. But she cleverly gives him an empty packet. After he discovers her dishonesty there is a scuffle. Gulley lets go of his painting, sending Sarah tumbling backwards over the bed. She goes down with a thud—head to the floor, feet up in the air.

I didn't want the audience to think Gulley had killed her so in a faint voice Sarah says, "It's mine, Gulley. It's mine."

We shot in a variety of locations throughout London, including a sequence outside Wormwood Scrubs Prison. My son was on holiday from school and I gave him his first job. Col allowed him to act as a third assistant director. He enjoyed the experience so much, he asked if he could finish with school and take a permanent job—reminding me that I'd done so at fifteen. What neither of us could foresee was that around a quarter of a century later his own son would make a similar proposal. And despite my best efforts to give Christopher a fully rounded education, he did leave when he was seventeen to become a camera assistant at Beaconsfield Studios.

Towards the end of principal photography my brother Derek tried to take his life. He had talked about it before, even making a few half-hearted attempts, but always leaving the door open for rescue. Terrifyingly he was more determined this time.

Only recently he'd returned from Cassis to his flat in Rathbone Place. Throughout his life he divided his time between London and the South of France.

He phoned at three in the morning. I was half asleep when I heard him say in a weak voice, "I've just taken an overdose, I'm on the way out."

Instantly fully awake, I said, "You idiot. Dial 999 and get help."

"No," he replied. " It's too late," then hung up.

I jumped out of bed, looking for my clothes and dialing the emergency service, at the same time explaining the situation to Beryl. Like a maniac I drove to my brother's flat. A policeman was waiting there. I was afraid he was going to say Derek was dead. Into my mind rushed a flashback of the policeman talking to my mother on the night my father had been killed.

"He's going to be all right," said the policeman. "He's in the Middlesex Hospital."

Breathlessly thanking him, I raced there.

A nurse said, "We've pumped his stomach out. He'll sleep it off now."

The relief was tremendous, but the whole thing was desperately draining—added to which a day's work lay ahead.

The next evening, I spent more time with Derek—talking things over with him in his flat. He had so much going for him, intelligence, good looks; I tried to convince him how much he had to live for and by the time I left he seemed to have settled down.

We were coming to the penultimate scene of the film in which Gulley's huge masterpiece, *The Last Judgement*, painted inside a derelict and condemned chapel, is going to be torn down by order of the borough council. The wall he had found for this vision was far too large for him to paint himself, so he has had to advertise for art students to assist him—each paying him sixpence an hour for the privilege. Real art students were hired as extras.

Bratby painted the wall, which was built on the back lot of Shepperton, completing it in eight weeks, one day before we needed it! We were heartbroken to have to destroy this work of art. But the script had been written and the story had to be told.

John Bryan had constructed the wall in brick without mortar in the center section so that when the demolishers' tractor crashes into it from behind, it would collapse easily and quickly. Of course, there could only be one take. If we didn't get it the first time round we'd have to build another wall and paint another picture—inconceivable!

The day arrived for the shot. Bratby was not on hand; he couldn't bear to see his work reduced to rubble.

As protection against unforeseen mishaps, I placed four cameras at various angles, two of them concentrating on the center. A special button was set up by the side of the first camera. Once pressed, a red light would blink to cue the tractor to move forward and knock it all down. I double checked to make certain everything was in order, said a prayer, rolled the cameras, and pushed the button.

I could hear the tractor begin to move. It hit the back of the wall, and the center came down perfectly—the rest started down as scripted. Then the most unexpected thing happened, something I hadn't planned, and couldn't have planned. One piece, about ten-feet square, remained upright for a few seconds as if the painting was refusing to be destroyed. Finally and very sadly it toppled and broke into hundreds of pieces. What an incredible piece of luck!

Amid the debris of the wall and the choking dust, Coker (Kay Walsh) hears a cough. She stumbles over the rubble, saying, "I'd recognize that cough anywhere." Out of the debris lurches Gulley. It was Gulley himself who had driven the tractor and destroyed his own creation.

Walking towards her, he explains, "Too much responsibility for those chaps, destroying a national monument."

He turns and walks away from the devastation. Coker calls after him, "Where are you going?"

"I'll be on my way. Fresh woods and pastures new. I need a new horizon."

The last sequence has him floating down the Thames on his leaky houseboat. Coker and Nosey chase after him along the embankment and watch as he floats beneath Tower Bridge and into the distance.

Coker says, "Old fool!" Nosey calls out even though Gulley can't hear him, "Michelangelo, Rembrandt, Reubens, Blake. . . . You're one of them, Mr. J-J-J-Jimson. Just so you know."

On the Monday of the last week of shooting, this charming young actor, Mike Morgan, suddenly became ill with meningitis. Within ten days, he was dead, cutting short what I think would have been an important career. It was another of those tragedies that will always remain with me.

In order to complete the film, someone had to be found who was able to imitate his voice convincingly for the required looping. To this day, when I watch the picture, I cannot tell which voice is Mike's and which is the impersonator's.

Tristram Cary had kept me apprised of his progress, so when we were ready to record, John and I sat anxiously in the control booth ready and listening. Muir Mathieson gave the downbeat to the seventy musicians for the two-and-a-half minutes title section . . . Before the end we knew we were in trouble.

"This is quite wrong," I thought—overdramatic and heavy—the opposite of what a comedy required. I looked at John and could see he felt the same. With a sinking feeling, we let the session continue until the lunch break while trying to figure out how to get something new at this eleventh hour. And we faced the unpleasant task of replacing Tristram. It was difficult not only because he was a fine composer, but also because we'd wanted to honor his father's wishes.

Tristram was obviously disheartened, but accepted the situation gracefully. The musicians were dismissed while Muir, John, and I sat down to discuss the dilemma.

I still felt Prokofiev had the right touch of arrogance and bombast that was Gulley, yet with a humorous tone beneath.

We transferred a recording of *Lieutenant Kijé* to a 35 mm sound track and ran it with the film on the Moviola. Using the leitmotifs, we underscored recurring elements in the film. Each time Gulley sees a blank wall and is inspired to create a painting on it, we used the same theme. The most majestic passage from the symphony was saved for tearing down *The Last Judgement*.

A new score was devised in a couple of weeks. The musicians were recalled. Muir once again raised his baton. This time we had our music.

I took a print of the completed film to New York for a United Artists preview. It couldn't have been received better. As we left the theatre, Arthur Krim said, "I don't know how you made *that* film from *that* script."

"That film was that script, Arthur," I responded.

A screenplay is not a novel; it's a blueprint. Only when one has studied a screenplay backwards and forwards can one judge what it will look like on the screen. Alec Guinness received an Academy Award nomination for his writing. Unlike Gulley Jimson, who is never satisfied, *The Horse's Mouth* was exactly what we had envisioned and more.

The picture was selected for a Royal Première in aid of Glebelands, a home for retired members of the cinema industry. The event took place on February 3, 1959, at the Empire Leicester Square in the presence of Her Majesty Queen Elizabeth and the Queen Mother. A contingent from United Artists flew from New York and were delighted to be presented.

In addition to our cast, an array of British and American film stars were in attendance: Sean Connery, Peter Sellers, Richard Attenborough, Maurice Chevalier, Peter Finch, Terry Thomas, and Lauren Bacall.

Afterwards there was an enormous party at the Mayfair Hotel. Peter Sellers played drums and almost every other celebrity, including Alec, performed. I encouraged my mother to come to the screening and the party, which she thoroughly enjoyed. After a few glasses of wine, when Renée Houston began an impromptu rendition of one of her music hall numbers, my mother couldn't resist the temptation of joining her on stage. They sang a duet together, receiving enormous applause. For a brief moment, dear Ivy was back in the limelight.

As the film was selected in competition at the Venice Film Festival, John Bryan, Albert Fennell, and I flew over for the occasion and spent a week at the lavish Excelsior Hotel on the Lido. Halfway through, the UA representative told us that Alec was going to receive the best actor's award, the coveted Volpe Cup. "You've got to get him over here," I was told. I phoned and pleaded with him to come for just twenty-four hours. Typical of Alec and his disregard for publicity, he refused. The UA man was right. Alec won.

Alec Guinness: I was terribly pleased when I did the script of *The Horse's Mouth*, kind of while waiting to do a terribly boring film somewhere else. I gave it to Ronnie to read, and he encouraged me. He was marvelous about that. He pushed it through because it was a bit of an oddity. I don't think anyone really wanted to do it. However, he managed to get things going for which I will always be grateful.

· 21 ·

Tunes of Glory

𝒯wo years later a similar conversation took place between Alec and me—I was in Venice while he was at home in Petersfield. This time the film being honored was *Tunes of Glory*. I begged him not to be stubborn and come over as he had been tipped to win again.

Independent producer Colin Lesslie had handed me the superb script by James Kennaway, adapted from his own novel. James had served with the Gordon Highlanders after the war and *Tunes of Glory* is about the soldiers he knew and his experiences with them.

Acting Colonel Jock Sinclair is an up-from-the-ranks officer, who has earned the respect and love of his men on the battlefield. Now, in peacetime, he has been running the regiment in a less than orthodox manner. Colonel Basil Barrow, a desk soldier from Sandhurst and of an elite military family, arrives at the barracks to assume command. Antagonism between the two men is immediate and intense. The narrative is both a psychological and emotional duel. In the end, they destroy each other.

"I think this part is right up your alley. I hope you think so too," I said in the note I sent to Alec with the script. He called me back, "Barrow is too similar to the Nicholson character I played in *Bridge on the River Kwai*. If you'd let me play his counterpart, the red-haired boozer, Sinclair, then I'm your man."

Knowing he could play anyone he set his mind to, my response was "All right, Jock Sinclair is yours."

With his involvement, the film became a joint venture between United Artists and City Entertainment Corporation, Dowling's company, which still had one more picture owed on the Korda-Guinness contract. Colin Lesslie and Albert Fennell were to be joint producers.

169

I met Kennaway and admired this feisty, intelligent, and free-spirited Scotsman immediately. We worked on the final script together, and in so doing, established a firm friendship.

We thought it was a good idea to use the factual regimental base he had depicted in his story as the principal location, Stirling Castle in Argyllshire and also to enlist the Argyll and Sutherland Highlanders as the men. Therefore, he, Colin, and I went to Scotland to meet with the Commanding Officer. He was gracious and said he would be delighted to help, but we would have to work around their usual routine as well as pay a fee to defray the various regimental costs. Naturally we agreed. He then asked us to come back in two days giving him time to read the script.

Duly we returned and were ushered into his office, which was empty. But there on his desk, alongside our screenplay, was a paperback copy of Kennaway's novel with a lurid cover—Jock holding a bottle of scotch with Mary, his actress friend, sitting on his lap. This racy scene was neither in the book nor our script. It was a cheap marketing ploy.

When the colonel came in, he appeared visibly upset. "I would never allow the Argylls to participate in a film where the colonel is presented in this manner," he said angrily.

Ultimately we placated him enough for him to agree we could use the exterior of the castle if it were not specifically named or recognizable.

Alec and I discussed who should play the part I'd originally offered him. Who would complement him, yet not be smothered by Sinclair's boisterous character?

He suggested Johnnie Mills.

"Johnnie has always played 'lower deck' characters," I said. "Do you think he could play upper-class, university-bred Barrow?"

"He's a good actor," was Alec's response, and, of course, he was absolutely right.

Both men looked forward to working together again more than a decade after playing Pip and Herbert Pocket in *Great Expectations*.

We cast Kay Walsh as Mary Titterington, a stage actress and Jock's former mistress.

The only other female part to fill was Jock's daughter Morag. I contacted Dennis Van Thal, who had recommended Stephen Boyd for *The Man Who Never Was*. Like all the best agents, he often visited repertory companies spread across England where a lot of good acting talent could be found.

His strongest recommendation was nineteen-year-old Susannah York. Since she had never made a film, we couldn't risk casting her without a screen test. Obviously not quite understanding the opportunity we were offering, she initially seemed reluctant to travel from Derby to Shepperton. Recently she'd married actor Michael Wells, and they were appearing up there in a pantomime.

Because of her inexperience with film, we wanted her to have every advantage and so Alec agreed to make the test with her, a most generous and unusual offer—normally they are made without stars.

Susannah York: After it was done and I was on the train going home, I suddenly realized, "My God, I've just done a screen test with Alec Guinness." It was a difficult scene, and he was very helpful. "Susannah," he'd say, "Try not to press so hard!" and I'd say, "Yes, Alec, so sorry." We'd do it again, and I'd do it the same because I didn't have any technique then. Alec bore manfully with my onslaughts. And so did Ronnie, who was patient with me.

The result showed her unquestionable talent. John Fraser was then cast as her love interest. The regiment of fine character actors we assembled included Dennis Price, Duncan Macrae, Gordon Jackson, and at least two dozen more.

Christmas Eve 1959 was probably the brightest in my career. I was on top of the world, thoroughly enjoying myself. Carol singers—children and chaperoning adults—arrived at the front door of Mount Fidget carrying -torches and bells and singing the traditional melodies. Beryl brought out a tray of cocoa for the kids and a tot of brandy for the grownups. Adding to the festive air was the fact that it was my son's birthday.

The phone rang.

Christopher went to answer it, leaving Beryl and I at the door to say goodbye to our visitors.

"Ronnie," he called from the sitting room. "It's for you." When I took the phone from him, he had his hand over the mouthpiece. "It's Johnnie Mills' wife, Mary. She seems a little upset."

"Hello, Mary. Happy Christmas."

"*Tunes of Glory*," was her response.

"Yes, we're all delighted with the whole project. Isn't it wonderful, Johnnie playing Barrow?"

"That's why I'm phoning. Johnnie can't possibly do the film if his credit is going to be below Alec's." She continued in an unseasonable tone, "Johnnie's always received top billing, and that's how it has to be."

I assured her we would sort it out so that she and Johnnie would be happy and she seemed satisfied.

For several days, we were in a deadlock situation. Neither Alec nor Johnnie could agree which of them would have top billing. Eventually the crisis was solved. They tossed a coin. Obviously Alec won.

Alec Guinness: One of the things I asked and Ronnie went along with was at least a two-week rehearsal. It was a very literate script, a brilliant script. Actors are better when they have a chance to work together. Unless one has worked in theater it is hard to understand how great it is to rehearse without a camera and without the whole crew around. It paid huge dividends. We had good actors. They began to dovetail together in a way in which I don't think they would have if they'd come in on the odd day now and then.

We marked out the shape of the sets and positioned stand-in furniture and props. While every important scene was covered in continuity, the cast got to know one another well. Alec and Johnnie were in friendly competition and I was the beneficiary. Since they hadn't worked together for many years, each was striving to outshine the other.

John Mills: Ronnie loves actors and appreciates them and knows their difficulties. On *Tunes*, he was a treasure. Rehearsals went brilliantly. They were marvelous for Alec and me. Ronnie said, "Barrow is right up your street, but one thing I can suggest. You have a rather nice voice, a soft voice, but the character has to be hard. Do you know Field Marshal Montgomery?" I replied, "I certainly do. I did shows for Monty just before D-Day." It was his voice I used in the film.

"I photographed you on *In Which We Serve*," I said, "and you didn't look too bad. I produced you on *Great Expectations*, and that worked all right, but I've never directed you. You must wonder what the hell I'm like in that area." I went on to make him a promise: "Johnnie, if you produce the magic I know you're capable of, the camera will be in the right place at the right time to take full advantage of what is assuredly going to be a great performance."

With the Argylls not available to us, an alternative regiment had to be procured—a good choice would be the Territorial Army, which is like the National Guard in America. We located a well-trained Scottish unit, which had added advantages—they had a splendid pipe band and they could wear kilts with the appropriate flourish.

Some of the cast had to learn how to wear these pleated skirts, and sit without keeping their legs apart—which a Scot would never do. Duncan

Macrae, who played Pipe Major MacLean, was very helpful in showing our Sassenachs—a disparaging term for Englishmen—the way to maneuver themselves and use other Scottish paraphernalia.

We invented our own regimental tartan, choosing muted colors of red, green, and gray, asking Berman's, the costumier (now called Angel's), to create 100 kilts and matching trews.

This was one of the few times the writer was on the set with me throughout. They can often be difficult when their view of how a scene should look doesn't match the director's. But James joined us in a dual capacity—as screenwriter and as technical advisor for regimental protocol.

Susannah York had no sense of her own importance. There was a chair with her name on it waiting for her between setups, but she always found somewhere else to sit, a box, a stool, the floor.

I reminded her, "You're one of the stars of this picture and you must behave as such and sit in your designated chair!"

She had a slight crush on handsome James Kennaway. They were both Scots and got on very well. Nothing more would have come of it, but to reinforce that, James received a letter from his mother, "Be kind to a young girl on your film named Susannah York. She's your cousin."

Part of the film's strength is that the two main characters are not black and white. There are times one dislikes Jock for his crude, rough behavior and bad treatment of both his actress friend Mary and his daughter. There are other times when you can see his vulnerability. Although Barrow is the more sympathetic of the two, there are instances when he, too, evokes our disdain.

One highly dramatic scene ends with a confrontation between Barrow and Sinclair. Barrow has arranged a ball at the barracks to which every important person in the town has been invited. The evening is intended to be a dignified occasion. Barrow has rehearsed with his men orderly traditional dancing and specifically forbidden unruly behavior, such as raising the arms above the head, and making whooping noises. Jock Sinclair encourages the men and the locals to break the rules. Their dancing and music becomes louder and more animated—men are twirling young ladies, and laughing. Barrow becomes enraged and touches his temple, trying to keep hold of his rigid control. His defenses fail; shaking with anger, he orders the pipers silenced, and tells the guests to go home.

The scene went extremely well. Alec and Johnnie were great, the extras were great. I said, "Cut! Print! Thank you, everyone." And started to move to the next shot when the soundman beckoned me. Evidently the needle had gone over the top of the scale during Barrow's rage and the sound might be slightly distorted. He asked for a second take as a safety measure.

John Mills: It had been a bloody good take. But Ronnie came over to me and explained why we had to go again. I said, "I really don't want to. It should sound a bit over the top, anyway." To his undying credit, he went to the soundman and said we would not do another. He might have said, "Come on, Johnnie, let's do it again." But if I had, I couldn't guarantee that it would be as good as the first and Ronnie knew I'd be worried about that. I thought he displayed tact and understanding. He showed that he made the decisions on the set.

Having punched a young fellow officer, Jock's behavior brings him up on charges. Barrow is determined to have him court-martialed. In exchange for not being prosecuted, Jock Sinclair promises he will behave impeccably from now on. He even suggests the two men could form a friendship. "We'd make a good team," he says.

Against regulations and his better instincts Barrow releases Jock from custody. The latter rejoins his colleagues at one end of the long mess table while Barrow is left at the other. Jock makes no attempt to honor his promises, and instead defies the colonel by singing with his chums knowing it will act as a slap in the face. Barrow again loses his composure.

Anne V. Coates: I wanted to start the scene with Johnnie, and Ronnie thought we should start with Alec. I cut it both ways. Ronnie had the good grace to say he liked my way better. It sounds like a simple thing, but it's really important to a scene because where it starts can change the balance of all that comes after it, as well as change the balance of all the other cuts.

Music and sound effects were tremendously important. In the scene where Barrow commits suicide, Sinclair and an orderly enter the bathroom and discover the body. The orderly retreats from the room, leaving Jock alone, washing the blood off his hands. There is a sound that accompanies the action, a slow electronic hum. The noise becomes more intense, louder and louder, until it reaches its climax. Jock, greatly affected by the suicide, leaves the scene. "It's not the body that worries me, it's the ghost." The door slams shut and the sound cuts off sharply. This auditory device is evocative of Sinclair's state of mind—his horror of an event he knows he prompted.

In the final sequence, he is on a dais in the barracks' assembly hall. As he tells the men his burial arrangements for Barrow, he goes into a near insane description of how he thinks he should be given the funeral of a Field Marshal. His words have a musical background. At first we hear the beat of the drums and the commands of the officers to the regiment marching with the gun carriage through the town. Jock says, "We'll have all the tunes of glory: *Scotland the Brave, Flowers of the Forest, The Black Bear*." His voice intermingles with the complicated musical score, which uses each tune he names played on bagpipes.

Jock's mind is disintegrating. The sounds, the commands, and the music represent what is happening inside his head. We reintroduce the electronic humming noise from the suicide scene. Jock cuts off the sound by banging his stick against the blackboard. Halfway through his distraught speech, two of his officers, Gordon Jackson and Dennis Price, quietly signal to the rest of the men to leave. Jock continues unaware the assembly hall has all but emptied. To the beat of a muffled drum, he slowly marches across the dais until he reaches the wall. He puts his head against it. Jock Sinclair is a completely broken man. He has not only destroyed Colonel Barrow, he has destroyed himself. He puts his cap over his face to hide his emotions.

The two officers know something must be done. They move onto the dais to comfort him. Jock says, "Oh my babies, take me home." One on each side of him, they help him across the room, out to the parade ground, then into his jeep. The whole of the watching regiment salutes him. Jock leaves his post for the last time.

Malcolm Arnold: I was concerned that there was so much dialogue, so I asked Ronnie "Where are you going to have music?" He replied, "There and there and there." We had one recording session, which was very difficult, especially getting the bagpipes in tune with the orchestra. I did the trumpet. The music for the last scene in which Alec goes mad was made up of the bagpipes and strings *sur pontecello*, which means on the bridge. I don't think the film could have been better. I told Ronnie I wanted *Tunes of Glory* to be the best bloody film ever made.

Tunes of Glory premièred in New York on December 20, 1960. And it was the official British selection for that year's Venice Film Festival. Albert Fennel, Colin Lesslie, and I attended. While we were there, we heard that Alec was again going to win the Volpe Cup for best actor.

Reluctantly he agreed to come over, on condition that his agent, Laurie Evans, could accompany him.

"By all means, bring him along," I said.

At the Italian border, Laurie was stopped from entering the country—his passport had expired. We contacted the British Embassy and after a lot of persuasion got him a special pass. Alec took the inconvenience badly; he was irritable and blamed me for everything.

The next evening we were led the two hundred yards from the Excelsior to the theater by a band of pipers, cheered by a large crowd who had gathered to watch the festivities. The film was screened and hailed a triumph. Next morning Alec left for England. The rest of us remained.

On the last day the awards were announced. "The Volpe Cup for best actor goes to. . . ." We knew. . . .

"John Mills for *Tunes of Glory*."

When I recovered from cardiac arrest, I headed straight for a telephone to inform Alec before the press got on to him.

"I'm terribly sorry," I said over a crackling connection, "but Johnnie got the award."

Alec replied, "Of course. So he should have."

When the film was released, I received a telegram from Noël Coward:

"Dear Ronnie, Tunes of Glory is impeccably acted and impeccably directed. Congratulations. Love, Father."

Also in the mail was a letter from Alec. In part, it read:

"Ronnie, the time has come for you to be very careful about what you do next. Don't accept something you don't believe in, even if it means you have to sell Mount Fidget."

Of all my films, *Tunes of Glory* is the one I care about most. Looking at it today, I find the performances and the production not dated in any way. It is a story that will always have something to say to each generation—a satisfying and rewarding experience.

My next film is on the low end of my estimation and is mentioned solely on the basis of an extraordinary talent, Yul Brynner, and because it moved me towards one of the most memorable experiences of my life—so much for Alec's advice!

The script of *Escape from Zahrain* was flawed, but Yul Brynner had a charismatic and persuasive character and I liked the idea of working with him. And it gave me another go at Hollywood.

Although a Paramount production, it was originally to have been shot on location in the Middle East, but at the last minute, after I had already locked myself into a contract, the studio executives changed their minds rationalizing, "Who needs Arabs? We'll get extras." "And why go across the world for a desert? We have the Mojave right in our backyard."

I tried to get Ina Balin for the female lead, but she was busy on *The Young Doctors* for producers Lawrence Turman and Stuart Millar. Instead we engaged Madlyn Rhue. Also cast was the warmhearted Jack Warden, as well as Sal Mineo.

With a mediocre script and the truly unpleasant conditions of shooting a sandstorm just outside the forlorn Barstow, I, for one, couldn't have been happier when it was all over and editing could start.

However, even that had its complications. Only ten more days remained of my permitted tax-free six months in the US. If I overstayed, there was a grave danger of having to pay double taxation. So the studio concocted a plan whereby I would give editor Eda Warren enough work on a Monday to keep her busy while I hopped over the border into Mexico.

Living in Rosarita Beach, Beryl and I had a lovely time from Tuesday through to Sunday. In this odd way editing was completed, but I was not able to remain in the US for the music recording and dubbing.

Besides my friendship with Yul, the only good thing about *Zahrain* was it put me in the right place at the right time to accept a film that would bring me back to England with one of the great talents of the twentieth century.

· 22 ·

Judy Garland

$\mathcal{S}$ometimes a single incident can change the course of a life. Ina Balin, an actress I'd never actually met at that time, had unwittingly introduced me to the two producers who were to offer me my next film. And years later, when the world around me would shatter, it was Ina who became the most instrumental in helping me put it back together.

Larry Turman and I had met in my efforts to get her for *Zahrain* and subsequently he and his partner Stuart Millar thought of me for a film they were developing with United Artists to star Judy Garland. Understanding my work permit predicament, they came to Rosarita Beach in Mexico to hand over an original screenplay called *The Lonely Stage*, by Mayo Simon. It was promising, but as is so often the case, it needed more work.

Of course, I'd heard Judy could be difficult and many said she ate directors for breakfast—and more often than not wanted them fired. But here was I, an arrogant Englishman, convinced my manners and tact could overcome any difficulty that might arise.

On one of my editing days on *Zahrain* at Paramount, Turman and Millar scheduled a meeting with Judy at the Beverly Hills Hotel. It was a friendly get-together and Turman called the following morning to say Judy had been impressed and had approved me as her director.

Just before my return to England, in fact on the last available day in the US, Judy and I met again. She selected a small Italian restaurant where she thought she wouldn't be recognized. This occasion was as warm as the previous one.

Judy was a woman with immense energy, yet with a vulnerability coming through her eyes. I was absolutely elated to have the opportunity of making a film with someone of her talent, and said as much as we parted—she towards her home and me towards the airport.

178

"I'm looking forward to it, too," she smiled as her driver helped her into the car.

I began working on the script with Mayo Simon in London. The film would be shot entirely at Shepperton and on various locations in that area, including two important sequences at the London Palladium.

Turman and Millar had already cast Dirk Bogarde. Judy and Dirk were close friends and he was particularly helpful in getting the script into its final shooting state—the dialogue he wrote suited Judy's personality, giving life and depth to her character. His contribution was nothing short of enormous but he refused to take screen credit.

By late spring, 1962, the script was ready; the sets were ready; I was ready and Judy arrived in London with her three children—Liza, sixteen, Vincent Minnelli's daughter, and Lorna, ten, and her younger brother Joey, the children of Judy's estranged husband, Sid Luft. I found out later that she had smuggled them out of her Los Angeles home in the middle of the night because Luft was threatening to take Lorna and Joey away from her, charging her with being an unfit mother.

She declined the country home we had rented for her in Esher and nearby the studio, feeling it lacked the security she needed to be safe from Luft. Until we could find her a safer haven, the producers' executive assistant, Marion Rosenberg, arranged for a suite at the Savoy Hotel. Some days later she found her a house in London near Kensington Palace, where Judy felt suitably protected.

She seemed happy with the amenities accorded a star of her rank—her suite of dressing rooms at Shepperton, her house in Kensington, plus a vintage Rolls Royce with a chauffeur. And the London High Court made her children its temporary wards. Even so, she constantly feared Luft's arrival.

In many ways, *The Lonely Stage* is a reflection of her own life. The consummate performer and a woman with a child custody situation, Jenny Bowman is a singer who comes to London for a series of performances at the Palladium. Once in the country, she contrives a situation whereby she can reunite with her former lover, David (Dirk Bogarde), who is a doctor. They have a son, Matt, played by Gregory Phillips, whom she had previously given up in order to pursue her career. The penalty was that she'd promised never to see him again. Now, after fourteen years, she asks David if he will allow her one visit. The subsequent reintroduction to her son, who is unaware she is his mother, and her desire to build a relationship with him, provides the complication.

Dirk went to the trouble of rehearsing with Judy at his country home, "Nore," in Hascombe, Surrey. It is good to have leading players supporting each other and no one could have been more loyal to Judy than he was. Joking that they were a team, Judy suggested—we'll be MacDonald and Eddy. "No," Dirk reminded, "I don't sing. Bogarde and Garland." "Not a chance, buster." Judy was adamant, "Garland and Bogarde."

Back in Hollywood, Academy Award-winning costume designer Edith Head had created a variety of outfits for her, but by the time they arrived, many had to be altered or new ones hastily stitched together.

Marion Rosenberg: It wasn't that Judy didn't like Edith's costumes. But she had put on so much weight, mostly around the middle, that they had to be let out. Judy was absolutely in love with Emilio Pucci and insisted on having him design for her. The problem was that one of his signatures was that he cut on the bias. It was almost impossible to make her look good in that cut. The red dress she wears when she sings is an absolute disaster. But she wanted Pucci come hell or high water and she got him, although he was never credited.

We were completing a few days of makeup tests when Judy's agent, David Begelman, came to London to ensure she was happy, settled in, and prepared for work. He and I met in Judy's dressing room, and after an initial polite conversation he announced, "I can see you're all set here so I'm going back to Hollywood."

"No, you're not," she said. "Not until I've started. Not until I say I'm okay."

"I have other clients, Judy."

"I don't care how many clients you have. You're staying here!"

I thought she was right—he shouldn't leave her at this moment. For the first time, I began to sense her insecurity. She needed him badly.

Once outside the dressing room, I ventured, "You know, I do think you should stay."

The look on David's face said everything—if only I could have read it clearly at the time. Without a word, he conveyed, "You poor schmuck. You don't know what you're in for!" He left the next morning.

Prior to principal photography, we recorded the songs she would subsequently perform to playback. She chose them all, her judgment unerring about what suited the story. And she was guaranteed to give her fans what only she could deliver.

Her sessions at the recording studio became an event. Loving the buzz of an audience, she invited everyone she knew. Even Christopher couldn't pass up the opportunity of hearing her sing. This took place at night—Judy's best time. Her captivating power came alive then. After what can only be described as a series of spectacular miniconcerts, her adrenalin kept pumping, thus making her practically useless in the morning.

Mort Lindsey: I had just completed more than thirty-five concerts with Judy, including the big one at Carnegie Hall in 1961, when I was assigned composer/orchestrator for Ronnie's film and went over to England. I prepared the big numbers. A friend of mine, Jack Parnell, put together the orchestra, but they couldn't get her to come in to record until she heard the orchestrations. As soon as she heard what we did with the songs it was an incentive for her to work. She told me that my arrangement of "I'll Go My Way by Myself" was the most favorite one in her whole life. She never put musicians through anything. She loved them. She respected them.

There were a lot of long dialogue scenes between Jenny and David, which we continued to rehearse for a week before production. Sometimes on a set that had already been constructed, sometimes around a table in an office or on an empty stage. As it had happened on *Tunes of Glory*, by the time we came to film those scenes, the actors felt comfortable with the situations and each other.

Shooting commenced at the London Palladium, familiar to Judy, who had been a headliner on its stage many times. She sang "Hello, Bluebird, Hello," a 1926 song by Cliff Friend, to the playback she had made earlier. Dirk gave her a small-jeweled bluebird pin to commemorate the occasion. She wore a short navy blue dress with a spangled jacket—the long shots showing off her terrific legs. Judy loved being back on that stage. One could see it in her energy and excitement.

As we finished the day's filming, she bestowed the nickname "Pussycat" on me. From then on, when I was in favor, she would say, "We're all right, Pussycat, aren't we?" Giving her a hug, I would reply, "We're all right, Judy."

From the Palladium, we moved into the studio with Judy and Dirk playing beautifully together and the atmosphere on the set was upbeat with a lot of laughter between actors and crew. Our star was renowned for her great sense of humor.

By now I'd become confident that the stories about her temperamental outbursts were exaggerated. But gradually, a day here, a day there, things started going wrong. Someone from her entourage would phone my assistant director Colin Brewer to say, "Miss Garland will not be in today." There was no excuse given, she simply would not be in. On the days she did arrive we never knew what type of mood she'd be in. When in good form, there was no one who could touch her.

More and more, crew members began posting what we termed "Whether reports." "Whether" Judy was in. "Whether" she was calm or frantic.

Part of the time while things were going well, I was Pussycat. At others she would say in a voice loud enough for the entire unit to hear, "Get that God-damned British Henry Hathaway off the set!" Hathaway was a highly-credited American director with the reputation of a bully.

Lawrence Turman: I recall one occasion when Judy wouldn't come out of her dressing room. Colin Brewer said, "It's my fault. I went in and asked her in the wrong way to come on the set." Ronnie said, "No, no. It's my fault because at the end of the last take, I did so-and-so." Then I'd say, "Guys, you're both wrong. I was the one complaining about the letting out of the costume." That's what she did to people. Everyone blaming himself for upsetting the apple cart, but I don't think it was calculating on her part. Judy required the highest maintenance possible, and it was all we could do to survive the picture.

I learned a lot from working with her, particularly about helping actors who are insecure. One must build their confidence. I remembered what Alec Guinness had taught me and would praise Judy before moving to the next setup. In hindsight, maybe I wasn't verbally enthusiastic enough to boost her self-assurance and therefore her trust in me. But one would have had to be a psychologist to understand that. When the film started, I knew little about her early history—how she'd been given drugs by the studios to keep her going, which ultimately led to her lifetime usage.

How many times did I hear her say, "Shoot around me. I won't be in"? I tried to explain to her, "You've got to be here. You're in almost every shot in the film."

Professionally, she knew it was so, although emotionally she was unable to make the commitment to herself or the production. Usually after a non-appearance drama, Judy would arrive at the studio the following day and do a one hundred and eighty degree turnaround, behaving as though nothing had been amiss. Then all was right in our little world at Shepperton—until the pattern started over again.

I found myself relying more and more on Dirk's friendship with her to try to keep her relationship with me amenable, but inadvertently my alliance with him made things worse.

Dirk liked a Guinness in the morning and often asked me into his trailer either for a chat or for us to work on a scene together. Judy, sadly, in her insecurity, presumed we must have been talking behind her back. I could see her through the window of the trailer hovering, thinking we were cooking up something between us. She was threatened by our rapport. So much so that I was told she circulated rumors around Hollywood that Ronnie Neame and Dirk Bogarde were an item.

In Hollywood, star trailers have private bathrooms. This was not the case in early 1960s Britain, however, and Judy took it as an intentional personal affront. So instead of walking into the studio loo, she reacted like a spoiled child and began utilizing her wastepaper bin as a toilet. The problem was, who would be assigned the job of lavatory attendant? By this time I was overwhelmed by so many other difficulties, I told my crew, "I'm not going to get involved with Judy's chamber pot!" In the end it was handled by either the property department or by wardrobe, both complaining bitterly.

Sunday was my day off. Christopher, who was still living with us at Mount Fidget, and I took morning trips to a local pub to have a pint of beer together—father and son, talking over the previous week's events. He had begun his career in the film industry and was working at Beaconsfield Studios on *This Sporting Life* starring Richard Harris.

Returning home we enjoyed a traditional English Sunday lunch with Beryl, and then for me an early night. Those country afternoons were respites from the unsettling days at the studio.

The script called for Jenny and David to visit their son Matt one weekend at a boy's boarding school. In his teens, Christopher had attended The King's School, Canterbury, and Beryl and I had paid him many similar kinds of visits. Now it would make the perfect location.

The school, with its picturesque medieval buildings, was founded over fifteen hundred years ago within the precincts of Canterbury Cathedral. From the cathedral's Bell Harry Tower one can look across the expansive countryside to the sea.

Permission to use King's had to be obtained from two very important gentlemen. One was the Dean, the Very Reverend Hewlett Johnson—known as the "Red Dean" because of his public support of communism. The other was the headmaster of the school, the renowned Dr. John Shirley, D.D., after whom the cathedral was irreverently nicknamed "Shirley's Temple." Both read the script and gave us their blessings.

Not being associated with the film industry, they clearly couldn't have understood how much was involved. Perhaps they thought we would come down and take a few pictures and be gone.

Our shooting took place during term time, so, with the real students hard at work, extras had to be employed. Back in London, a call had been put out for available boys, who we would dress authentically in school blazers and ties. But our young fellows turned out to be a bit rough round the edges and behaved badly compared to King's more gentlemanly scholars.

A conflict started brewing. During a break in lessons, the real students came to watch us film and didn't like what they saw. They thought our young actors would give their school a bad name, especially by smoking in public.

They went straight to the school captain and he in turn got on to the headmaster.

"This behavior must stop immediately," John Shirley demanded.

The Red Dean arrived on site a few minutes later. He was aghast to see the crew laying a camera track down a pedestrian pathway. "People are going to trip over these things and injure themselves," he sputtered as his mind calculated the cost of insurance claims against the cathedral. "We never expected anything like this."

We were certain both men would shut down production.

If things weren't tough enough, Judy chose that moment to throw one of her tantrums. She was having an audible, flaming row in her trailer with her most loyal friend, Dirk. To emphasize some point, she chucked her breakfast eggs and bacon at him. It was all to do with him being unable to stay with her and the children at a local hotel that evening because of an appointment in London.

Somehow I appeased both the Dean and headmaster. Perhaps the offer of a generous donation to the library helped and a promise that our boys would stay in their coach until they were needed for filming.

Then I turned my attention to Judy, who, astonishingly, stepped out of her trailer, happy, smiling, and ready to work. The sequence was finished without any further ado and the following Monday found us back at Shepperton.

It is traditional in British public schools to put on an annual play, often at the end of the winter term. This was the next scene to be shot. Since it was a boys only school, boys also played the female parts, just as they had in Shakespeare's day. Everyone would have expected us to have chosen *As You Like It* or *A Midsummer's Night's Dream*, but we decided on Gilbert and Sullivan's *H.M.S. Pinafore* because this gave Judy an opportunity to sing.

Also an entertaining twist would be if our boy, Matt, played one of the girl's roles. In some ways it was déjà vu—me playing Juliet at Hurstpierpoint. Of course, as Americans, Turman and Millar were puzzled by this very English tradition.

Every attempt was made to ensure authenticity, slightly ragged performances and all! A group of boys who could sing were brought in for Saul

Chaplin's version of "I Am the Monarch of the Sea"—Judy accompanying them on the piano and singing along. This was the only musical number shot live, rather than to playback, Saul doing the actual keyboard work at the side of the set while Judy mimed. It was a special day for her, she loved what she was doing and again it showed. Happily, during this studio period, we had several days of harmony and peace:

"We're all right, aren't we Pussycat?"

"We're all right, Judy."

One evening after shooting, about three quarters of the way through the schedule, I went to the Shepperton bar for my usual end-of-the-day scotch. Colin Brewer joined me and mentioned that Judy had decided not to go back to London, but was staying at an inn in the village so as to be near the studio for an early call the following morning. Great, I thought. As I was leaving, Col called me to the telephone and mouthed, "Judy."

I took the phone with trepidation, expecting the worst—she was going to tell me she wouldn't be in the next day.

"I want to see you immediately."

"You mean now?"

"Yes, right now." She thought nothing of preempting the plans anyone else might have. "I'll expect you in ten minutes."

I hung up and dialed Beryl, who commiserated with me. I can't say I moved quickly from the bar to the car!

When I arrived at the Ship Inn, the barman directed me to her room. Climbing the red-carpeted stairs, I could only think, "What now?"

Judy's voice came in response to my knock.

"Come in."

She was propped up in bed with a bottle of Blue Nun *liebfraumilch* on the night table, and a glass of the wine in her hand. It was the only alcoholic drink she was allowed since an earlier bout of hepatitis.

The room was a square box with a small wardrobe, a bed, and one modest chair for me—not the setting for a big film star.

"Order a drink from the bar and sit down and let's talk." She refilled her glass. I had expected trouble, but instead, she was friendly and cheerful as we chatted about the film and how well it was going. All the while I was wondering why I was there. A double scotch was delivered, and she refilled her wine glass again.

"The local doctor is coming to see me in a few minutes," she announced.

I thought nothing of that because Judy was always seeing doctors. Another scotch for me, another wine for Judy. A knock at the door and I admitted the expected man.

"I'll say goodnight, Judy," I said excusing myself. "See you in the morning."

"No! Don't leave, Ronnie! Go downstairs and get another drink. Come back when the doctor leaves."

I sat at the bar, watching the ice melt in my glass. I still couldn't help wondering what was coming next.

Twenty minutes later, fuming with rage, the doctor came down. "I can't get through to that impossible woman. She thinks she knows more about medicine than I do. My patients don't tell me what they need. Good night."

Back up the stairs I trudged.

"Stupid man!" She spat out the words as I sat down again. "I know what I need. I know myself better than anyone. Get me another doctor, Ronnie."

"Judy, it's 9:30 P.M. We're in Shepperton, not London. I don't know a doctor."

"There must be another in the area. I *need* a doctor . . . now . . . or I won't be able to work tomorrow!"

Once again, I descended the stairs and located the hotel manager. Duly impressed that Judy Garland was staying at his establishment, he arranged for his personal doctor, who was a friend, to come round.

Climbing the stairs, a little more slowly this time, I informed Judy. Within minutes the phone rang, "He's here," she announced as she replaced the receiver.

"I'll have a word with him before he comes in to see you," I said and went down the familiar seventeen steps.

Being completely frank, I told him. "Miss Garland must be on set at 8:00 A.M. tomorrow morning. She's just seen one doctor, and he walked out on her. I don't quite know what to do. But, could you please be very tactful?"

As I turned back to the bar to await the outcome, I found myself thinking, "God knows what's going to happen. There is nothing to shoot without her." But by now, I'd had a good deal of scotch, and somehow it didn't seem to matter as much. I was starting to look at the evening more lightheartedly.

We'll never know what happened between Judy and this doctor. Perhaps he understood the vagaries of the picture business or perhaps he had a personality capable of ministering to difficult patients. Whichever way, he was all smiles when he came down.

"I think you can stop worrying. She's fine."

I traipsed my way up again. She too was all smiles. I gave her a big hug, and she gave me her words of approval, "We're all right, Pussycat."

After another half an hour, completely drained, I was able to extricate myself, but with difficulty—in her desperate need for attention, Judy made it clear she wanted me to stay and comfort her for the rest of the night.

The next day she arrived promptly and for five more days we had absolutely one hundred percent professional work from her. Moving easily from set to set, we even began to catch up on the schedule. One of the strongest scenes in Judy's career was filmed during this period.

After two rehearsals we shot the first long take. It is the evening of Jenny Bowman's performance at the Palladium. She sprains her ankle and is taken to the emergency ward where she asks the hospital staff to call David. Shortly he arrives. Realizing she is late for her performance, and indeed, has no intention of going to the theater, he pleads with her not to let her audience down. A short lull. Then he offers her some coffee.

"I'm full," Jenny retorts, "full to the brim of the whole God-damned world."

"Jenny, it's a sell-out. You promised. They're waiting. . . ."

"Let them wait. To hell with them. I can't be spread so thin. I'm just one person. I don't want to be rolled out like a pastry so everybody can have a nice big bite."

As the drama progresses, her emotions change from anger to tears, and what ultimately transpires between Jenny and David is a kind of nonphysical love scene. The words fitted Judy and her state more closely than any of us could have imagined. Dirk picked up the dialogue:

"Darling I don't give a damn who you let down. . . . There is something I haven't been able to say to you."

"Don't say it, if you say it now. . . ."

"I love you."

Normally, a sequence of this length would be a day's work, with several cuts. But, I realized something was happening. Something not planned. Something I'd never get anything like again. The room was filled with such emotional intensity that the unit became caught up in the moment. It was magic! Instead of cutting the camera where originally intended, I kept it running. . . . Nodding to the grip to keep tracking forward. . . . Closer and closer to Judy and Dirk. Quick to understand, Arthur Ibbetson signaled to an electrician, to put a diffuser over a light that was on the top of the camera before it became too bright for a large close shot.

Dirk, who must have had tremendous peripheral vision, realized what was happening and adjusted his physical closeness to her, all the while listening to her and modifying his own dialogue accordingly. Judy became so personally involved that the words took on a special meaning for her far beyond the character as written. Tears were streaming down her face, her nose was running; her voice was choked with feeling. It was as if there was no camera. Judy was using this situation as a catharsis for everything that was taking place in her own life.

The poignancy of the scene revolves around the fact that they both know from the start that no matter how much love there is between them, their relationship is over. The only meaningful and lasting one Jenny has is with her audience. In the end, David persuades her to go back to her life in the theater and to stand on the stage alone.

When I finally said "cut," everyone on the set was visibly affected. The crew, who had little reason to like Judy, found themselves in tears.

Andrew Lloyd Webber: In *I Could Go On Singing*, the sequence between Judy Garland where she lets her inner self go is an unforgettable example of Ronnie's skill and instinct. He had such sure command over his team that he was able to keep the cameras rolling when Garland took off into unscripted flight.

After this incredible sequence, Dirk and Judy went home very satisfied with their performances. I was on a high and felt everything was now going splendidly.

But, suddenly something occurred that devastated Judy—Marilyn Monroe had taken a fatal overdose. In many ways Judy's life and Marilyn's had run parallel. Both were unquestionable stars, but both were fragile and were substance abusers. Furthermore, they equally knew the benefits and consequences of being adored by millions.

"This need never have happened," Judy exclaimed angrily, "someone should have been there to rescue her. She shouldn't have been left alone."

Marilyn's death hit too close to home. Turman and Millar told me much later that on two occasions early on in the production, Judy had staged her own halfhearted suicide attempts, mainly with pills; she also hit her head against some tiles in her bathroom.

A few days later, she seemed to have bounced back from her depression—laughing on the set once again with Dirk and Liza. Liza had been with her all the time, and was a tremendous support to her mother. We had three or four happy days, lulling us into a false sense of security. Then one morning, at 3:00 A.M., the phone rang. I knew who it was.

"Yes, Judy."

"I won't be coming in today."

"Oh, Judy, please, darling. You must come in."

"Liza is more important to me than your fucking film. Shoot around me."

"I can't shoot around you. I have nothing else to shoot."

Slowly more awake.

"What's Liza got to do with it?" My voice still gruff with sleep and frustration.

"She's flying to Israel this morning, and I'm going to the airport to see her off. And that's final."

Now fully awake, I was able to think.

"What time is the plane?"

"Eleven o'clock."

"Let me send the makeup team to you at home. Go with Liza to Heathrow and see her off, then come on to the studio—it's only twenty minutes from the airport. You could be there by 11:30. I'll somehow do a few inserts or something to keep us going until you arrive."

"I may never come in again." She rang off.

I immediately phoned Col.

At the studio the next day, the unit waited. Dirk wasn't on call, just Judy, Aline McMahon, who played her dresser, and Jack Klugman who played her manager. At 11:30 A.M. no Judy.

I asked Col to ring her home. "Tell whoever answers that Miss Garland has got to be in the studio by two o'clock or else we'll report the whole matter to United Artists in New York."

At 2:30 Judy arrived. She walked straight up to me and said, "You shit. You could have given me the whole day off."

"I've already told you, Judy, there is nothing left to shoot without you. You have to be here every day until we finish the picture."

I took her through one of the key scenes in the story. Jenny has returned to her hotel to try on some hats. As she puts one on, she tells her dresser that she loves young Matt, who still doesn't know she's his mother, and intends to go on seeing him, despite her promise to David.

The rehearsal went beautifully. Her hairdresser twirled a final curl, and we shot the first take.

"Okay, Judy, that was fine. We'll do just one more."

Like so many actors, she tended to get better and better each time.

"If that was fine, why do you want another one? You're not going to have it unless I know what was wrong."

I wasn't trying to antagonize her, but by this point in the production, the crew was on edge. I was on edge. Perhaps most frustrating was that I could see glimpses of her brilliance coming through.

"Judy, you know as well as I do that sometimes you do something even better when we shoot again, and besides, we need two printed takes for editing. But since you're making such a fuss, there's no longer any point in going again. You certainly won't be any better."

"No," she said. "We'll do it again."

"Judy," I said, emphatically, "we will *not* go again. We'll do the close ups."

"Then you'll do them without me."

She headed for the door, with one of the hats still on her head. As she was about to exit, I said rather loudly. "Get the producers on the set."

She paused, turned as in a choreographed scene.

"That's right! Get the producers to come in and save you. You won't see me again until I'm treated like a lady!" And she walked out.

I still sometimes wonder if it really happened. But it did, and she was gone. She said it with more finality than all the other times. I was physically and emotionally exhausted. Judy could do that to just about anyone.

A few minutes later I went to her trailer and knocked.

"Who is it?"

"Ronnie."

"I don't want to see you."

"Please, Judy, open the door."

The dresser opened it and then slipped away. Judy was taking off her makeup. I knelt down beside her to be at her level.

Taking her hand, I said, "Judy, we both want to make a good film, don't we? Please let's be friends. In only another few days, it'll all be finished."

This time she yelled, "I don't want to talk to you. Get the hell out."

I heard from several members of the crew that she later boasted, "I brought Ronnie to his knees."

Jack Klugman: It was authority she had problems with. She may have felt they were always trying to corral her. She loved her fellow actors. She was rebellious against producers, directors. But never did an artist give more. Even when she was tired, she gave it all she had. If she trusted you, she was as gentle as could be. If not, she had the sharpest tongue.

Next day there was no Judy. By now, Turman and Millar, although sympathetic to my plight, had the responsibility of getting on to Arthur Krim in New York.

"She wants you off the film." I wasn't surprised and told Arthur I'd willingly resign if he thought it would help get the picture finished.

He then asked, "Are you prepared to carry on no matter what?"

"Yes, of course. If I have your support."

"Could you complete without her?"

"It's nearly possible," I said, with considerable uneasiness. "Maybe if Dirk does a narration for some of the scenes." Who was I kidding? "But, Arthur, there is no way we can complete the film without Judy singing the last song scheduled for next Monday at the Palladium."

"Okay, we'll send her a telegram through her agent: 'If Miss Garland isn't at the London Palladium Monday morning, the production will be closed down, and there will be a lawsuit.'"

Hoping for the best, Colin called a thousand extras, most of them from Judy's fan club.

Early on Monday morning everyone was there. No Judy.

We had to vacate the theatre by 5:30 P.M. for the scheduled show that night.

I was desperate. And extras were waiting for their idol. Three cameras were ready to roll. An entire unit was on hold.

Eventually we turned round onto the audience. And Ronnie Neame played Judy, miming the song to her playback and doing all the movements we had planned for her. The enthusiastic and noisy audience reactions were shot. At least something had been achieved.

Suddenly the makeup man, Harold Fletcher, approached me and whispered, "She's in!"

I called Colin over, "Ask her to come on stage, and I'll show her what we've blocked out." Onto the set she came, hair in curlers. All of us could hardly believe she was actually there!

"Hello, Judy," I managed cordially.

"What do you want me to do?" she asked.

I showed her.

"That's okay, Pussycat."

It was as though this terrible week had never happened.

I went on to explain where we were going to cut David into the scene. In the script he has accompanied her to the theater only to wait in the wings until he is sure she is standing on her feet again. Once satisfied, he leaves. And Jenny sees him walking out of her life forever as she finishes her song, "I Could Go On Singing."

Judy, in a short black dress, completed the scene as brilliantly as anything she'd ever done. Miraculously we were out of the Palladium on schedule.

The last shot of the movie was filmed on a lovely sunny day on the lawn at Shepperton Studios. The entire unit was there. It was a simple exterior close shot. Once done, I quietly said, "That's it, Judy, darling. It's finished. It's really finished."

She repeated, "It's really finished." She looked at me, and then took in the whole unit for a few seconds. With a smile she said, "You'll miss me when I'm gone!"

Her parting line was not sympathy seeking, nor was it expressed with rancor. Given the emotional roller coaster ride we had all been on, it's hard to explain why, when she left that set for the last time, many of us were in tears.

The song "I Could Go On Singing," composed by E. Y. "Yip" Harburg and Harold Arlen became the title of the film. Although not an immediate success, over the years it has become a cult movie. Fans still watch it over and over to see vintage Judy at her sporadic best, unscripted emotions blended with sparkles of her remarkable talent.

And all these years later she was right. My goodness, how we miss her.

· 23 ·

Ron-Pon

$\mathcal{R}$oss Hunter, a producer known for his pristine sets and heavily gauzed camera lenses, and I, a director who had been trained in realism, made an odd combination for *The Chalk Garden*, a film based on the play by Enid Bagnold. Ross had established his reputation in Hollywood with a series of lush dramas, *Imitation of Life*, *Magnificent Obsession*, and predictable comedies like *Pillow Talk*. Most of his films had large audience appeal and were consequently big box office hits.

The play, produced by Irene Selznick, opened in the fall of 1955 in New York with Gladys Cooper playing the lead role of Mrs. St. Maugham. In the spring of the following year it began an extended run at London's Haymarket Theatre with Dame Edith Evans taking over the part.

Ross had contemplated turning it into a film for a long time, but didn't get in touch with me until early in 1963. I had seen it and confess to thinking he was not the right casting as producer for this specialized piece that would inevitably have a smaller audience than his usual projects. However, he expressed a desire to do something more prestigious and because I liked the subject very much, I agreed to work with him.

As the film was to be shot in England, Ross came over to choose locations and organize the casting with me. He had decided on Gladys, but Dame Edith's agent contacted me about the possibility of her playing the part. Understandably both women regarded the role of Mrs. St. Maugham as their own.

"You know," I said, "Dame Edith is a very important actress in this country, and even if you're set on the idea of Gladys, as a courtesy, you should at least meet her."

A few days later, we arranged a morning appointment in Ross's elegant apartment at the Dorchester. Sweeping into the suite precisely at eleven came the regal, somewhat intimidating Edith Evans.

193

"Good morning to you, Mr. Hunter, and to you, Mr. Neame," she said in her imperious voice. Fixing her eyes on Ross, she added, "I know you are an American producer, Mr. Hunter, and I've heard about you."

After this slightly ambiguous beginning, our conversation rapidly became warm and friendly, as we spoke about a variety of topics—especially how she felt that the role was made for her. "It really shouldn't go to anyone else!" she told us in no uncertain terms. "It's my part."

At the end of about half an hour, something odd occurred. Edith had got it firmly into her mind that she was to be Mrs. St. Maugham.

"You know," she concluded as she rose to leave, "I believe I'm going to enjoy working with you Mr. Hunter. Just give me a call when you want me to go for wardrobe fittings and I will be there. Thank you. Goodbye to you both." She left as majestically as she had arrived.

Ross turned to me in amazement, "What happened?"

"I've a feeling you just cast Dame Edith."

Ultimately he was happy with the choice, but Gladys Cooper was bitterly disappointed, blaming me for having sabotaged her—in reality a very savvy seventy-five-year-old grande dame of the English stage had hoodwinked us and literally cast herself!

Years later in Hollywood, Robert Morley introduced me to his mother-in-law. Gladys Cooper's only words to me were, "You're the man who did me out of *my* part in *The Chalk Garden*."

We had a fine screenplay by John Michael Hayes, although, as usual, we brought in someone else for additional dialogue. Despite the quality of the script, it still tended to be a piece of theater rather than film, therefore one of my tasks as a filmmaker would be to add the visual component.

Sandra Dee had originally been picked to play Mrs. St. Maugham's troubled granddaughter, Laurel, but had to bow out when she became pregnant. Hayley Mills took her place—a terrific choice.

Deborah Kerr, with whom I hadn't worked since *Major Barbara*, was now an important Hollywood star with several Oscar nominations. We cast her as the governess/companion, Miss Madrigal, and my old chum, Johnnie Mills, came along as the butler, Maitland. Felix Aylmer took the role of Mrs. St. Maugham's former lover, Judge "Puppy" McWhirrey.

Occasionally during rehearsals of the longer dialogue scenes this eminent old character actor would fall asleep, only to be reprimanded by Dame Edith.

"Stupid old man," she would exclaim, "quite unforgivable."

Exteriors were shot in several picturesque settings in Sussex—the outside of a period country home in Littlington, as well as locations in Alfriston, Beachy Head, and the White Cliffs of Dover. Ross couldn't apply his Hollywood touch to these very English areas, but when we returned to the studio, we ran into his penchant for lushness.

The very clever Carmen Dillon designed the sets. Her past credits included Laurence Olivier's *Hamlet, Henry V* and *Richard III*, as well as Anthony Asquith's *The Browning Version*—so she knew her craft. Appropriately, the interior of the English country house was slightly shabby with a lived-in look giving the impression Mrs. St. Maugham had spent many years there. But Ross started to change everything.

Carmen came to me in tears. "Ronnie, it's just awful what he wants me to do. He's ruining everything."

When I talked to Ross about it, he countered, "Who cares about authenticity. I can't put that tatty stuff on screen. The home belongs to a well-off lady and it has to be beautiful."

I commiserated with Carmen, but there was little we could do. Ross was the boss. She was disappointed, but, like a true professional, she carried on.

Edith was a joy to direct. She brought as much to a role as Alec did, but unlike him, she always expected to be the center of attention.

"I don't know anything about film," she would complain to me. "It's all so difficult. I mean am I supposed to stop on this little dot or that one? How can I possibly do so and concentrate on my lines?" In fact it was a ploy, she knew exactly where to position herself and she never missed her mark.

After Ross had seen the first day's rushes, he visited the set and gave a lively pep talk to the cast and crew. "You're all so good. The rushes are wonderful. Congratulations and thank you. You're really great." And he was gone.

Almost before the stage door had closed behind him, Edith said to the entire unit as if she were addressing the gallery in the theater:

"What else did he expect us to be?"

She and I would often sit together while waiting for the next setup, and we would chat, mostly about her. Out of the blue, one day, she said, "You know, I've never been a beautiful woman."

"You *are* beautiful," I told her.

"No, no, no," she protested. "I'm not beautiful. But in my long career in the theater, I've had to play many beautiful women. Do you know what I do, Ron-Pon?"

"Tell me."

"Five minutes before my entrance," she explained, "I stand in the wings, and I think *beautiful*. Then, when I walk on stage . . . I *am* beautiful!"

Ron-Pon remained her pet name for me throughout the many years of our friendship.

Not only was Deborah's performance meticulous, but also her demeanor towards Edith was one of patience and understanding. She stepped back, making Edith feel like the star, even though Deborah was the far more important film celebrity. I was terribly grateful to her for that gesture. It would have been impossible if my two leading ladies had competed for center stage.

Working with Johnnie and Hayley was a personal delight. Hayley was so good as Laurel and so professional. I'm sure Johnnie worked with her at home. The entire Mills family was—and still is—a closely-knit group.

Except for my disappointment with the clean, white, sterile decor, the shooting period itself was most enjoyable.

A director normally stays with a film right up to its delivery to the distributor, but, in the case of *The Chalk Garden*, I made the decision to leave after my director's cut. The reasons were personal. Beryl and I were considering a big change in our lives, and needed to concentrate all our efforts on that.

Therefore, unfortunately, I was unable to exert any influence on the final cut, dubbing, and music recording. Malcolm Arnold, who had done such wonderful work on *Tunes of Glory*, wrote a score under Ross's supervision and influence. Malcolm's ability was apparent, but it was overused—the film finished up with wall-to-wall music. To say the least, I was upset. Music can be an enormous plus to a film, an added dimension, but too much defeats the object.

In all honesty, even if I'd remained on the picture, I very much doubt anything could be achieved other than what Ross wanted. He was Universal's most successful producer and the studio would naturally back his decisions—he was where the money was.

• 24 •

Mister Moses

Long-term finances began to occupy my thoughts. As a child, my family didn't worry about money, but after my father's death I learned what it was like to be poor and during the war years we had all lived frugally. At age fifty-two, I still hadn't been able to save and was concerned that my slightly advancing age might soon put me out of fashion. I had watched it happen with my mother and wanted the security of knowing my own family could live comfortably into my retirement. Income tax in England in the 1960s had reached the extortionate level of eighty percent and it had become utterly impossible for those of us existing in a freelance capacity to save for the future. Many older directors and actors with whom I'd been associated ended up with nothing after working hard their entire lives.

We started to think about buying a property outside England where the cost of living was more affordable—Spain or Italy.

Four of us—Beryl, Christopher, along with his girlfriend Heather, and I—went to Monte Carlo. Christopher had been busy with his own career in films that year which included *The Wrong Arm of the Law* starring Peter Sellers, and a TV series, *The Human Jungle*. He had met Heather the previous summer and their relationship looked as though it might be serious.

From Monte Carlo we crossed the Italian border on our short way to La Mortola, a village of pastel colors near Ventimiglia. Friends of ours, the Crosbys, had recently retired there and become part of a substantial British colony. George, a retired Harley Street doctor, had a gentleness of manner and his presence befit such a role—belying this was his usual attire of shorts and colorful shirts and his constant puffing on a pungent, square-shaped cigar. His wife, Vi, had been an actress and she was the life and soul of the party, outgoing and witty.

197

The hillside overlooking the Mediterranean was strewn with villas—large and small—and the warmth of the people charmed us. As a result we were very much taken with the idea of settling there. Apparently, if we built a house and it was not deemed to be a luxury villa, it would be free of rates and taxes for the first twenty years. This meant if I was fortunate enough to make a few more films, we would at last be able to save.

Vi and George kindly let us have the guest quarters of their villa while we began to search for a suitable plot of land. Because of the geography and geology of the area, this was more difficult than had been anticipated. We often took a break from our task and went "abroad" to Menton—a ten-minute drive from La Mortola. French food made a change from pasta.

During the intervals he spent in the South of France, my brother often joined us. Derek still suffered from depression—feeling everyone was against him, or robbing him, even his friends. In retrospect perhaps he should have been on some kind of medication. I hugged him after each visit, making him promise to try and look on the bright side and not to do anything to harm himself.

One day, on our return to La Mortola, we found Vi and George in a state. Pointing up at the hill, George said, "There's been an accident."

"What kind of accident?"

"A car coming round the bend spun over and came off the road."

"Oh, my God. Was anyone hurt?"

"Fortunately not. The woman driver and her son walked away from it, but the car's a write off. Come and have a look."

We started up.

A few minutes later, as we stood a few yards from the wreckage, I turned to gaze out towards the Mediterranean sparkling in the Italian sun and suddenly thought what a wonderful position for a house.

Within days, our newly appointed Ventimiglian business manager, Trucchi, had located the four brothers who owned the property. Three were interested in selling; the fourth wasn't. Finally, Trucchi managed to persuade the stubborn sibling, and we became the proud owners of a piece of land on the Italian Riviera. This was the first of many little miracles Trucchi would work for us over the years.

Now we were faced with two tasks—selling Mount Fidget and finding someone to design our Italian home.

Mount Fidget sold almost immediately, the new owners agreeing we could stay on until able to relocate. My mother was still living at the Onslow Court Hotel, and agreed to come often to Italy, especially during winter.

On our first trip there, George and Vi had introduced us to Colin Colahan, a gregarious Australian-Irish painter and sculptor, who lived with his wife,

Ursula, just up the hill in the largest villa in the area. Twice married, he had been in Europe since 1934 and was best known as a "war artist." I always thought of him as a latter-day Impressionist—his paintings had a richness of color with a softness of light. Like everyone else in La Mortola, he seemed to dress like his perceived image of himself—floppy straw hat on top of his long white hair, paint-stained artist's smock and sandals.

Colin volunteered to assist with the designs and also find someone to do construction work. Everything seemed to be falling into place. A young Italian builder came along and within a week the land had been surveyed and pronounced safe. We had committed ourselves to an exciting journey that would last for several years.

During one of our stays there, Arnold Picker, then head of United Artists under Arthur Krim, asked me to fly to Hollywood to meet producer Frank Ross about a picture to be made in Africa. It was to star the handsome, all-American Robert Mitchum.

Mister Moses was from a novel by Max Catto—a sort of modern Exodus story. Several writers had had a go at the screenplay, including Charles Beaumont and my chum, James Kennaway. Even so I had my concerns. Frank Ross, a somewhat nervous man who compensated for it by sounding authoritative, assured me that whatever my worries were, they could be ironed out before we arrived in Kenya. He was extremely enthusiastic and, like so many producers, had an instinctive desire to be in control. What immediately caught my eye was the animated way he used his hands to express himself.

I wasn't so naïve as to completely believe him—that line about improving scripts was an old chestnut! But, a director wants to direct. And the temptation of working with Mitchum, as well as the excitement and adventure of filming an exotic location, proved irresistible.

Most of the logistics for preparing a unit for a three-and-a-half month location were left in the capable hands of line producer Richard (Dick) McWhorter, an even-tempered, jovial character who livened up a room just by being there. He and Frank Ross would be the only Americans on the unit.

Frank had already been to Nairobi to confer with the incoming government officials about the production. He knew there might be problems because the British had just given the country its independence and leadership had been turned over to Jomo Kenyatta, who would serve first as prime minister and then as president. December 12, 1963, East Africa once again belonged to the East Africans.

Fortunately, Kenyatta was a great film fan and, in fact, during one of his many long visits to England, had appeared as an extra in Zoltan Korda's 1935 film, *Sanders of the River*. As the first movie unit to film in the newly independent country, we were glad that Kenyatta was our friend in a very high place.

Dick and I traveled to Kenya to finalize the shooting areas, visiting a Masai village above Lake Naivasha on the shores of which we intended to build our own village. We met and took a great liking to the chief of the tribe, and he to us. There and then he committed his people to work on the film. It was explained—through an interpreter—that each warrior would be able to bring only one wife and just two children. But he, as chief, could bring four wives and eight children.

We arranged for five hundred to come down to the edge of the lake, where, under the supervision of set designer Syd Cain, they built a new village for themselves out of their usual raw materials—straw and cow dung. This encampment served as their living quarters as well as the main set.

A European unit on location for such a long period of time needs more comfortable lodgings, however the only decent hotels were in Nairobi, which would mean long-distance traveling each day resulting in a negative impact on our shooting schedule.

Dick McWhorter: Many British colonists, fearing the country's new independence, had left their property. One hotel, the Brackenhurst, only about an hour from our location, had run down to nothing. There were cottages that were actually mud huts with straw roofs. There was a big mess hall, a clubroom, and a nine-hole golf course overgrown with weeds. I suggested to Frank Ross that we fix up the cottages, which all had bedrooms, bathrooms, and fireplaces. We brought in carpenters and painters and got some machines to cut the lawn and restored the golf course so the unit would have something to do on Sundays. We installed a cutting room and editing equipment.

By the time I got back to London, the revised script was waiting for me—still unsatisfactory. Learning Arnold Picker would be in town within a few days, I made an appointment to see him at the Dorchester.

"The script's not good enough and, as you well know, the script is the picture. We're not ready to go into production. Please postpone until we have something better."

"We can't do that," he told me. "Mitchum has a pay-or-play contract and an established starting date of no later than the first week of January. We must go ahead."

"Then would you please release me?"

"You are a gentleman," he said, "you've signed, and I know you'll honor your commitment."

Once again I had taken a gamble by agreeing to proceed before being ready. I had only myself to blame, but at least persuaded him to bring in writer Monja Danischewsky to work first in London, and subsequently in Africa sorting out any final problems.

We had begun to assemble a small yet excellent supporting cast: Alexander Knox as the missionary, Ian Bannen as the colonial official, Raymond St. Jacques as Ubi, and good old Reggie Beckwith as Parkhurst.

For the role of Julie Anderson UA wanted a marquee name, Carroll Baker. She had been nominated for an Oscar for *Baby Doll* in 1956. In my opinion, although a fine actress, she was far too glamorous to be a missionary's daughter! I had in mind twenty-two-year-old Julie Christie, who had made two minor films (Christopher had worked on both) and the higher profile *Billy Liar*. But she was completely unknown in the States and therefore not marketable.

About ten days before the New Year, I flew to Nairobi, leaving Beryl to arrange the shipping of the furniture from Mount Fidget to Italy.

On December 24, Christopher celebrated his 21st birthday without me, but he does remember I phoned. As a gift, Beryl and I gave him a series of flying lessons at the nearby Elstree Flying Club.

Finally, on New Year's Eve, they left Mount Fidget for the last time and stayed at a hotel until the time came for them to join me.

That same evening, I was in a hotel in Nairobi waiting to meet Bob Mitchum. I'd heard stories about his bad-boy image—his heavy drinking, the wild parties, the women. We made our introductions and he appeared every bit as low key and charismatic as he was on screen. Enjoying our conversation and a couple of scotches, we had every intention of toasting in 1964, but as the evening progressed we couldn't keep our eyes open. By 9 P.M. we had passed out. In our enthusiasm we'd forgotten Nairobi is several thousand feet above sea level and had both become affected by the mixture of alcohol and altitude. Nonetheless we had started a lasting friendship.

Indispensable Colin Brewer was on the picture and I was glad to have dear Ossie back as director of photography. Os had suffered a tragedy, and there was no way I knew how to comfort him.

The previous March, he had been working on a remake of *Of Human Bondage* in Ireland—his wife, Connie, visiting him from London several times. After one weekend, he took her to the airport for her return flight to England. The following Wednesday he came into his hotel to receive a devastating phone call. Connie was dead. Apparently she'd had a brain hemorrhage that morning straight after taking their children to school.

Os and I had known each other most of our lives and through the years his family and mine had become very close. It could only be hoped that everyone on the unit would be able to help him through this difficult time.

Christopher, along with the rest of the crew, arrived in Kenya towards the end of the first week of January. By then he was experienced enough to be on a big production and Ossie had agreed that he could be the second assistant cameraman. Beryl arrived a few days later and everyone settled into their cottages at the Brackenhurst.

Christopher Neame: We drove out to the location on the day we arrived to see where we would be shooting and were rather disappointed by the terrain. It was like driving through a country lane in the south of England, except giraffes peered at us from the side of the road. Suddenly, we rounded a corner, and the bottom dropped out of the world. It was the Rift Valley. Taken aback, we drove excitedly down the escarpment to Lake Naivasha and were stunned by the enormous and vibrant Masai village that was to be our set.

Dick McWhorter gave me the keys of an aging Mercedes and suggested I take Colin, Ossie, and Pamela Davies, who was our script clerk, on the fifty-mile drive to the location. He said if we traveled together we could save time by talking about the day ahead during the journey. Other senior unit members were handed keys to equally ancient cars and given similar instructions. The offer seemed appealing because he added, "When we're not filming, the cars are yours to take anywhere." This was ingenious of Dick. He bought them, and then sold them at a profit after the production. He didn't tell us much in advance so we couldn't complain about it. And with us responsible for our own transportation, he also avoided hiring drivers—a great "mean man."

But it didn't all run smoothly. Kenya's high altitude affected the tuning of the cars, the air and fuel mixture was not right. The wretched vehicles wouldn't get up the escarpment that had to be scaled to get home at night. Frequently I got out of the Mercedes and, along with Col and Ossie, pushed it uphill while Pam stayed behind the wheel.

Dick McWhorter: When Ronnie and Ossie saw me back at the hotel, they would swear at me, saying, "Dick, you're putting in that damn cheap gas." But, in fact, I had put pumps at the location with the best gas I could find so they could fill up "on the house" anytime they needed to. Over the years, Ronnie, Ossie, and I have had a lot of laughs about those old Mercedes and "that cheap gas."

An important member of our cast, not overly concerned about the story, was an elephant named Suzie. She was shipped in from Johannesburg to the seaport of Mombassa and from there brought to location by flatbed truck. The script called for her to pull Mister Moses's caravan, but elephants don't *pull*, they *push*. Her trainer was doubtful whether he could ever change her inborn habits, but after three weeks she was obliging.

Carroll Baker: Bob Mitchum got along fine with Suzie, but she didn't care much for girls. I had to trudge alongside her and she had a habit of nudging me with her big wet trunk. Or I'd be standing and talking and one of those big ears would knock me down. Then she'd sneeze all over me. If you've never been the victim of an elephant's sneeze, you can't quite appreciate my predicament. Suzie was sensitive and lonely. She developed insomnia and they had to import a friend to keep her company.

With each day, our respect for the Masai grew. We admired their looks—tall and dignified—and their majestic manner. The greater part of Kenya's population is made from the Kikuyu tribe, who easily adapted to city life. The Masai, wearing their lovely yellow ochre garments, continued their tradition of living as nomads. They are an intelligent people with great integrity—proud and honest.

The men are taught from childhood to stand "at ease" on one leg, rather like flamingos, using their spears to balance themselves. We were amazed at their spear-throwing ability. After they had demonstrated their prowess and retrieved the javelin-like weapons, one would hand his to a unit member and gesture for him to have a go. Try as we might, we couldn't come close to their skill. The warriors laughed at our feeble attempts, and we laughed along with them. Their spears had a reminder of an earlier association with Britain—each bore the stamp "Made in Birmingham."

Shirley MacLaine came to stay with us for a few weeks on her way back to America from one of her many journeys, and became part of our family.

Shirley MacLaine: I became very interested in the Masai, and I went off and lived with them. I was present for the birth of several babies. From then on they began to follow me around because it was good luck to have a white woman on hand for the occasion. In fact, several children are named after me. They didn't call them "Shirley," but "Shudy"! I watched Ronnie directing amid the heat and the flies and the blood and the milk. He was able to overcome all this with the British stiff upper lip. Promptly at five o'clock, someone would come along with his glass of whiskey.

One scene called for a long shot of the whole tribe on the move across country, led by Mitchum astride Suzie pulling the caravan. We found the ideal spot, an area with rolling hills, about five miles from Naivasha. The unit drove there, but the Masai walked, as was their custom. I took my position on the top of a hill with the camera looking down into the valley while Col lined up the tribe below.

Colin Brewer: I communicated with Ronnie, who was about a half mile away, by walkie-talkie. The Masai were ready to move. They started on "Action" and then suddenly all went into a "V." Ronnie yelled through his walkie-talkie, "What's going on?" I went to investigate and found that one of the women had gone into labor. I told Ronnie, "You'll have to wait. It shouldn't be long." After half an hour, Ronnie was back on the radio. "Now, what's the holdup?" I had to tell him, "You're not going to believe this, but there's another woman having a baby." Both were delivered on the spot. Then they got back into the march and we continued with the shot.

Mitchum was patient, professional, everything a director could wish for. He was a quietly tough man, a heavy drinker, though not a Bob Newton. As an actor he was so relaxed that if you were not close by the camera you would think he was underplaying. I recall after the first sequence we shot with him and Carol, Frank Ross came up to me in a terrible state:
"He's just walking through it, Ronnie. He's not giving a performance."
"Wait till you see the rushes," I said. "He appears to be doing nothing, but in fact he's doing everything."

Ossie Morris: Bob's claim to fame was, "You don't learn your lines until you get in the car to go on to the location." He boasted that he could read the day's work and learn it within the hour from the hotel to Lake Naivasha and be word perfect upon arrival. He was true to his word.

We did have one moment of temperament. Our schedule called for Bob to report to the location for night shooting at eight P.M. Props were having great difficulty with a flame torch, which Mister Moses uses to frighten the Masai. In our film, and in reality, they are very afraid of fire. It took much longer than anticipated to get it to appear sufficiently frightening. As a result, Bob was kept waiting and, unfortunately, by midnight he was still waiting. I think I'd have been testy in his place.

Christopher Neame: Bob came out of his trailer, went straight to Ronnie, and bawled out a rather lengthy string of profanities that boiled down to: "You incompetent ass. What the hell are you playing at, keeping me hanging around all night?" Even though Ronnie was not the cause of the delay, he refrained from replying, or defending himself. The next night, Bob was there, as called, at 8 P.M. This time we were ready. Barely five minutes passed before he resumed his center position on the set. "Ronnie," he said—and we waited with baited breath—"I want to apologize to you and to the entire crew for last night." He looked around at us all. "I'm sorry."

Mitchum showed his caliber—we went back to work as if nothing had happened.

The film's title, *Mister Moses*, is derived from the fact that the Masai find a man (Mitchum) unconscious in the reeds at the side of the river. The Masai, knowing that a nearby dam will soon flood their village, reluctantly agree to leave, and put their trust in Mister Moses to lead them the two hundred miles to their "Promised Land." Making certain the tribe would not be able to return to their homes, a British official (Ian Bannen) sets fire to their huts—a climactic sequence that was left until the end of the Naivasha filming.

Before starting the scene, we explained to the Masai the possible danger, telling them to keep well away from the area. Knowing their fear of fire, we were confident they'd obey. The sequence was shot successfully and it was all over within the hour.

During the lunch-break the local fire brigade dealt with any remaining hot spots. The cast and crew were seated in the marquee and enjoying the now famous buffet prepared by our caterers—Dick was careful with money when it came to cars, but always made certain our meals were first rate. We were relaxing and discussing the day's work when we heard the most terrible explosion. Colin bolted from the table, followed by a few other members of the crew.

What had happened was that one of the acetylene containers used to start the fire had overheated and exploded—several jagged pieces flying out some fifty feet. A large piece of shrapnel struck a young Masai man, who, in spite of our warning, had slipped back into his burnt-out hut. He was killed instantly.

By the time Colin arrived on the scene there were twenty or so warriors around the body. They were upset and angry—blaming us for the death. Standing there, Col suddenly realized he was in great danger. He kept calm, expressing his sympathy. Then he turned his back on the warriors and came to tell me what had happened. I dread to think what might have occurred if any one of the Masai had accurately thrown a spear at him.

Everyone on the production was horrified and saddened. Perhaps I was the most taken aback because of my certainty that no one had been in danger—I'd been as careful as was humanly possible when dealing with explosives ever since the fatality on *In Which We Serve*. It was a one in a million accident, a piece of very bad luck.

A meeting with the elders was held there and then to find a way of expressing our sorrow and of compensating the young man's relatives. We agreed to follow Masai custom—eight head of cattle was delivered to his family. Small compensation for a life, it has to be said.

Once the location work was over I knew I'd miss these people. It was a privilege to have had the opportunity to know and work with them alongside a good cast and crew, and all of it in one of the world's very special pieces of scenery.

Beryl left for La Mortola and Christopher went back with the unit to London while the editor, Peter Weatherley, and I set off to Rome where we made the final cut. Once this was done I was anxious to return to La Mortala and see the progress made on the villa during our absence.

I arrived just in time for "the ceremony of the roof"—a tradition in many countries that calls for tree branches to be placed on the roof for good luck. To celebrate the event it was also customary to give a party on the site for all the builders.

We decided to call our home "Casa Yolanda," which was Beryl's middle name. We had the letters painted over the wrought iron gates that led to the house. But as "Y" doesn't exist in Italian and "J" is pronounced the same way, so it read "Casa Jolanda."

Our stored furniture was moved in and now only one piece of business remained. Having the villa inspected and counting on the official paperwork to read "non-luxury" and thereby freeing us from rates and taxes for many years. A large part of our financial future lay in the hands of the local examiner.

Trucchi proved invaluable by delivering a well-mannered gentleman for lunch. As this official began his inspection Trucchi took me aside and asked if he might offer the gentleman a little *gift*. I agreed.

The villa was duly recorded as a "non-luxury"—twenty years tax-free!

Soon we began to socialize—getting to know our neighbors and going back and forth across the border to France to see some old friends. We dined several times with David Niven (Nivey) who had a magnificent house on Cap Ferrat and he came to our new home. We also saw a great deal of Frank Launder, an old chum from Independent Producers, and his wife Bernadette.

One morning Vi came over to ask a favor. "My nephew is a composer and he's a genius. You have recording equipment and we haven't, you also have a better piano than our old blue-painted one. Could he do some work here?"

"Send him up," I said, then added perhaps unfairly, "but we all have genius nephews don't we?" The next afternoon, a polite fourteen-year-old arrived.

I'd been asked to direct an original musical that was hopefully being set up in England. Somewhat patronizingly I said to the young man, "I hear you are going to be a composer."

"That's right."

"Perhaps you'd like to write a song for my next film?"

"Oh, I would."

I'm sorry to say the musical never got off the ground but Vi's adolescent nephew did turn out to be a genius.

Andrew Lloyd Webber: To me everything to do with Aunt Vi was glamorous. She seemed to know everyone in show business. Among her many friends was Ronnie, who she had persuaded to build a rather grand villa almost next door to hers. I remember our first meeting well. The drawing room was full of photographs of the great and famous, the likes of Alec Guinness and Judy Garland. When I realized Ronnie was trying to develop a musical it was time to strike. Being a precocious brat, I naturally presumed that I could write wonderful songs for the movie. Thus, poor Ronnie was obliged to listen to my juvenile offerings, which he did with astonishing kindness and patience. He claims one of them was the tune that a few years later became "I Don't Know How to Love Him" from *Jesus Christ Superstar*. I truthfully cannot remember this, but I am absolutely sure that charming as he was to this long-haired teenager, he didn't think that in less than a decade we would work together when I composed the score for *The Odessa File*.

Mister Moses on location in Kenya, with Carroll Baker and Robert Mitchum.

Gambit with
Michael Caine
and Shirley
MacLaine.
Keeping Shirley's
eyes the right
shape was a
problem.

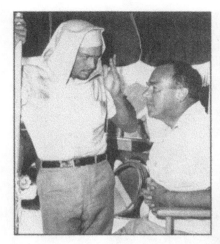

Escape from Zahrain: in the desert with Yul Brynner.

I Could Go On Singing, Judy Garland's last film.

Hayley Mills' birthday party on the set of *The Chalk Garden*: me, Deborah Kerr, Felix Aylmer, Edith Evans, Ross Hunter, and Hayley with her dad, Johnnie.

The Prime of Miss Jean Brodie with Jean and her girls.

Escorting one of those girls, Pamela Franklin, down the red carpet at the Cannes Film Festival.

Top: With Flicky and Gin Rummy.

Center: *Hopscotch* with Glenda Jackson and Walter Matthau.

Bottom: *First Monday in October*, at home with Walter.

The Poseidon Adventure with Jack Albertson and Shelley Winters.

The cast of *The Poseidon Adventure*.

With Donna and the CBE.   An honor from BAFTA.

Donna and I with Her Majesty the Queen and Prince Philip at BAFTA's fiftieth.

Top: Hayley Mills, Donna Neame, John Mills, and Andrew Lloyd Webber.

Center: "Hitch" is Man of the Year.

Bottom: At the screening of *The Card* for the London Film Festival, Alec and I reminisce.

Top: The last time I saw David Lean, with Donna and Peter Beale.

Center: Tony Havelock-Allan and I in Venice.

Bottom: My ninetieth birthday weekend, with Christopher, Gareth, Donna, and Prince Edward.

· 25 ·

Gambit

$\mathcal{B}$ored with her lifestyle, through a series of misadventures, Madame Yes becomes a pirate on a ship loaded with guns and ammunition heading for the Middle East. The perfect role for someone unconventional and free-spirited—Shirley MacLaine.

Dale Collins' novel *The Mutiny of Madame Yes* could, in my view, be turned into a good film, so I contacted the Mirisch brothers in Hollywood. They read it and were enthusiastic, agreeing to engage Monja Danischewsky to work with me on the screenplay and when Walter Mirisch told me Shirley had expressed an interest, we naturally wrote with her personality in mind.

I flew to Hollywood with the completed work, but to echo Gulley Jimson, "It wasn't the vision I had, not what I meant." Therefore, it never went into production.

Just as I was making arrangements to return to Italy, my current US agent, Arthur Parke, phoned to say that a producer on the Universal lot, Robert Arthur, was anxious to speak with me. When we met at the studio that afternoon, he told me he was in serious trouble with a production shooting in Europe called *A Man Could Get Killed*. The cast and crew had fallen out with director Cliff Owen who had left in the middle of production. Robert explained the problem had been a clash of personalities. Currently the film was on hiatus as the unit was moving from Portugal for interior shooting in Italy. He asked if I would step in.

"What makes you think I'd be a good replacement?"

"Both James Garner and Melina Mercouri know about you," he told me, "and would be delighted if you'd join them."

The film also starred Tony Franciosa and Sandra Dee.

208

By July 1, 1965, I was in Rome speaking with cast members to find out more about the problems, re-reading the script and looking at what had been shot so far. In a matter of days we were on a stage at Cinecitta.

Melina, with her distinctive accent and low raspy voice, was a real professional—she alone made the film worth doing. Other than her husband, Jules Dassin, I was one of a very small number of directors who worked with her. She liked to spend time with her director and often asked me to join her for dinner. Although I was extremely fond of her, her strong personality made me wary. She used to say, "Ronnie, I think you are afraid of me." The truth was that after a day's shooting, I was tired and preferred to return to the hotel the company had arranged for me just outside the city. But yes, perhaps I was a little afraid.

Despite the usual existing problem when directors are replaced, everything proceeded smoothly enough except one, a night scene when my two highly talented but volatile leading men turned on each other—it had already been intimated that James and Tony Franciosa did not get on!

The action was a fight between their two characters. Suddenly Tony yelled, "You shit. You're really hitting me." In that instant they both lost control and it became a nasty brawl with them going at each other with such ferocity that the crew had to pull them apart. In the final cut it added realism, but at the time it was most unpleasant.

Universal flew editor Alma Macrorie to Rome for the editing. I was delighted to have the opportunity of working with this gifted lady, but in the end, the finished film was disappointing. The only memorable thing about it, for which I can't claim credit, is Bert Kaempfert's theme song, "Strangers in the Night," which became one of Frank Sinatra's most popular hits.

On my next visit to Hollywood, I met Leo Fuchs, a former stills photographer, who aspired to be a producer. Universal was about to give him the opportunity. He'd presented the studio with a short story by Sidney Caroll entitled *Who Is Mr. Dean?* and then Sidney was also asked to write the screenplay.

By the end of September I had been contracted to direct it. Through a delightful set of circumstances, Shirley MacLaine was signed to play the lead. Perhaps it was our destiny to make a film together whether it was called *Madame Yes* or *Gambit*, the now retitled name of Sidney's script. All we needed next was a good leading man:

Shirley MacLaine: We had seen Michael Caine in *The Ipcress File*, and I just loved his acting and what he did, and I asked Ronnie if we could use him. Michael remembers that I was responsible for bringing him to Hollywood. It was the time of some of the clubs like The Daisy, so Michael had his experiences with Hollywood babes.

Michael was one of the hottest young actors around—the year before he had been nominated for an Oscar as *Alfie* and had also appeared as Harry Palmer in *Funeral in Berlin*—but he had not yet made a film in America. Thankfully Universal had the foresight to sign him up as our antihero.

On his first-ever visit to California, he was booked into the Beverly Hills Hotel but no one bothered to advise me he was there. Thus he had been basically on his own for his first two weeks. Shirley eventually found him, and from then on he got along fine without anyone's help. After awhile he moved into a well-known apartment hotel, the Sunset Tower.

When he came to my luxurious office, his first comment was, "This is the life, Ron." After we had relaxed and felt at ease with each other, he asked if he could use the phone to call England.

"Be my guest," I replied, as I vacated my chair.

He settled behind the desk, and had a long chat with his girlfriend. "Ron," he said as he hung up. "This is a bit of all right over 'ere."

Michael is down-to-earth and jokey and can slip from cockney to upper crust without missing a beat. He has the ability to play the consummate gentleman or the complete scoundrel and be utterly convincing as both. The greatest compliment I can pay him is that he is a "chameleon" like Alec Guinness.

Alvin Sargent's input on the final script was invaluable—his dialogue and understanding of the nuances of character improved the story immeasurably. *Gambit* was his first feature film and, as they say, the rest is history (Oscars for *Ordinary People* and *Julia*).

We wanted our film to be different from the glut of comedy heist movies already in release and Shirley, who contributed to every aspect of the film, was the one to come up with a way of grabbing the audience.

Shirley MacLaine: The whole first part of the film had dialogue for my character. My muse visited me, and I had a revelation. "Why don't we just have this first part silent?" Ronnie went along with my idea completely. I don't say a word until twenty-seven minutes into the film.

With Shirley's idea and Alvin's understanding of character, we were able to craft an excellent script. The film introduces the audience to Harry Dean (Michael) and Nicole Chang (Shirley) as Harry fantasizes with her about how easy the heist of a valuable art object would be. Through his eyes we see exactly what will happen. Twenty-seven minutes later, the audience is brought back to reality and then follows the actual robbery where everything goes clumsily and completely wrong.

Alvin Sargent: Michael Caine is the best kind of person to write dialogue for. There's something musical about his delivery. Shirley is rather playful. Ronnie is a focused workman, no anxiety to his work, an iron fist in a velvet glove. For about two months, I was writing while they were shooting, and I remember running up to the stage to deliver revisions to him.

Herbert Lom was cast as Ahmad Shahbandar, the wealthiest man on earth. We had worked together before on *The Golden Salamander* and had kept in touch ever since. He is amicable and an intellectual, a moderate man with a passionate temperament.

Herbert Lom: Shirley was charming and very formal, calling me "Mr. Lom" for the first few days. Then she heard me rehearsing with Michael Caine, and I used a couple of four-letter words. From that day on, she called me "Herbie."

Shooting commenced in December 1965 and almost immediately we met our first and almost only problem. Shirley, playing a Eurasian, had her eyes taped back to give her the right look. But under the heat of the lights the tape kept coming loose—three or four times a day a right or a left eye needed makeup repair, each occasion costing us thirty minutes.

When I went into the commissary, at the end of the second week, I walked past the table where the studio management, in their navy and gray designer suits, lunched. Practically in unison they raised two fingers to indicate I was two days behind schedule. At the end of the third week, three fingers. We were up to five when I decided to end their sign language. "The reason I am a week behind is because of Shirley's eyes. Remove the problem and I'll keep on schedule."

The next time I passed they used their hands to wave a conciliatory hello.

Michael Caine: There is a different working relationship at Universal versus the studios in England. Hollywood is a much more structured, businesslike affair as if run by accountants. You didn't see that in England. We're all very laid back, a bit inefficient although our crews are as good as Hollywood's. It's the administration. We don't feel fear from the top, from the suits.

From the outset Shirley and I thought it would be fun to give an end of week party for the unit, so every Friday evening, the prop department placed a tree by the stage door. In the morning, as each member of the unit came in, he or she would clip a few dollars onto its branches. At about four o'clock, one of the propmen would collect the money and purchase a keg of beer, some bottles of wine, and some food. Once Shirley took it upon herself to bring in an entire feast. Everyone looked forward to these gatherings when we could come together as a family.

Both of the stars are similarly dedicated to their craft, and neither are self-centered or egotistical—as a result one could talk to them without climbing through layers of gauze. Equally they enjoyed having a bit of fun.

Michael Caine: There was an incident about panty hose. I didn't know what they were. They were fairly new at the time. I couldn't figure out how Shirley got in and out of them. It had all been garter belts and stockings up until that point. Then I suddenly realized—I'd already done Shakespeare—so they were tights. I'd worn them myself, and I told Shirley how I kept them up. If they got a bit saggy, what you do is get a coin and twist it round in the elastic at the top and then tuck it back in itself and it tightens the whole thing up. Ronnie called them passion killers, and I agreed with that.

It was certainly a happy film, however, I must admit some days it became frustrating when Shirley, Herbert, and Michael got into laughing mode. Their humor was vastly entertaining and I realized it was a way of keeping their energy high and of relieving tension, but I had the responsibility of delivering a film that was already behind schedule. Shirley was the ringleader and there was one occasion I had the awkward task of having to ask her to stop being funny.

Shirley MacLaine: Ronnie wasn't the only director to tell me to quit making jokes. Every director tells me that. I make jokes with the crew and whomever I'm playing with. I do that right up to the time the camera rolls. The movie business is a big joke anyway. Now that I'm directing, I let the actors make jokes then I let the camera roll when they don't know it.

In a clever move that has become more elaborate over the years, the Universal Tour began taking star-struck, camera-toting tourists around the lot and, if Michael was in his dressing room, he would hear one specific young guide saying through his bullhorn: "On your right is Michael Caine's dressing room. And next to his is Shirley MacLaine's. They are both starring in *Gambit.*" This happened three or four times daily. Finally Shirley became so annoyed she took her name down and put up "Zelda Glutz."

So exasperated did he become that Michael seriously considered reporting the guide to the studio management. But he never did. He now says he's glad, because several years later that young man became one of Hollywood's most powerful agents—Michael Ovitz. Michael Caine eventually signed up as one of his clients!

Shirley had a wonderful costume designer named Jean Louis. He had fashioned clothes for many famous leading ladies, including Doris Day, Loretta Young, and Greta Garbo. One of his dresses adorned Marilyn Monroe when she sang *Happy Birthday* to Jack Kennedy. He actually had to sew it round her.

Jean was French, very religious, soft spoken, and diminutive. When someone asked him if Monroe, who used to have her fittings in the nude, was a natural blond, he blushed bright fuchsia and answered, "I didn't look."

Jean and his wife Maggie had been living in Malibu, but were in the process of relocating to Montecito, which is an elite suburb near Santa Barbara. (Santa Barbara doubled as the French Riviera in *Gambit*). Many actors and other celebrities live or lived there, including Bob Mitchum.

Around this time I attended a party in the hills overlooking the ocean in a beautiful home when I noticed Jean speaking in French to a young blonde girl—presumably French herself. Soon I learned she was an American studying at the university. Her name was Donna and although our meeting was for a fleeting moment, the image of it would come back to me more vividly later in life.

After the completion of *Gambit*, I had only a few days in which to return to England for Christopher's wedding on April 3, 1966. He and Heather had become engaged just prior to *A Man Could Get Killed*. Heather's mother and father had long since parted, so my future daughter-in-law asked if I would escort her down the aisle. In a sort of way I gave away both the bride and the groom! The service was held at Fulmer Church and the reception was an elegant affair at the celebrated Compleat Angler in Marlow. On their return from a short honeymoon, the couple moved into Dobins Cottage, a tiny place adjacent to our old home, Mount Fidget.

I returned to the States for a *Gambit* publicity tour of the East coast. It was all pretty exhausting—getting on a plane in one city, getting off in another, arriving at a radio or television station and talking about the film and the stars to a battery of journalists. The questions were always the same. It was after this tour that I stopped giving interviews, unless absolutely necessary, because of being misquoted—invariably an unpleasant experience.

One of the reporters baited me:

"Are movie stars, like Shirley MacLaine, difficult?"

I think I answered something like, "Everyone can be difficult sometimes, even Shirley." I'm equally certain I added, "But Shirley is a consummate professional and it's always a pleasure to be around her."

The headline ran, "Ronald Neame says MacLaine is difficult."

Perhaps because I rarely give interviews, few people know who I am. Those appearances and interviews I have enjoyed were ones not arranged by a studio, but given willingly to friends—but even then I have been burned.

Recently, I had the sad task of leading a memorial for Alec Guinness. Several people got on to me about him and, out of admiration and respect I cooperated. A reputable newspaper in London asked about Alec's participation in *Star Wars*. I said, "Alec probably took that film for the money, just as I took *Poseidon*. We all do that sometimes." The outcome:

"Neame Says Guinness Sold Out for Money."

In the case of Shirley, I am happy to say she forgave me and we have continued our friendship. In fact, over a wonderful meal she had prepared at her house in Malibu, we even talked about making another film together. We never got around to it in this life, but I am looking forward to the distinct possibility in the next.

Shirley MacLaine: I always liked Ronnie's diplomacy and sense of kindness, but underneath it all, he is very shrewd. His experience in every level of filmmaking is quite obvious. Both personally and professionally there are several dimensions to him. It's really Ronnie on the screen. He'd probably have made a very good actor. He is an actor. Not only does a director have to play all the parts, he has to be able to finesse what the characters are really feeling in relation to their frustrations.

Gambit was released in New York and Los Angeles in December 1966. It was generally well received, but wasn't as financially successful as any of us had hoped. There were several similar films being released at the same time—*Topkapi*, *Ocean's Eleven*, *The Jokers*. Nonetheless, I maintain it was a good script, and I'm proud of it. Also it helped my career in the sense that although I may not have been "a hot property," I certainly became "a warm one."

We welcomed a new Neame to the family on March 8, 1967, when Heather gave birth to my first grandchild, a boy, Gareth Elwin. Now, thirty-four years later, he is the Head of Independent Drama at the BBC in London—a fourth generation of Neames to become part of show business.

After his christening in Fulmer Church, Beryl and I returned to Italy. But shortly I was off again.

"Do you know a director who is available to take over a film that's in trouble?" was the urgent question put by Richard Zanuck of Twentieth to my agent Christopher Mann. I was asked if an immediate assignment on *Prudence and the Pill* would be of interest.

Richard Zanuck: I kept getting calls from cast members that things weren't working well. There seemed to be a lack of communication between them and the director, Fielder Cook. I'm not blaming him; those things happen. I went to London but, unfortunately, after talking to everybody, including Fielder, I realized I was on a hopeless mission. There was almost an open rebellion by cast members. I don't understand it because they were all lovely people. It just wasn't clicking. I told Fielder we would have to close down. It was one of those sad conversations. I had no idea who was going to come in. I just knew we couldn't continue.

A Man Could Get Killed had taught me that taking over a film could prove to be time wasted, so I was less than enthusiastic at first. However my interest increased when Mann told me my chums, David Niven, Deborah Kerr, and Dame Edith were involved—as well as Judy Geeson. The editor was Norman Savage and Wilfred Shingleton, from *Tunes of Glory*, was the production designer. After some discussion, we agreed that I'd leave for London.

Producers Ronald J. Kahn and Kenneth Harper met me at the airport on a Friday morning and whisked me off to Pinewood to review the situation. There I met with the cast and crew to hear about their frustrations— and screened what had already been shot, which didn't seem at all bad. Also I insisted on meeting with the director, which was arranged for the Sunday morning.

Exhausted, I returned to the *pied-à-terre* in St. James's, that Beryl had found for us. She had suggested the idea of getting a small place in London as we could more easily visit Chris and Heather, and also it would be convenient if a film brought me back to England. I must say it was good having a foothold in my own country again.

Fielder Cook had directed television as well as features, and I knew his work. He told me the problems he had with the production centered on the casting of Irina Demick, a French girl. Her role as David Niven's mistress was not large, but there were insurmountable difficulties—her acting was mediocre and her English inadequate. Fielder had told Darryl

Zanuck "Either she goes or I do." But she was Darryl's *protégée* and recasting was out of the question!

"Under no circumstances will I continue," Fielder told me, and then added, "I'm very glad it's you who'll take over."

With the proviso that I should have no screen credit, which I felt belonged to Fielder, I accepted the job. In the end the Directors Guild of America insisted that its contractual terms with the studios be upheld and the credit was ultimately given—I couldn't waive it.

Richard Zanuck: Not only did Ronnie decide to do it on short notice, but also we barely missed a day. We were up and shooting in no time, which I always thought was miraculous. It was worse than starting from scratch. Like coming in and taking over as captain of a ship as it's going down. Only someone as highly skilled as he is could have done it. I'd never seen that before—or since. It was a wonderful thing he did for me personally and for the studio.

Irina Demick had been assured her role was secure and she accepted me, especially when I offered her an idea.

"You know there isn't time for you to learn English, and your accent is part of the problem. What I can do is read your lines into a tape recorder, you can listen to them, hear how the words should sound, and then repeat them until you feel comfortable."

The process is something I'd never ordinarily do with an actor, but I must give Irina credit—she was conscientious and made a great effort to improve. With the cooperation of the rest of the cast and crew the production proceeded smoothly.

Judy Geeson: I'd never met Ronnie. He was tremendously comfortable with David and Deborah, who were also old friends and loved each other. During read throughs they would have tears in their eyes from laughing so much. In this relaxed atmosphere, the first thing Ronnie did was become friends with you. At once, we felt we could trust him. He would say, "What do you think Fielder would do? Where was he taking you with this role?" He became the father figure, taking care of the children, who are the actors.

I was on my own during this film, as Beryl had remained in Italy. One Saturday I walked from St. James's to lunch with Bob McNaught, who had taken an office in Christopher Mann's Park Lane suite. As he was in preproduction, he and his assistant were at work.

She was a pleasant and attractive person with an engaging personality, but I gathered from our talk that she wasn't part of the film business, simply glad to be able to work with Bob on a short-term basis.

Over lunch he told me her name was Felicité Philipson—her friends calling her Flicky. She had been divorced a few months earlier and had to earn her own living.

When we returned to the office, I chatted with her and she mentioned she had never been to a film studio. I suggested that Bob bring her along to Pinewood. When they arrived a few days later, I introduced them to the cast and after they'd spent a couple of hours on the set, Bob needed to return to his office. Seeing that Flicky was enjoying her visit, he asked if I would drive her back to London later that evening.

As we pulled up at her place and she stepped from the car, I said, "I'm sure we'll meet again," not realizing those few words would change the entire direction of my life.

At the top end of King's Road where fashionable shops burgeoned is an area called "Sloane," which became the name of a society of women, including Flicky, who were known for their discernment when it came to clothes, restaurants, and a whole outlook on life. Slender and of good height with long dark hair, her personality would come alive through sparkling brown eyes. She was one of those people who needed to laugh—and what is more infectious? We saw one another more often over the next few weeks and found we enjoyed each other's company enormously—more than I had any right.

Prudence and the Pill resulted in a light, rather clever comedy, although based on a totally incorrect premise about how "the pill" is packaged—our pill was in a bottle like aspirins and that was essential for the plot. In spite of all the complications, it turned out to be a financially successful picture and a surprise hit for Fox.

· 26 ·

The Prime of Miss Jean Brodie

If one has been singled out for youth and beauty, growing old can be particularly difficult. The years since Curley's death had not been kind to Ivy. She found it terribly hard to cope with the loss of a second husband—she was lonely and becoming bitter, sometimes taking out the unhappiness on those around her. I wondered if it had been wise for her to come back to England, where she was still questioned about years past. She would often ask, "Why can't they just go away and leave me in peace?"

When she visited us in La Mortola, she seemed to take comfort from the sunshine and occasional lunches with Derek. Apparently she had been to Glebelands, the film industry retirement home, several times and spent hours with her old show business friends. Now she expressed a desire to live there herself. I told her it wasn't practical, because people who went to Glebelands had no financial support, whereas she was assured of continued maintenance. She insisted it was the ideal place, so I promised to see what could be done.

As the Royal Command performances of *Oliver Twist* and *The Horse's Mouth* had been successful fundraisers for the home, its board of directors knew of me. Back in England, I explained Ivy's position to the gentleman in charge of admittance and he came up with a solution. If a bed-sitting room in the main house could be endowed in her name, it would be my mother's for life. To this day a plaque above the door reads "The Ivy Close Room."

With my mother settled into her new accommodation, I felt more relaxed about being abroad. Christopher and Heather, now pregnant for the second time, and little Gareth, came to stay with us in Italy for a winter holiday.

After Christmas, I was hoping to get back to work and as if in response to my wishes, Christopher Mann asked, "When will you next be in London?"

From the tone of his voice, there was obviously something he had in mind. Dick Zanuck was about to pay me back tenfold for taking over *Prudence*.

The producer of *The Prime of Miss Jean Brodie*, Bobby Fryer, was a likeable man, whose background had been theater rather than film—he had several Tony winning Broadway productions to his credit including *Mame* and *Sweeney Todd*. I very much wanted to do *Brodie*, my interest stemming from having seen the play once in London with Vanessa Redgrave and again in New York with Zoë Caldwell.

Richard Zanuck: Ronnie seemed the logical, wonderful choice. He had the right temperament; he understood the characters. He was perfect casting. We were thrilled that he liked the idea of directing it.

Maggie Smith had already been contracted to play the eponymous and persuasive schoolmistress and I was looked forward to working with her.

As one of the four Brodie girls, eighteen-year-old Pamela Franklin was signed as well. Her character, Sandy—wise beyond her years—ultimately destroys her teacher.

Composer-lyricist Rod McKuen had also been selected. My initial thought for the music was something traditionally Scottish until I heard his main theme, *Jean*, which won me over instantly.

Wendy Hiller and Celia Johnson were considered for Miss McKay, the conventional headmistress, with whom free-spirited Miss Brodie eventually has a powerful final confrontation. Both ladies I'd worked with and knew each was eminently qualified, but we had to settle on one—the decision was Celia.

Several girls were auditioned to find the other three to play prominent roles as members of Brodie's inner circle. Jane Carr had done the tragic, stuttering Mary McGregor on stage at Wyndhams Theatre, and I knew she was right. And I selected Diane Grayson as Jenny, and Shirley Steedman as Monica. But the American contingent didn't concur.

It seems that Fryer and coproducer James Cresson had tested some more glamorous young girls in Hollywood. But it was essential to stand my ground. "You're wrong to try to idealize these girls, Bobby. They must be realistic characters."

As I spoke, haunting memories came back of Ross Hunter's approach to films. Whether Bobby saw my point of view or whether he thought I would walk will never be known, however he eventually agreed to go along with me.

Maggie's husband, Robert Stephens, was picked for Teddy Lloyd, the school's married art master and Miss Brodie's lover. And Gordon Jackson, again wearing a kilt, joined us as the music master, Gordon Lowther.

Another seventy-five girls were needed to fill the classrooms and calls were put out to all the acting schools and agencies. Assistant director Ted Sturgis made arrangements for audition rooms in London. He was a solid rock of a man, with a ruddy complexion and bulbous nose, whose innate sense of humor, unapparent at first, grew with his confidence. Not two seconds elapsed after opening the doors before we were inundated with about four hundred young girls, and another four hundred doting mothers.

Hastily retreating to an inner sanctum, I discussed with Ted and the casting director how we could possibly deal with them in the one morning allocated. Quickly we devised something I still think was ingenious. Ted would arrange the hopefuls into groups by age and bring in about twenty at a time, beginning with the youngest.

In came the first lot.

"Good morning, girls."

"Good morning, sir," they chorused back.

"You all want to be in this film, don't you?"

"Oh, yes," came their reply in unison.

"You all want to act?"

"Oh, yes."

"You know I am the director and you will have to do whatever I tell you?"

"Oh, yes."

"Good! Now, when I was a boy at school, my friends and I thought girls were silly because they always giggled. Do girls still giggle?"

Some of them did by way of affirmation.

"Well, now we're going to find out which of you can giggle, the loudest. When I count to five, I want you to start. Are you ready?"

They began on cue—some tittered nervously, others let out chuckles, and some actually offered the most delightful level of laughter. The choices were easy—those uninhibited enough to laugh on command could probably take direction.

I asked Colin Colahan (from La Mortola) if he'd like to paint the various oils of the characters to be seen in Teddy Lloyd's studio—including one exposing Lloyd's obsession with Brodie. Colin jumped at the idea, as it would mean a sojourn in England. One of the key pictures was a self-portrait of Teddy with his wife and five children. Colin chose to depict them in descending order of age with the youngest seated on a chamber pot. My grandson, Gareth, at eighteen months played this important role.

As always, one of the clauses in my contract stipulated that I could choose my secretary—I asked Flicky to join me. At Pinewood, I introduced her to production supervisor David Anderson's secretary, Caroline, and hoped she would help Flicky during the first, often hectic days of production. Flicky was energetic and bright enough to pick up the routine quickly.

On arriving home early one afternoon, I received news that Derek had once again attempted suicide—this time more desperately than before. He had jumped off Waterloo Bridge into the Thames and had been picked up by a police rescue launch before being driven to a mental hospital on the outskirts of London. I went there immediately. After several days, the doctors persuaded him to undergo shock treatment. They convinced us both it was a last effort to help him cope with his depression. The procedures completed, he complained bitterly that his brain had been damaged—yet before he returned to France we played chess and, as always, he beat me soundly. Who knows whether the treatments helped, but there was one small miracle—he never attempted suicide again.

Now I had a film to get on with.

On our first day, I discovered Maggie was not a morning person.

"Good morning, Maggie," I said cheerily.

A muffled reply such as "Grumph."

On the second morning; "Good morning, Maggie," with an added "darling." More spluttering, guttural sounds in response.

To hell with this, I thought, I'm not going to be rebuffed when I'm just trying to be friendly, so I offered no welcome for the next two days.

On the fifth morning, catching me completely by surprise, she came and sat next to me. "'Ello," she said—it was kind of an acceptance speech.

Jane Carr: Maggie became our genuine Miss Brodie. We were hers for life and hung on to her every word. In one of the picnic scenes she was battling for attention with a particularly noisy bird that seemed to squawk every time she said a line. When Ronnie said, "Cut," Maggie, in that inimitable voice of hers said, "Shoot that fucking bird." I was so surprised that she swore and, of course, terribly amused, but wasn't certain I should be seen laughing.

In one sequence, Pamela Franklin's character, Sandy, poses in the nude for Lloyd in his studio—an act of rebellion on her part against the role Miss Brodie has envisioned for her. I'd given a lot of thought to the conclusion of the sequence. While exchanging dialogue with a man who is very much captivated by her, she gets back into her clothes, covering her perfect figure with dreadful woolen stockings, a shapeless jumper and glasses—turning her from a butterfly back into a caterpillar, thus bringing the art master sharply down to earth and reminding him of the repercussions of his attraction.

We had three highly dramatic moments between Maggie and Celia Johnson—the kind of scenes directors wish they could have in all their films. The first occurs when Miss McKay reprimands Brodie for spending weekends with the music master (Gordon Jackson) at his manor house overlooking the sea, taking her "gells" with her. The second concerns a love letter purportedly written to him by Miss Brodie, but actually concocted by two of Brodie's "set." The third, the shortest and most emotionally charged, has Miss McKay dismissing her—an act that leads to the final altercation between Brodie and her protégée, Sandy.

Maggie and Celia, both consummate actors, played these scenes brilliantly and coped with the extended dialogue without interruption. My responsibility was to create movements for them to take the weight off the lines. Maggie and I both had strong opinions about the outcome of this emotional sequence. Sandy confronts her teacher and tells her that she was the one responsible for Brodie's dismissal. Once the girl has departed, Maggie wanted to remain in the classroom and say softly, "Assassin." I wanted her to follow Sandy out as far as the top of the stairs and shout after her, "Assassin! Assassin!"—an echo to be added later for dramatic effect.

Maggie told me in no uncertain terms what she thought, but when she couldn't persuade either Bobby Fryer or me, she relented with dignity and played it our way.

Towards the end of shooting I received a call from Glebelands to say that Ivy had fallen and broken her hip. Although terribly inconvenient to her, I was assured that the damage was rarely life-threatening and we just needed to be patient until she was up and around again. Over the next few months, I took every opportunity to visit her in the nursing home at Goring, Oxfordshire, where she'd gone for convalescence.

With the studio work completed on *Brodie*, the unit went on location to Edinburgh for a short period, filming at Greyfriars Churchyard, Candlemaker Row, and Crammond Village—all dressed as they would have been in the 1930s.

As a resident alien in my own country, I started the *Escape From Zahrain* routine again. Monday through Thursday I would edit with Norman Savage and then Thursday evening I'd set off from the studio for London Airport, leave my car there, fly to Nice, pick up my newest car, an Alfa Romeo, and drive across the border to Casa Jolanda. On Monday mornings at 5:00 A.M., I'd leave Italy and be back in the Pinewood cutting room by 8:15 A.M., ten minutes before Norman arrived.

The film was ready for its first preview in Los Angeles, which Zanuck had arranged and I was back at La Mortola preparing to fly over there when

I received a call from the nursing home in Goring. My mother had passed away peacefully on Wednesday, December 4, 1968, at the age of 78.

That Sunday I flew to England. My brother was not stable enough to attend the funeral held on Monday at Golders Green Crematorium. From there her ashes would be taken to Glebelands. A few months later they were interred in a little churchyard nearby where my family held another private service. Both gatherings were small and far removed from the crowds that had admired Ivy Close so long before.

Immediately after the service, I took a flight to Los Angeles. Norman Savage accompanied me and was a great support in my sadness.

I met with Dick Zanuck before the sneak preview at the Village Theater in Westwood. He advised me that it hadn't been officially announced, adding, a word of warning, "British films are not always well received in this part of the world, so don't be disturbed if some people leave."

He was absolutely right—as the main credits came up about two dozen people walked out, but within five minutes those who'd remained became interested. At the end there was enthusiastic applause.

After the preview, I left Norman to deal with some editing details and returned to England. Flicky picked me up at the airport and we celebrated the film's success over dinner—it was a warm and welcoming homecoming after an unhappy departure.

The Prime of Miss Jean Brodie marked the third time a film of mine was selected for the Royal Command Performance. A few hours before the actual screening, Ralph Bromhead, chairman of the Special Selection Committee, informed me that one short scene was inappropriate for the Royal Family. Three of the girls are in Teddy's studio looking at a sketch of a nude male torso. It wasn't the sketch the Committee thought offensive, but the line of dialogue in which Teddy uses the words "pectoral muscles." The giggling girls think it refers to something lower on the male anatomy. We thought the scene innocuous, but we made the cut—later restoring the "offensive" words for general distribution.

The evening papers—most probably fed by the Twentieth Century Fox publicity department—picked up the whole episode.

As the Royal couple arrived at the theater, the principals, various dignitaries, and Beryl and I stood in the receiving line. Prince Philip, closely following Queen Elizabeth, shook hands and exchanged a word or two with everyone. When my turn came, I waited for him to extend his hand. He didn't.

"You are the director of this picture, aren't you?" he asked, looking me straight in the eye.

"Yes, sir." I was pleased he knew who I was.

"Do you think we're all children?" he asked somewhat irritably. "Removing a scene in case we're offended is really very silly."

I attempted an explanation. "I must apologize, sir, but it wasn't anything to do with me—I was instructed by the committee that arranged this screening."

As he moved down the line, he repeated, "Well, I still think it's very silly."

The film was an invited entry—out of competition—to the 1969 Cannes Film Festival. Beryl, Pamela Franklin, and I went to the screening.

Brodie received two Oscar nominations. Maggie won for Best Performance by an Actress, but Rod McKuen's "Jean," nominated as Best Song although reaching number two in the charts, lost out to "Raindrops Keep Fallin' on My Head."

· 27 ·

Scrooge

$\mathcal{A}$ndré Hakim had informed me that Darryl Zanuck was looking for a vehicle to star his latest French protégée and sent me a script, asking if it might be a possibility. It wasn't. But, just by chance, I'd read something called *Hello Goodbye*, which had promise, and coincidentally the lead was a French girl. I sent it to André as an alternative and he passed it on. Darryl liked it enough to negotiate a buyout from the original producers.

As I'd been able to work with one of his former ladies with a modicum of success, he felt comfortable with the idea of repeating the experience. The problem was I hadn't met Geneviève Gilles and no one told me Zanuck would be on the set at all times. Had they, I'd have been more chary of accepting.

Casting included Michael Crawford, later to star in Lloyd Webber's *The Phantom of the Opera*. Curt Jurgens was signed to play the Baron to Geneviève's Baroness. And to my delight, I was able to persuade John Bryan to take a break from producing and join me as set designer. In addition to the four films we'd made together, John produced *The Spanish Gardener, There Was a Crooked Man, Tamahine,* and several others. He had stayed an integral part of my life whether we were working on a film or not, but knowing he would be by my side reinforced my decision to accept *Hello-Goodbye*.

During preproduction, John and his wife Janie stayed at the Carlton Hotel in Cannes while I returned each evening to Italy. Together we started looking for locations in the area, including Nice and Marseilles. In view of what was about to happen, it is ironic that he and I were able to reminisce about our unsophisticated youth during lunch at the Negresco. I recounted a dinner I had hosted with Elia Lopert and his family when his daughter had ordered steak tartar. Trying to be polite I had asked, "How would you like it, medium or rare?"

Laughing, John countered by recalling the time Beryl, Christopher, and I joined him and Janie and their children, Richard and Rosemary, for a summer holiday in France. "I can still see the group of us staring at the dish I'd ordered when trying to be adventurous," he said. "None of us had a clue what bouillabaisse was, and the children especially, who would have preferred bangers and mash, were quite disappointed when the table became crowded with dishes of floating fish."

On Sunday John and Janie were to come over to La Mortola, but unfortunately it was teeming with rain. When the phone rang at around 10:00 A.M., I said, "I bet that's John saying they're not coming because of the weather."

In fact it was Janie. And she was barely articulate, her voice reflecting her desperation. "Something terrible has happened. John has had a stroke and been taken to hospital. He's in a coma and I don't know what to do. Ronnie, please help me."

Numb, I found it hard to speak as I told Beryl what had happened. Within an instant I was driving as fast as possible across the border towards Cannes. Gathering my thoughts behind the wheel, I remembered how John was forced to leave a film a few years earlier because of a cancerous kidney that had been removed. I wondered if his illness might have returned.

At the hospital, I sat with Janie while the doctor gave us the news. John's condition was very grave and he would probably not survive. We were both in a state of shock.

"Can you get him back to England immediately?" the doctor asked. Somehow we would.

I was able to get in touch with Stuart Lyons, now head of Fox-British, to ask his help. Within three hours, he'd arranged a chartered jet to take John and Janie to Heathrow. I drove back to La Mortala to get Beryl and we booked a commercial flight from Nice that arrived in London alongside the Bryans. John went straight to hospital by ambulance—us following. We stayed with Janie until he was settled in and then went to get some sleep at our St. James's flat. She phoned early the next morning.

"We're back home. I don't know what the doctors have done, but John is conscious and lucid and he wants to see you."

I found him sitting up in bed, as bright as usual.

"My goodness, you gave us a scare," I said trying to keep a smile on my face.

He knew he would not be able to continue on the picture and was interested in who would replace him.

"That's the last thing on my mind."

"It should be the first," he said with a look of admonishment. "John Howell would be a good choice."

We chatted on for a while as if nothing was wrong and then said our goodbyes.

On my way out, I said reassuringly to Janie, "He seems fine. Maybe there's been some dreadful mistake."

She shook her head, "No." Her face told the whole story. "It's just a matter of days."

And, in fact, John died only two days later on June 10, 1969, at the age of fifty-eight. He is buried in the churchyard next to Shepperton, his favorite studio, within the sound of the mill from the carpenter's shop where he spent so much time. It was absolutely the proper resting place for him. I'll never stop missing him.

John Bryan was the doyen of modern art directors. If you go through the list of top designers, you'll find that practically every one of them worked under him, including John Box, Ken Adam, Terry Marsh, and Peter Lamont. When he designed a set, there was only one place for the camera to go. He would say, "Two lines in design that should be avoided, the vertical and the horizontal." His sets were invariably in perspective—this allowed for the most extraordinary compositions.

After the funeral, I had to return to Cannes to continue preproduction. Over the next two weeks, twenty-five members of the English unit joined me, including Flicky. She shared a house in the hills behind the town with an assistant in the art department. And I moved into the Carlton for the duration of the production.

Darryl had spared no expense on the more than two dozen gowns in which to show off his inamorata, including some so sheer they caused lively conversation among the crew. He had also made arrangements to borrow thousands of dollars worth of jewels from Van Cleef and Arpels to adorn her. Geneviève certainly looked beautiful, but she couldn't act her way out of a paper bag.

From the moment the camera started rolling, Darryl, with his mandatory cigar, positioned himself next to me, monitoring every move and every word. "Perhaps we should do this," or "shouldn't we try that?" At first one thought, here is a man completely besotted, but when he went to the extent of diving into the lake in which Geneviève had to swim to ensure it was safe, one started to get the impression that Darryl was suffering from some sort of mental illness. This was not what should be expected from the president of Twentieth Century Fox. Surely he ought to have been attending to his duties in Hollywood rather than leaving his son Richard to hold the fort

On one occasion, when we were doing a close shot of Michael Crawford, and Geneviève was positioned off-camera to give him her lines, Darryl settled himself into a vantage point from where he could observe her clearly. At the end of the third take, I said, "Great, Michael, that's a print."

We were about to move to the next setup when Darryl came up behind me and whispered in my ear, "Ronnie, she was much better in take two."

"Yes, but we weren't shooting on her."

"I know," he said, "but take two was really better for Geneviève."

This was not going to be a viable working arrangement.

Early the next morning, I called Chris Mann in London who said, "Don't do anything until I get there."

He arrived the next morning to negotiate my exit. Darryl could obviously see this was coming and had already contacted his friend, Jean Negulesco, to take my place. Mann demanded I be paid for the entire production because Darryl had broken the contract by not giving me working conditions normally granted a director of my standing. Reluctantly Zanuck agreed, but with a stipulation—I was forbidden to say anything to the press, or indeed anyone else, about what had occurred for one year. The penalty was forfeiture of payment.

The crew gave me a farewell party during which Michael Crawford approached me and said he would be willing to walk off the picture if I said the word. I was touched by his gesture, but told him not to leave. Saying goodbye to Darryl, he shook my hand politely,

"You know Ronnie, you'll never work for Fox again."

"Yes, I know, and I'm very sorry about that."

Dick Zanuck: *Hello-Goodbye* was a nightmare. It was one of the factors that led to the internal disruption between my father and myself. I felt sorry for Ronnie because I knew what he was stepping into. It was doomed from the start. In a strange way, it was the same situation, but from a corporate standpoint, that led to the rupture between my father and me which eventually led to my leaving the studio. Ronnie was the professional trouper through it all. He did the best he could. It was an awful experience.

Of course Flicky left with me and flew back to London while I drove to Casa Jolanda. As had been the pattern throughout most of my career, when one door closed, another, usually more beneficial, opened.

"Ronnie, this is Gordon Stulberg," came the American voice over the telephone. "I'm chairman of Cinema Center Films. I read in the trades that you've left the movie in France."

"Yes, that's true. It just wasn't working out."

"As far as I'm concerned, it *is* working out," he said enthusiastically. "Can you come to New York tomorrow to meet with Leslie Bricusse and producer Bob Solo? Leslie's written the script, music, and lyrics for a musical version of Dickens' *Christmas Carol*. We'd like to talk to you about it."

Dickens was right up my street. This great author was stepping into my life again and it couldn't have happened at a more perfect moment.

The following evening I was in Manhattan meeting with Leslie, who had nearly completed the script, entitled *Scrooge*. He had also been given an executive producer credit, although Jere Henshaw would oversee production. There had been previous screen adaptations of *A Christmas Carol*, including the quintessential version starring Alastair Sim, however this would be the first in color and the first as a musical.

Casting the lead character proved tricky. We needed an actor who could play Scrooge as a young man as well as an old one. I learned that Leslie had asked Albert Finney, but he had turned it down without having read a word.

In August 1969, a month before I was signed, the problem appeared to be settled when Richard Harris accepted the role. He was starring in a film being shot in Israel—something called *Bloomfield*. But when shortly it ran into trouble, he took over as the director and felt obliged to remain through the postproduction period. Thus we had no Scrooge again.

Flicky started work as my assistant at Shepperton, and each day I looked forward to being with her. In trying to express why it was I cared about her, I'd have to say we certainly shared the same sense of humor, she was good company, and had the capacity of being able to mix and get along with everyone. Unquestionably though, our relationship was beginning to put a strain on my marriage.

Terence Marsh—who had won an Oscar for the magnificent sets on Carol Reed's musical *Oliver!*—designed for us an ingenious composite of Victorian London's Cheapside. Streets ran along all four sides of the rectangular stage—and one down the middle connecting to alleyways. The top was the town square and the bottom a series of warehouses.

Terence Marsh: The set at Shepperton was on the biggest stage in use in England at the time. In order for it not to look like a set, I wanted to slope the street so the houses would have some steps up to them, railings, different levels. This is much more expensive to do because there was so much rostruming. As it was Christmas, the ground had to be covered in snow and for that we used some firefighter's foam and mostly Epsom salts because it has such a nice sparkle. The actors and dancers walked on it, sending up dust, which is hardly visible. After inhaling this "fog," everyone seemed to be running to the toilet more than usual—Epsom salts are taken to cleanse the system!

Ossie Morris, who had himself been nominated for an Oscar for the musical *Oliver!* was the director of photography. And, once again, I had Maggie Furse as costume designer—by now an expert on period pictures. She enhanced every character in the film as well as the overall look of the production.

Many of the cast were regulars: Gordon Jackson, Kay Walsh, Dame Edith Evans, and Alec Guinness.

Kay Walsh and Maggie Furse, who had once disliked each other, had now become friends. They had a lot in common. Each was immensely talented—and both had loved David Lean.

Ian Fraser was arranging and orchestrating the music. He had previously worked with Leslie and his partner Anthony Newley and so knew the ropes. Anytime there was a problem with music or lyrics, Ian received revised material over the phone from Leslie, who, after a few weeks in England, had returned to America.

Ian Fraser: Like Irving Berlin, Leslie could not write music. He would sing or play on a keyboard, and I would write out the melody, harmonize it and take it from there. Basically, I put the songs down on paper and hopefully made them sound good. With me was a wonderful gentleman, Herbie Spencer, whose experience with Hollywood musicals went back to *Alexander's Ragtime Band*. We worked hard—there was a tremendous amount of music and it didn't stop very often.

Choreographer Paddy Stone began rehearsing some fifty dancers and singers and quickly caught on to what I had in mind. So many musicals are staged as if through a proscenium arch, but I wanted to move three hundred and sixty degrees around the performers. It's the advantage film has over theater. Understanding my determination to make the dialogue scenes blend with the musical numbers, Paddy succeeded brilliantly in integrating the two as a whole.

There was less than a month to go before our starting date and we still had no star! Clearly the picture would be cancelled unless a name could be found acceptable to the American financiers. Their strong recommendation was Rex Harrison. Even so, there was a problem; *The Lion Touch*, a play he was doing in the West End would not have completed its run in time for him to join us. So desperate were we that we decided to buy out the last two weeks of his contract. Negotiations were successful and he was duly signed on December 12, 1969.

The casting plot thickens. Albert Finney's production partner, Michael Medwin, had accepted the role as Scrooge's nephew. Naturally Michael had a copy of the script, which had been sent to the office he shared with Albie. One day, the latter casually picked it up from the desk where it was lying and began reading. We received a call:

"I've changed my mind. I've just read your script and, if the part is still available, I'd like to play Scrooge."

"Wish you'd told us before," one of us answered with a touch of exasperation. "We've just signed Rex Harrison."

"Dammit, it's my fault. If anything changes, I'd still love to do it."

Everyone agreed he was our best choice, but what could be done about Rex? How could we gracefully withdraw from our agreement? I'm afraid we behaved rather badly.

"Rex, we're very sorry, but as it turns out we are unable to put up the money to buy you out of the show," we explained lamely. "We have to start the picture, we can't wait. We're all terribly sorry."

Another member of our cast who had originally refused the role was Alec Guinness—but he ended up playing Marley's ghost to perfection. He had to be outfitted with a harness so he could fly with Albie. Alec hated the contraption and much later I learned he'd developed a double hernia from swinging in it. Typical of him, he didn't say anything at the time. After completion of the film, he had surgery followed by recuperation in a nursing home. By bizarre coincidence, I too had a hernia and found myself in the same place in a room opposite his. The postoperative days were so painful we couldn't laugh at the absurd circumstances in which life had placed us.

Alec Guinness: I didn't want to do *Scrooge*, but Ronnie can be very persuasive. I thought it was a rotten part and that sort of fantasy stuff in the middle of the film is not Dickens. However, he went on and on about it, and I accepted since it was only going to be a very short bit of work and I had nothing particular to do at the time.

The story describes the Ghost of Christmas Past as an apparition, strange and weird. If we'd taken the author at his word, it would have entailed an enormous number of special effects, which had to be avoided. So we changed the character entirely. Our ghost became a *grande dame*—Edith Evans.

Kenneth Moore was Christmas Present. Moving around became a tricky job. He had to wear a huge velvet cloak with a pile of heavy jewels.

The part of Christmas Future was simpler, a faceless black figure taken on by choreographer Paddy Stone.

To round off the casting, Shuna, my second grandchild, was brought along by Heather to be the babe-in-arms of a beggar woman. She bawled through the entire scene, which was in character as she was supposed to be poor and starving. After her brief debut, she was taken to my trailer where her mother and Flicky plied her with sweets to calm her down. That was Shuna's one and only foray into film.

All the musical numbers were prerecorded for lip-synching to playback. One potential problem was that although inherently musical, Albie is no musician in the true sense. Yet he does have a natural talent for acting a song. He would be talking and then he'd be singing. The transition wasn't apparent. His voice was pitched so that when he went into melody, it was as though it hadn't happened. And his sense of rhythm and timing is impeccable.

In many instances he would want to dance around more than we had planned, or I wanted to extend a piece of business during a song and there wasn't music to cover it. Fortunately, Ian was on the set most of the time and able to help.

Albie came up to me one morning with his makeup man, George Frost. "Ronnie," he instructed, "show us your hands."

"What in the world for?"

"We want to see what an old man's hands look like."

That really hit my pride and I was highly insulted. Albie, at 34, must have thought I, at 58, was just a few months away from my pension.

Scrooge's last song comes when he realizes he's not dead and not in Hell, but safely at the foot of his four-poster bed with the sheets tangled around him. Repenting, he sings:

> I'll Begin Again
> I will build my life
> I will live to know that I've fulfilled my life.

Ian Fraser: Albie said, "I can't lip-sync this one; I've got to act it." We decided to hardwire an earpiece under his wig, down his back, and under his gown. The wire went out of the picture and into the room where I was at the piano. We shot it live to my accompaniment. When I scored the picture, we added the orchestra to his voice. All this put more pressure on Ronnie because it had to be done in one shot. The result gave the song a wonderful presence, the feeling of "now."

Ronald Searle, known for his *St. Trinian's* series, produced a great set of drawings as a background to the opening titles. And then it was finished.

The day we screened *Scrooge* for the distributors, they went into rhapsodies. The première was held on November 30, 1970, at the Dominion

Theatre, Tottenham Court Road as a charity show for the Variety Club of Great Britain. In attendance were HRH Princess Margaret, Countess of Snowdon and the Earl of Snowdon along with Dickens' great grandson, Captain Peter Dickens. Gordon Stulberg flew in for the event.

The postscreening dinner was held at the Café Royal and featured a Dickensian Christmas feast with all the trimmings. Flicky helped organize the occasion, which proved an awkward evening in a personal sense since naturally I had brought Beryl with me. She was aware Flicky was my assistant on the film, and she may well have begun to believe there was something between us. That evening, I sat at a table with my wife and visiting dignitaries while Flicky was at another table at the far side of the room. My dilemma was reaching epic proportions.

In terms of the picture, however, it is still viewed with pride. My vision of the story, with its dialogue and music tightly integrated, worked well, and it was great fun to direct. It has gone on to become a perennial holiday treat.

The Academy of Motion Picture Arts and Sciences honored *Scrooge* by nominating it for Oscars in the categories of art direction, set decoration, and costume design. Leslie Bricusse was also nominated for music and lyrics for "Thank You Very Much" and Leslie, Ian, and Herbert W. Spencer were nominated for original song score.

Scrooge had come to terms with his ghosts, but I still had to confront my own. Something had to be done about my double life, but I didn't know what or how. One night in London at our St. James's apartment, I couldn't sleep. After tossing and turning in bed for hours, I slipped on my dressing gown and went into the living room. I'd not been there long when Beryl came through, obviously concerned.

"What's the matter, darling?"

I knew the moment had come.

"I've fallen in love with Flicky. It's wrong. I hate myself, but it's happened. I don't know what to do."

As ever, she was dignified in the face of adversity.

"You'll have to make up your mind. It's either her or me."

"I know," I said miserably. "All I can say is that I care about you deeply and never thought anything like this could happen."

The outcome was that we decided on a trial separation while I sorted out my feelings. I moved into the Carlton Tower Hotel near Sloane Street and, after a few days, found a service flat behind the Dorchester, where I remained for three months, agonizing over what to do.

True life is stranger than fiction. Shortly after I was unpacked, Christopher joined me. Heather had recently presented me with my third grandchild, a girl named Emma, but sadly she and my son were unhappy together and had decided to part. The Neame men had gone from a home life of solidity and predictability to living like transients. As for me I was a director, not knowing which direction to take.

The only contact I had with Beryl during this period of soul-searching was through Christopher. Flicky tried her best to be supportive by not influencing me one way or the other, although by now we loved each other very much.

I came to a decision—I must give my marriage another chance. Beryl and I had spent forty years together, going through the good times and the bad. My conscience and sense of what was right would not let me walk away.

To help us to start afresh, we moved into a new London apartment. We were spending six months of the year in England and needed an extra room that could serve as an office, as well as a space for visiting grandchildren. Consequently we acquired a twenty-eight-year lease at 14 Chesham Place, just off Belgrave Square, and I gave Christopher the flat in St. James's Place.

· 28 ·

The Poseidon Adventure

$\mathscr{T}$he excitement in Gordon Stulberg's voice was evident from the first syllable: "I've just been appointed president of Twentieth Century Fox." He then went on in a more serious tone, "But I'm in trouble. What are you up to?"

"Nothing at the moment."

"Maybe you can help. I'm leaving for Los Angeles tomorrow evening. Would you be able to fly to New York and meet me at Kennedy Airport, then we'll continue on to L.A.? I'll fill you in on everything when I see you." He paused before saying. "I really need your help, Ronnie."

Gordon was a highly experienced and successful lawyer, an Ivy League type who sported V-neck sweaters. He knew how to present a compelling argument, to flatter or cajole, whichever was needed. As he was speaking, I started to reason that a location film might be exactly what was needed to stabilize my situation.

"Tomorrow? I suppose so."

"Good. You may be in California for a while, so pack accordingly," he advised. "I look forward to seeing you." He hung up somewhat abruptly, possibly to prevent me from changing my mind.

Beryl helped me pack hastily. I would send for her as soon as things were finalized.

I met him as planned and we boarded the plane to Los Angeles. This usually urbane and reserved gentleman was uncharacteristically fervent about his new position; he even boasted about it to the flight crew—such was his elation that he could have flown without the plane!

We ate dinner in the aircraft while he filled me in on the situation. "I've inherited a picture already in preparation called *The Poseidon Adventure*. It's from a novel by a Brit, Paul Gallico. Do you know it?"

I knew Paul but not the novel.

235

One of Gordon's problems was producer Irwin Allen. "He has had a serious disagreement with the director who's left the production. I have to decide whether to go ahead or cancel."

We arrived in Los Angeles after midnight and were met by a dark-haired stocky man, the very gentleman who had been the topic of our in-flight conversation.

From the moment Irwin said, "Good evening, or is it good morning?" I sensed he quite clearly didn't like what was happening. He couldn't understand why Stulberg had brought this Limey interloper all the way over and was seriously considering appointing him the director of *his* film.

Gordon was whisked off to his home by car, leaving me in Irwin's hands. As he deposited me at the entrance of the Beverly Hills Hotel, he said, "I'll send a car for you first thing in the morning. We'll talk the whole thing through."

For the next two or three days, he and I had an uneasy relationship as I met the major part of the unit he had assembled: production manager Sidney Marshall; personal assistant Al Gail; unit production manager Hal Herman; assistant art director Ward Preston; and someone who was to become very important to me, production designer Bill Creber, an easygoing man with a sharp mind, who makes Jimmy Stewart seem like a fast talker.

Bill Creber: About six weeks before we were going to begin, the studio decided they wanted a stronger director, and Ronnie came in. We were all a little miffed because Gordon Douglas was a friend, and we said, "Why do we need this new guy?" Just to make conversation during one meeting, I said to Ronnie, "Two of my favorite films were made by a British director." "Oh, which ones?" I told him, "*The Horse's Mouth* and *Tunes of Glory*." Ronnie laughed and said, "I'm glad you like those. I directed them both." I was so embarrassed because I should have known. But he knew it was really a sincere compliment, and we became, as he would say, "great chums."

Irwin and I agreed to get on together, and that I'd remain in Los Angeles for six weeks while we worked on a new script. At the end of that time, the studio bosses would decide if the film should move ahead or be canceled. By mutual agreement we brought in Stirling Silliphant, who had won an Oscar for his screenplay *In the Heat of the Night*. Production Manager Sidney Marshall often sat in with me to work on the script with Stirling, as did Irwin. Stirling received the credit, but it was a joint effort.

During this time, Irwin had started casting, invariably consulting me prior to making a final decision. Soon Gene Hackman was signed, Ernest Borgnine,

Red Buttons, and many of the other principals. Irwin could be persuasive when it came to convincing stars that a particular part was right for them.

Even though the actors were in place and the sets were being built, we still didn't know if *Poseidon* would actually go into production—everyone involved was on tenterhooks waiting for the front office decision.

The moment finally came to present our script to Gordon. "We have the screenplay that will make a great film," said Irwin, never one to understate.

In a less effusive British manner, I supported him, adding, "I think it's reasonably good."

Gordon wanted to send it to his official readers and asked us to return later in the week for their evaluation.

Only two days passed before he phoned Irwin, "I'd like to talk with you and Ronnie. Can you come right over?"

Off we went to the executive building, readying to congratulate ourselves on what we thought he was about to say.

He was cordial and we exchanged pleasantries.

"The reaction of my readers is not good. They think it would be a disaster to proceed. Others who've read it don't particularly like it either. The bottom line," he said with conviction, "is I'm going to cancel." As further justification, he continued, "At the moment, Fox cannot afford to spend five million on such a risky project."

Irwin and I were astounded—it was the only time I saw him anything but upbeat and in control.

After working a month and a half on the script, I was keen about the project—yes, it had its limitations, nevertheless I thought it would be a highly satisfactory film for audiences around the world. Furthermore, it was crazy, in my view, not to continue as the studio had engaged the unit, built the sets, and already spent nearly a million dollars.

"Maybe you're being a little hasty," I said. "Why don't we all take the afternoon to think about it? We could come and see you again this evening when we've got over the shock."

Always the gentleman, he agreed. "By all means. But I doubt I'll change my mind."

I left Irwin in his office, as close to tears as I'd ever seen a producer.

Returning to my own, I shuffled papers and thought about what to do on my return to Europe, which was much more imminent than it had been at lunchtime.

At five o'clock, I was in Irwin's office and insisted he open his tightly locked liquor cabinet. I had a stiff scotch and unexpectedly he joined me. Thus fortified, we left for the meeting.

Gordon reemphasized his position and then suddenly Irwin played his trump card.

"If I can get two million, five hundred thousand absolutely guaranteed from outside, will Fox come in with the other half for fifty percent?"

This was one of the few times I appreciated Irwin doing the talking. All afternoon I'd been bemoaning my fate while he was out doing what he did best—getting finance.

"Two gentleman you know, Steve Broidy and Sherrill Corwin, have agreed to guarantee any loss Fox might incur on the picture up to that figure."

Gordon was as surprised as I was at this turn of events. "If this is a genuine offer, we'd certainly accept it."

"It is genuine," Irwin responded.

He was really in his element at this conference, and I shall always admire him for the action he took that day.

Later I heard how he had acquired his winning hand. In the afternoon, with unit production manager Hal Herman in tow, he had crossed the street to Hillcrest Country Club and marched straight into the members' lounge. Here he found Broidy, head of Motion Pictures International, and Corwin, head of Metropolitan Theatres Corporation, (his friends of many years) engaged in a game of gin rummy—probably for serious stakes.

"I want to discuss what I spoke to you about on the phone," he interrupted as they were dealing a hand.

"Never mind the details," Broidy said. "We're in. Now, go make your movie!"

"But," Irwin blustered, "let me tell you the details."

They again waved him away.

That was the end of the conversation.

According to Hal, he had to pull Irwin aside before he talked himself out of the deal.

Signed off on a deck of cards, *The Poseidon Adventure* was "green lighted" with shooting to commence in April 1972.

Until this moment, I had been so engrossed in preparing that there'd been little time to think about my personal life. Picking up the phone to call Beryl, I told her everything was set and, as I'd be in Los Angeles for close to a year, she should bring enough to be comfortable.

We rented a house on the corner of Hillcrest Drive and Santa Monica Boulevard in the heart of Beverly Hills and only fifteen minutes from the studio. It didn't have much personality, but Beryl warmed it up with knick-knacks and family photographs. Both of us were trying very hard to restore our marriage.

Even so, my emotional ties to Flicky were stronger than I'd realized. We had reluctantly agreed not to meet or talk on the phone, but during the weeks and months, I began to communicate with her via a cassette recorder. On the early morning drive to Fox, I would describe the route. "I'm passing Santa Monica Blvd., where I see the park area along the road where people jog." Or I'd tell her about what was happening at the studio. I tried not to, but in the end I admitted how much I missed her.

Regardless of my private turmoil, ahead of me was a terribly complicated picture with myriad challenges, Irwin not the least.

He was one of the most controlling producers ever, in both the positive and negative sense. In some respects, he was the worst type—a frustrated director. Though in my case he knew he had to be cautious since the president of the studio had brought me in.

One of our early disagreements occurred when he said he wanted the film shot based on storyboards prepared by *his* sketch artists. Or put another way, shoot the whole thing the way Irwin saw it.

"I couldn't possibly do that."

"Why not?" he countered.

"Because when I get actors on the set and begin to rehearse, all kinds of interesting things happen—the unexpected may develop into something exciting. It may be the same scene as written, but the emphasis could change for the better."

Irwin persisted over the next couple of days and in a moment of exasperation, I expressed my frustration to Gordon.

"Do you want me to take him off the production?"

"Good gracious, no! It's his picture. I suppose I just wanted you to know my feelings."

Trying to calm things down, I suggested something I would have done anyway—using storyboards for action sequences and where stunts were involved. Naturally it was important for everyone to know exactly what we were planning. "But," I stressed, "not when it comes to dialogue and characterization and storytelling. I must have the freedom and flexibility to deal with that my way."

Irwin found it hard to face what he perceived as defeat, so he arranged for his artists to see my rushes and draw the setups *after the fact*. Displaying them on his office walls, he could tell visitors, "This is what I've been doing."

Then there was the occasion when the first unit moved from the big ballroom set to another stage. I left him in charge of picking up the fifteen or so shots still needed of stunt people falling. Immediately he took this as an opportunity to turn himself into the director and called in as many members of the press as possible to visit *his* set. He also had a short film made of the shooting of the picture, featuring himself at the camera. It is partially for these reasons that the movie is known today as "Irwin Allen's *The Poseidon Adventure*."

Carol Lynley: I know it was very difficult for Ronnie although he and Irwin were a good match. Irwin supplied the chutzpah and Ronnie supplied the technical know-how and the on-set dealing with actors. It was just Irwin's nature to try to take credit for everything. I don't think he singled out Ronnie. He would have done that to anybody. But he knew he needed him to get the movie done. They were definitely an odd couple.

Fortunately I had the unit firmly behind me, Bill Creber quickly becoming one of my greatest allies—his support helped keep me afloat.

Irwin had an unwritten rule that we would lunch together, but sometimes I liked eating with my other friends on the unit, especially Creber and Preston, the assistant art director, also Sidney Marshall.

On several occasions, in order not to offend Irwin, it became necessary to sneak out of the back door of the stage where my chums would be waiting in a car. I would jump in, and we'd be off to enjoy an hour at our favorite nearby hole in the wall.

I don't want to imply that we didn't socialize. Often Beryl and I spent evenings with him and his girlfriend Sheila (who played a small part in the film and later became his wife). With a flair for entertaining and a love of good food, he gave lavish parties at Chasen's. It was at one of these evenings I met and became friends with Groucho Marx.

During production, Irwin had his eye on everything and certainly knew how to keep the picture on time and budget. Each morning during shooting he held a meeting with the production department to ensure everything was efficiently organized. In many ways he was a tremendous help.

The shooting schedule was well organized and one of its strongest points was to allow filming in continuity—every director's dream. Furthermore, it meant the actors would have the opportunity to build their characters as the story unfolded.

The only time it was necessary to slip out of continuity for a few days was on location aboard one of the greatest of all oceangoing ships, the *Queen Mary*. Like her sister ship, the *Queen Elizabeth*, this luxury liner and former World War Two troop carrier was now converted into a tourist attraction, moored in the harbor at Long Beach, California. At 6:30 A.M., with the help of several members of the studio fire department, the storm sequences were filmed. Five or six enormous fans blew up a gale as they hurled water across the decks. Not only did it appear real, it felt real!

These watery shots had to be completed prior to the arrival of busloads of sightseers, at which point the unit moved to a lower deck for cabin and companionway scenes.

Once back at Fox, and in a more manageable environment, filming went along at a good pace.

To give the audience the impression of being at sea, the camera had to be pitched and rolled continuously—the rhythm fluid, almost subliminal. This was achieved by mounting it on a baby Chapman crane, separated from the rostrumed sets. Along with the normal pan and tilt mechanisms, it was rigged with a cross-tilt device, the cumbersome extensions almost surrounding the operator. The effect it produced was spot on.

Before long we got to the sequence in which the ship overturns—with a hundred extras at the heart and soul of it. Often extras are treated with a lack of respect by production crews—they are considered uninterested in what's going on, leading to boredom and lethargy. On the first day they were called, I set about putting this straight, enlisting their support.

"You're going to be working with me for quite a few weeks," I said after introducing myself. "I want you to know how important you are to this film and in particular to the sequences we are about to shoot." By now I had their attention. "But I can't expect your full cooperation unless you know what the film is all about." I then explained the storyline and their roles in it.

There was a round of applause. I gave them the respect they deserved, and, in return, they gave me their enthusiasm and best efforts.

The principals were all seasoned actors. As the story progresses their characters become more frantic and desperate, also dirtier—continuously the cast was hosed down and smothered in nasty goo. Each took to the unpleasantness well and, except for the most difficult pieces of action, did their own stunts. Understandably there were temperamental moments—with ten of them, this averaged about one a day! Along with Ernest Borgnine, the only other member who never lost his calm was young Eric Shea—he seemed to enjoy everything thoroughly. Then came the afternoon when it was my turn to lose my temper telling the shamefaced lot of them, "This little boy is more grown-up than all of you put together!"

Shelley Winters is a real trouper—a perfectionist, and serious about her job. I liked her from the start. She has an opinion about everything and these opinions are based in lively conversation and intelligence. There was one incident, however, that caused a problem.

In the midst of shooting a scene that takes place after the ship has capsized, Shelley suddenly yelled "Cut!" There is an unwritten rule that no one *ever* says, "cut" other than the director. Shelley knew this.

"What was that for?" I asked, as the entire unit stared at her.

"There's a piece of paper on the floor that shouldn't be there."

"Shelley, the floor isn't in the picture, and *you* don't say 'cut.' That's my job. Don't ever do it again."

She accepted my reprimand good-naturedly. However, to this day she still blames me for one significant detail—claiming that I asked her to put on forty pounds. But I'm convinced this was her choice because she would do anything she felt was right for her character.

After a particularly touching scene with Jack Albertson, who was playing her on-screen husband, Shelley had to climb an enormous Christmas tree. When she can't quite get past some of the rigging, Gene Hackman, the leader of the group trying to escape the upturned ship, comes up beneath her and shoves her posterior to get her through. Later she's dragged up a steep slope to a higher level. It was really gutsy of her!

Her most difficult stunt, an exceptionally demanding one, occurred during the scene in which she rescues Hackman.

In order to get to the engine room, the survivors dive into an area that has filled with water. One of them has to lead, pulling a rope through to the opposite side of the bulkhead for the others to follow.

Mrs. Rosen (Shelley's character) says, "I have prizes as a swimmer. I've been a lifesaver. Please let me do this."

Gene's character, as scripted, agrees to let her, and she dives in, but becomes trapped. He rescues her. But once they get to the other side, she suffers a fatal heart attack.

Just before we were to shoot the scene, Gene came to me. "It doesn't work."

"Why not?"

"There's no way I would let that old woman dive in first," he observed. "It's just not believable."

"Do you have a suggestion?" I asked.

As with many good actors, he had thought the problem through and knew the solution.

"I should refuse to let her. I should say, 'I'm going to do this, not you.' Then I get stuck and she saves me. The scene finishes the same. But that way, it's truer to both characters."

It was an excellent idea and clearly the correct way to go.

Immediately I called Irwin to come to the set and explained the situation. He agreed and we decided to talk to Shelley about it. Not unexpectedly, she blew her top.

"This scene is the only reason I agreed to do the film. Now you're taking it away from me and giving it to Gene. I will not do it his way."

The idea was argued back and forth among the four of us. It was all very unpleasant and we were soon in a deadlock situation.

Then I made a stupid remark, "This is the worst morning I've had since I worked with Judy Garland!"

That did it. Insulted, Shelley walked off the set!

She headed, in high dudgeon, straight for Gordon Stulberg's office in the executive building, charged up to a startled secretary, who told her he was in a meeting with the company's directors.

Regardless, she stormed into the boardroom. And there she was, covered in goo, her dress torn, her face smudged, and her hair a mess. She must have stunned those pinstriped gentlemen as she blurted out, "They're destroying my part."

Meanwhile, someone, probably Irwin, got on to her agent, while I worked on a scene in which she did not appear.

About an hour later, we heard Shelley's distinctive voice calling from the entrance of the stage, "I'm back! I'm ready to go! When do we do it?"

It was explained to her that we had rescheduled the scene.

"Oh, okay," she said nonchalantly as she headed over to sit with Jack Albertson.

Ernest Borgnine: Jack Albertson, God bless him, was the most wonderful man. He always wore glasses in between takes. But he'd take them off when the camera rolled. I'd tell him "You hang on to me when we go up these ladders." So he did. He always had a hand out towards me. He had a gin rummy game going on throughout the picture with Shelley. He won thousands from her that she never paid. She insisted on playing another game, saying, "I'm going to win all my money back." But Jack would take her to the cleaners every time.

Two days later, we did the scene Gene's way. Shelley rescues him and they come up the other side of the bulkhead. Everything flowed beautifully, including Shelley's beige chiffon costume that had the skirt stitched underneath into a culotte-like arrangement so it wouldn't float over her head.

She was a good swimmer and had been coached on how to hold her breath for long periods of time by a member of Jacques Cousteau's team. Consequently she was able to do the scene one hundred percent convincingly.

Shelley Winters: I didn't get a sense of how dangerous our stunts were until I saw the completed picture. After the underwater scene with Gene, he said to me, "You were trying to drown me!" I said, "I didn't think you'd notice." The on-screen heart attack was very difficult. I always play music to help me reach the state I need to be in for a scene and Ronnie gave me the greatest gift a director can give an actor—he made me feel secure. When that happens I can risk doing something I wouldn't normally do. He was the only "gentleman" who ever directed me, and I give him all the credit for my Best Supporting Actress nomination.

Even after Mrs. Rosen dies, there were a few shots in which her body is on screen and Shelley would have to remain still and silent—as difficult for her as any stunt!

"No breathing, Shelley, until I call 'Cut!'"

Red Buttons and Carol Linley shared a terror of heights. In one scene they had to climb a steep ladder, but they had their doubts.

"We could, of course, use doubles," I told them, "although that would mean we couldn't move in for closeups."

I've never known an actor to refuse a closeup.

They looked at each other and decided their fear would make their performances more realistic. As they climbed the ladder, which went up two decks, some twenty-five feet off the ground, with a water tank below—they were indeed convincing!

Red Buttons: If I get above the second floor, my nose bleeds. For the scene, I didn't overcome my fear. I just held on to it and it helped me in my performance. It gave me a certain edge. The fear of not doing it submerged the fear of doing it. It has really become a cult film. In my nightclub act the joke is, "Do you know why Shelley Winters dies in *Poseidon Adventure*? Because she tried to talk underwater." It always gets a scream.

One of the laughs in the picture is the altercation between Stella Stevens and Ernie Borgnine, playing husband and wife. They climb the tree and join the group to find a way to safety. Stella was wearing a tight slinky white evening dress, not fashioned for climbing. Gene's character tells her to take it off. Ernie's character is aghast at the suggestion, but she sheds the dress and puts on his tuxedo shirt, which almost adequately covers her. I owe Ernie and Stella an enormous debt of gratitude for the fun they brought to the situation.

Stella Stevens: I didn't wear anything under that gown—it was designed to be worn nude. After I take it off and put on Ernie's shirt, I put on underwear for the climb though. My shoes were platform with a high heel, which were strapped on. Going up the Christmas tree, I could hook the arch of the shoe in the limbs of the tree. I couldn't have done it in bare feet. Even though I had three pairs of those shoes, the more bedraggled and worn they became, the more I tended to wear the same ones so they would be authentic and look just right.

When Ernie suggested an amusing bit of business, Gene wasn't happy, "What are we making here, a comedy?"

"No," I replied, "but with any film in which there is continuous tension, there have to be a few laughs to relieve it."

Although we socialized often, Roddy McDowall and I hadn't worked together since he was eight years old on the "quota quickie" *Murder in the Family* along with Glynis Johns. He maintained his professional demeanor throughout production and gave a first-rate performance.

Like the rest of the cast, Pamela Sue Martin was terrific to work with.

Pamela Sue Martin: I was eighteen, alone, and in this mega-film. In one scene I was supposed to scream at the sight of a dead person, and was really nervous about it. Gene Hackman took me off to another sound stage and had me practice. He helped me through it. He took me under his wing and gave me a sense of confidence. And I remember Shelley being very mother-like. Ronnie recognized I was homesick, which was so sweet of him. I was homesick for the first five years I was in L.A.

I had been careful about any possible danger on the set. So I was naturally concerned about a stunt that occurs as the ship turns over. A man hangs from a table on the floor of the now upside-down ballroom. When he can no longer keep hold, he drops to his death through a glass skylight in the ceiling thirty feet below. Stuntman Ernie Orsatti practiced the feat in a gymnasium pool under the exact conditions he would face on the set. When the time came for him to take the fall, he knew exactly what to do. He did it perfectly in one take. Because stunts like this are dangerous, stuntmen are paid extra for each take. Ernie was somewhat disappointed when we only did it the once!

There was a sequence that caused trouble near the end of production when Gene has to rescue the boy. A track had been constructed at a forty-five-degree angle with a corridor built on top—this structure was like a train heading downwards into the water in a huge tank on the Fox lot. Wearing chest-high waders for ultimate protection, the camera crew and I were at the high and dry end of the corridor, Gene and Eric Shea at the soon to be flooded low end. On screen we would not see the angle—it would appear as an ordinary corridor filling with water.

The action then called for them to swim and escape to an upper deck—with the set stopping its descent before they were completely immersed. But, despite our careful plans, the set didn't stop! And everyone ended up in the tank, camera and all. Half-drowned and with our waders filled with water, we climbed out looking like a squad of Michelin men!

Hurriedly, the film magazine was released from the rescued camera and rushed to the lab where the footage was again submerged in water before being placed directly onto the developing machine. Every frame was saved.

While we were shooting in the studio, special effects expert L. B. Abbott, along with Bill Creber, had the complicated task of filming the miniature *Poseidon* in a huge tank on the Fox Ranch at Malibu. Their results are remarkable—especially considering the model was only twenty-five feet long.

Added to the many technical problems Abbott had to resolve was the fact that the real *Queen Mary* traveled her own length in fifty seconds. Our model traveled its own length in five seconds. In order to create a sense of reality, the camera was cranked at ten times normal speed (240 frames a second), which meant that, on film, the model also took fifty seconds to travel its length. The ship and in particular the water looked uncannily real.

The final sequence—the rescue—is somewhat disappointing. The original intention was that the survivors, once emerged from the ship's hull into daylight, would see rescue ships surrounding them. This big sequence was supposed to be shot in Los Angeles Harbor. Unfortunately, we had to settle for a small part of the hull built on the back lot. A helicopter lands and takes the grateful survivors away to safety. We had, quite simply, used up our budget!

When we came to the cutting room, editor Harold Kress made an enormous contribution, especially in the capsizing sequence in which he assembled more than a hundred shots into a cohesive, exciting whole. He put this jigsaw puzzle together on his own and then brought me in to see it. "It's so good," I told him, "We don't need to touch it."

During editing, I discovered there was a problem with the first twenty minutes. We spent two reels introducing and developing the characters—

terribly important if we were to care about them later on. However, it would be difficult to hold on to an audience impatient for action. Somehow we needed to make the first two reels more prescient. My son, Christopher, who was in Los Angeles at the time, came up with the solution. At the beginning of the picture a title reads:

"At midnight on New Year's Eve, the *SS Poseidon*, en route from New York to Athens, met with disaster and was lost. There were only a handful of survivors. This is their story . . ."

The title required the audience to be attentive while the exposition was presented, as they would then be intrigued to know the characters and speculate which of them would come out alive.

John Williams had been contracted early on to compose the score, which turned out to capture the power of the picture and still retain a melodic element. Also a song, to be lip-synched by Carol Lynley, was needed, but we weren't sure exactly what it should be. Just a week before principal photography had commenced composer-lyricists Joel Hirschhorn and Al Kasha came along.

Joel Hirschhorn: Ronnie said he wanted something positive, so the title came first. We thought of a ballad but not so ballad-like that the song wouldn't have a tempo. "The Morning After" was not only an integral part of the film; it was also a hit record—sung by Maureen McGovern. But she isn't heard in the movie. The singer we hear is Renee Armand, who was a good voice match for Carol Lynley.

While the *Poseidon* was sinking and the actors were going through their paces, my future was still uncertain. The pressures of filmmaking kept my predicament at a distance for much of the time, however my arm's length contact with Flicky continued.

At one point, I wrote a long letter telling her we should end the whole thing once and for all. I took it to a post box in Century City, not far from the studio, and placed it in the slot. But I couldn't let it slide away. Returning to my office, I tore it up.

The director's cut was finished and the music recorded.

The première was held at the Egyptian Theater on December 12, 1972. I didn't stay for it, instead going back to England, which, from a professional standpoint was the biggest mistake I could ever have made. Contractually I was entitled to "A Ronald Neame Film" credit immediately after the main title, which Irwin had found hard to accept. However, without in any way wishing to underestimate his tremendous contribution to the film, it was unfair of him to change its position to after the cast credits—thereby diminishing it. Had I remained in Los Angeles this would never have happened. But my heart ruled my head.

On our return to the Chesham Place, Beryl and I had a quiet, civilized, but heartwrenching conversation and then we parted. Fortunately, in spite of it all, we maintained a close friendship. The time we had shared together will always be part of us, and the family we created is a continuous statement of our love.

After I'd been in England for around six weeks, Gordon phoned me from Los Angeles. "Ronnie, I'm calling to tell you that *Poseidon* is going to make more money than all the rest of your films put together."

I laughed. "You're joking. It's not possible."

"Wait and see. It's going to be the blockbuster of all time."

I had contracted for five percent of the net. I suppose, in hindsight, because of my strong position with Fox, I could have insisted on a percentage of the gross. So be it—at least with the picture's immediate success the money came in at such a pace that the accountants didn't have time to prepare a second set of books!

As things turned out, neither Broidy nor Corwin, our guarantors, had to put their hands in their pockets—they never even visited the studio during production. Each of them, sharing fifty percent of the gross with Irwin, made millions.

Although I was the one who fared least well financially, *The Poseidon Adventure* earned me what is laughingly known as "F. U. money" and thereby allowed me to buy yet another car—a Rolls-Royce. There was an irony to the film's success—only a short while earlier Darryl Zanuck had told me I'd never work for Fox again!

The Academy honored the film with nine nominations—Shelley Winters for Best Supporting Actress and Bill Creber for Art Direction. It also received mentions for Cinematography, Set Decoration, Costume Design, Sound, Editing, and Original Dramatic Score. And Al Kasha and Joel Hirschhorn took home Oscars for their song. The Academy also gave L. B. Abbott and A. D. Flowers the first ever Special Achievement Award for Visual Effects.

Looking at the film today, these effects are still magnificent—and they were all created without the aid of computers.

As a film, it's purely escapist fare, and still has a strong audience—playing as it does on television around the world. Not long ago the *Queen Mary* hosted an evening for the cast and 450 fans who came for autographs and memorabilia. And recently, the American Film Institute added *Poseidon* to their "100 Years—100 Thrills" listing. I never would have imagined in my wildest dreams that thirty years later there would still be this interest.

· 29 ·

Losses and Gains

$\mathcal{I}$t was right that Beryl should keep everything, including Casa Jolanda and Chesham Place. And thanks to *Poseidon*, I was also able to give her financial comfort for life.

Within a few weeks, carrying only a suitcase, I moved into Flicky's small Chelsea townhouse, settling into a routine of seeing chums, dining out, going to films and the theater, and playing gin rummy, a game she loved so long as she won! We shared a tremendous warmth and compatibility.

Several times our close friends Debbie (a writer friend I'd met in Los Angeles) and her husband David Pochner came to stay with us. With them we went to Ascot and drove at weekends to a thatched cottage Flicky and I purchased in the Hampshire countryside. Except for shadows from the past, these were happy days; however, I realized at some point I needed to make another film.

Fred Zinnemann's *The Day of the Jackal* had deservedly been very well received and when British producer John Woolf approached me about a film from the same author—*The Odessa File* by Frederick Forsyth—I was extremely interested. (John Woolf was the son of well-known tycoon C. M. Woolf, the man I'd gone to see during *Major Barbara*.)

Essentially a true story, it tells of a secret organization of former SS officers accidentally discovered by a young German journalist.

It wasn't an easy screenplay to write. Kenneth Ross, who had scripted *Jackal*, and I spent three months straightening out the intricate plot into a simpler cinematic line—tussling all the way, particularly with the denouement.

Once completed, Woolf and I went to Hollywood to present it to the film's financiers, Columbia. While there we scheduled a meeting with Jon Voight, who was considering, and ultimately accepted, the role of Peter Miller, the journalist. Jon, I was told, had a reputation for being difficult, however from the moment we met, any fears about having to deal with another temperamental star rapidly faded. He was earnest, precise, and extremely cooperative.

Even though I still had some script reservations, Columbia approved it, which meant we could start preproduction in England and Germany immediately.

Having been raised in a military family, Flicky was well organized about everything. She made time for her friends, but never seemed to have enough for herself, in particular her health. Several months earlier she had been to see a doctor who had told her she needed further tests, which she had put off. Before I left for Hollywood, I'd convinced her to get them done. On the evening of my homecoming, I asked, "How did things go at the doctor's?" I was taken aback when she replied, "Not well." She went on to explain that she needed an operation as soon as possible. "I have uterine cancer." It was a desperate shock to both of us and although we tried to be brave, we were aware of her condition's gravity since her own mother had died from the same cause.

She was admitted to Guy's Hospital and underwent a hysterectomy. As soon as permitted, I went to her bedside to wait for her to regain consciousness. Her first question was in a whisper, "Am I going to make it?"

"Of course, you're going to make it. You'll be absolutely fine."

The surgeon told me she had been given eleven pints of blood during the operation. "I needed to go deeper than I'd anticipated, but I'm sure we got it all." And then he added in a reassuring voice, "Eight times out of ten, these operations are successful, so the chances are good."

While Flicky was in the hospital I heard that Noël had died in Jamaica. "Goodnight my darlings. I'll see you in the morning," were his last words. A few months later, David Niven, Christopher, and I went to his memorial service in London at St. Martins-in-the-Fields. Even though in the heart of the West End, the inside of the church is intimate, ideal for such an occasion. With Noël's vitality and drive I'd always imagined he would live forever.

Jon Voight's mother in *The Odessa File* called for someone readily able to evoke sympathy. Maria Schell, the Austrian actress, with whom I'd worked on *The Magic Box*, was the obvious choice. And, having played many villains in the past, her brother, Maximilian, (Oscar and Golden Globe winner for his role in *Judgment at Nuremberg*) was cast as the war criminal Eduard Roschmann.

Next an original song was needed for the opening night sequence, as Voight is listening to his radio while driving through the Christmas decorated streets of Hamburg. To enhance the holiday atmosphere, the actual song would be played while we were filming—meaning it had to be written and recorded up front. My suggestion to Woolf was that we engage Andrew Lloyd Webber to write the score, the same young man I had gotten to know years before in Italy.

Andrew Lloyd Webber: Tim Rice and I wrote a good song called "The Christmas Dream" which was performed by Perry Como. When Tim composed the lyrics he put in what we considered an innocent line, "All we need's a little snow." The Americans thought it was about drugs so it was basically banned. Neither Tim nor I had any idea that snow was slang for cocaine—clearly neither did Ronnie!

The song would be played over the main credits and, after a chorus or two, be interrupted by an announcer making the shattering statement: ". . . This is Washington. We have just received confirmation that President John F. Kennedy is dead following a shooting earlier today . . ."

With this pronouncement, the date of our story is established—November 22, 1963.

Flicky was determined to be well enough to work on the production—and she was. We celebrated the New Year's Eve of 1974 in Hamburg with the entire unit—a lovely start of filming party. Ossie was there. He'd been remarried for several years and had brought his second wife, Lee, with him on location. Vividly I remember standing there with them at a hotel window several storeys up. Watching the celebratory fireworks light up the sky, he turned to me and said, "It's strange, Ron—the last time I saw Hamburg, I was thirty thousand feet up in a Wellington bomber."

Everyone worked well together, but there was occasional unease because of the film's sensitive subject matter and the fact that over half the unit was German. There were two men who never spoke to each other; one was a former SS officer who became technical advisor on the concentration camp scenes; the other a Jewish consultant, a Holocaust survivor, who conferred with us about the behavior of the prisoners. His parents had been sent to the gas chambers, and the severe physical abuse he had suffered during his internment had left him with a bad limp.

Alongside assistant director Colin Brewer was his German counterpart, a man who had been in the Hitler Youth Movement. With Col's help and that of casting directors Renate Neuchl and Jenia Reissar, we set about gathering together extras for the concentration camp scenes.

Simon Wiesenthal, the famed Nazi hunter, was also a consultant. On first meeting him in London, I was struck by the fact that such a mild natured man of slight stature had, almost single-handedly, taken on the enormous task of seeking retribution for the millions of Jews who had suffered so horribly during the war. He was also to be portrayed as a character in the film, and for this role a German actor, capable of recreating his special qualities, had to be secured. Initially I thought Israeli Shmuel Rodensky's accent was too heavy, but his slow, studied manner of delivery made him absolutely right casting. He gave the character depth and sincerity—completely understandable and convincing.

Although the part of a passport forger is small, it is one of those pivotal ones. None of the Germans we auditioned seemed right. Knowing I could count on her judgment, I phoned my agent and old friend, Anne Hutton, (formerly with Christopher Mann) in London, for a suggestion. She recommended Derek Jacobi. He joined us in Munich and, as expected, did a superb job.

All directors look for something special to bring to each sequence of a film. On *Odessa*, I needed to make our own black-and-white newsreel footage for a wartime flashback in which Roschmann (Max Schell) shoots and kills the journalist's father. The way the authenticity was achieved was by rehearsing the action of the sequence and then bringing in three hand-held cameras to shoot it live. I gave the camera operators general assignments: one for close-ups, the second for long shots and the third as a roving eye, then let them loose. They occasionally got in each other's way, but we dealt with it by judicious editing. The finished sequence has the immediacy of an actual newsreel.

Once our locations were completed in Hamburg, we moved to Munich, a long way to the south and equally as cold. But happily much of our work was shot inside the stages at Bavaria Studios. On those occasions that we did work outside, Flicky set up shop in a warm trailer, and in between takes members of the unit would visit us for an always available cup of coffee.

On our days off she and I would drive into the town and relax—simply to adjust our focus away from the film. On one of these occasions we went with Colin and his wife.

Colin Brewer: I had promised Hazel a mink coat for her birthday. Flicky was very sweet and modeled some so Hazel could see how they looked on another woman. Ronnie gave his approval as to which one he thought was best. But it must be said, he's not a person to go shopping with—he can't wait to get away.

By now Flicky was looking well, happy, and relaxed—the horrible recent past behind us.

As scripted, Jon Voight's character hopes to get information about his father's death and attends a reunion of the Organization Siegfried, the secret group of former Nazi officers. This was filmed in a beer hall filled with 200 real army veterans recruited by advertisements in the Munich newspaper.

In the scene two former officers of the brigade make speeches. Some of the Hitler quotes from the second of them were controversial. "One day we will rise again! One day Germany will become what she was! This will be a great day! One people! One Germany! One leader!"

Cautiously I filmed the scene at the end of the day because of uncertainty about how the ex-army extras would react to an evident Nazi sympathizer. They were entirely opposite to what I'd anticipated.

"If someone had made that speech in 1963," they said, "he would have been arrested."

To help lighten the serious, often harrowing content of the film, we held Friday evening parties on set. They started out simply enough, but as the unit became better acquainted, the event became more involved. One week set designer Rolf Zehetbauer and his art department dressed a nearby stage as a beer hall. Another week, John Woolf and his production team hosted an elaborate do. And, on the last day of shooting, the studio gave us a fancy dress affair. Compliments of the wardrobe department I came as King Farouk of Egypt, complete with moustache—Flicky was my Arab princess.

In the spring, as the weather in Germany warmed up, we returned to Pinewood Studios for editing, having completed fourteen weeks of filming.

The Odessa File is an acceptable film but it isn't as good as *The Day of the Jackal* because the necessary exposition required too much dialogue. Also, there was the language problem. We had Germans who were supposed to be speaking German, speaking English instead—many with a strong accent. Probably that's why the film is better in the German "dubbed" version—strangely it was more successful there than in any other country. To this day, I get more fan letters for this movie than any other. Except *Poseidon*!

Frederick Forsyth: I think the film was very successful in terms of its translation from a novel to the screen. If they had taken it from page one, scene by scene, it would have been a five-hour movie, and it wouldn't have had the tension. An author doesn't have the color and movement and the whole range of things the filmmaker has. It did follow the storyline pretty damn closely, the pace had to be kept up, and it was. Every salient point is there, nothing was distorted. Ronnie got it all in somehow.

Once the picture was delivered to Columbia, Flicky and I went in high spirits to the States on a promotional tour preceded by a première at the San Francisco Film Festival on October 16, 1974.

When we arrived at the Palace of Fine Arts, I was surprised to see the studio had staged what I thought was an overly-aggressive promotional stunt—standing at ease in an open truck was a group of men wearing brown shirts and swastikas, a large Nazi flag draped over the side.

"Columbia has gone too far," I remarked to Flicky. "This is in extremely poor taste." Everyone else thought so too. But with a bombardment of shouting and offensive gestures we soon realized these were genuine neo-Nazi protesters, calling the film "offensive."

Flicky loved Hollywood and since my career often brought me there, we decided to buy a place of our own. We found a house in one of the canyons with views of the Pacific, the mountains, and the San Fernando Valley. Once settled in, we traveled back and forth over several months between London, the English countryside, and Hollywood until Frank Yablans at Twentieth Century Fox offered me *The Other Side of Midnight,* based on the Sidney Sheldon novel. I signed to direct for a spring 1976 start.

It was another of those situations where one writer followed another, trying to bring the novel down to an acceptable length. Daniel Taradash and Herman Raucher finally created a decent enough script.

We were in California when without warning something alarming happened. Flicky awoke noticing that her ankles were seriously swollen. I immediately phoned my agent, Phil Kellogg, who referred us to a doctor.

"Bearing in mind her history, I think some tests should be done at once," the latter recommended. She was admitted to Cedars Sinai Hospital where she spent several laborious days undergoing these tests, all of which proved negative. But the Cedars' doctor did suggest that when we returned to England, she should see the surgeon who had performed her hysterectomy. Waiting was not an option and within days, we were back in London.

More tests.

I was with her when the doctor broke the news. The diagnosis was not good, the cancer had returned and gone into Flicky's lymph nodes.

"How long have I got?" was her first question.

"As it has been a year since your last operation, I'd say you have another four years, perhaps five."

"Not to worry too much, darling," I said. "That makes us level-pegging in terms of expectancy and, if we try we can both beat the odds, and live a lot longer."

Because *The Other Side of Midnight* was in full preproduction, I had to leave her at the Chelsea house and make a quick trip to Paris to choose locations, and then to Hollywood to sort out some details.

It was desperately worrying to be away from her, but I had a contract and shooting was imminent. The decision about what to do for the best was made for me when I received a phone call from Flicky's brother, himself a doctor.

"Ronnie," he said in a voice foreshadowing what he was about to tell me, "things don't look good. She doesn't have four years; it's more like four months. I think you should come home."

Producers Frank Yablans and Martin Ransohoff were more than generous and accepted my immediate resignation. Charles Jarrott took over the picture.

In the short time I'd been away, Flicky had deteriorated. The doctor told me there was little they could do but in a last ditch hope chemotherapy was started. She entered King Edward VII's Hospital for Officers, just off the Marylebone Road. Admittance to this special facility was allowed because her father had been an Army colonel.

I sat with her day after day, week after week. Her brother and sister-in-law came from the Midlands for a few days. As they were saying goodbye, Flicky remarked, "I don't suppose I'll be seeing you again." After an awkward silence, she added, "I mean on this trip."

For another three weeks, I stayed with her and tried to keep her room a cheerful place, even setting up a bar for visiting friends. She and I had always enjoyed a gin and tonic before lunch, but soon she stopped drinking and ate less and less.

I had called in my own doctor, Brian Piggott, who had looked after my family for years, to see if he could offer any other prognosis. He walked with me down the hall: "It's really very bad Ronnie. The morphine has been increased to ease her pain. She'll sleep a lot now and won't be able to talk much when she's awake."

I went back into her room. She smiled and said, "Hold my hand."

She closed her eyes and slipped into a coma. Ten days later she died. Felicité Philipson was only thirty-nine.

We had known one another for seven years and she had made me happier than I ever knew could be possible. Now I was alone not knowing what to do next.

On my arrival back in California, Ina Balin (who I'd contacted for *Escape from Zahrain*), became my strength, helping me to rebuild my shattered world. Her brother Richard and his wife, Rochelle, as well as my other friends rallied round—each of them leading me through the crisis. I couldn't seem to face the task of removing Flicky's clothes so they did it for me.

Beyond being a wonderful actress, Ina was a remarkable woman, who had recently gone to Vietnam to help evacuate orphans during the war. She ended up adopting some of the children herself and a film was made of her dedication to their rescue.

One evening after the Balins had left I found myself wondering, "What am I doing here?" I was sixty-six years old, thousands of miles away from England and the thing that made the most sense was to sell-up and go home.

Harry Saltzman, who, with his partner, "Cubby" Broccoli, produced the original James Bond films, came to see me about a film he was planning. When I told him of my contemplated departure, he gave me some advice based on personal experience. "Don't make any decisions for one year. You've been happy here. In twelve months you may feel quite differently from the way you do now."

I took his advice and more than a quarter of a century later, although I often visit my family in England, I still live in the same hillside house.

A man on his own gets invited to dinner parties and I was fortunate enough to be included in many social gatherings. Ina introduced me to a friend of hers, Natahlie Paine. When we met, Natahlie was deeply involved in preventive medicine and had established a medical foundation. Her particular interest was adrenal cortical extract; a substance she firmly believed could cure almost anything. For a time, I became her guinea pig, being injected daily with something or other—I supported her foundation and even served on its board of directors. Perhaps I owe my longevity to her efforts.

With Natahlie a normal life regained ground. We remained companions throughout the next few years, and she was alongside me when I returned to filmmaking. She also helped when I began arrangements to enlarge the house by adding a second floor. And eventually a country kitchen was constructed by knocking down some interior walls.

"They need a director badly, and I'm designing the sets" were the words that launched me into the next film. My colleague from *The Poseidon Adventure*, Bill Creber, added, "I've talked to the producers, and they're keen to meet you."

Theodore Parvin and Arnold Orgolini told me the film's story. It was based on scientific studies done a decade earlier about an asteroid that circles the earth on a regular basis. The fictional element enters when the meteor shifts onto a collision course with earth and the two great powers, Russia and America, have to work alongside each other to save the world. The only solution is for them to point their united arsenal towards the heavens at exactly the same time. But if one failed to do so, the other would be vulnerable to attack—mutual trust in a cold war situation. This strong social and political conflict appealed to me and I accepted *Meteor* in the same spirit and high expectations that I had accepted *Poseidon*.

The impression given to me was that Parvin and Orgolini were the only producers, but that was not the case. Fellow producer Sandy Howard had put together the finances and was very much a part of the team. I had heard of his successful *A Man Called Horse*, but what I didn't know were the exploitive titles of some of his other pictures—*Death Ship, Crunch,* and *City on Fire.*

To help sell the film, Sandy created an elaborate color brochure with illustrations showing the devastation the meteor would cause when it struck Manhattan, Hong Kong, and the Alps. The booklet was immense with everything anyone would ever need to know about meteors. Much later, I learned that the young woman who had been engaged to put it together was the same blonde student I'd met fleetingly at Jean Louis' party in Santa Barbara during *Gambit*. More than ten years had passed since then and Donna had graduated and joined the workforce.

On the strength of this brochure and Sandy's charm and persuasive personality, Warner Bros. committed $4,000,000 to the production. Additional financing for distribution rights came from Run Run Shaw in Hong Kong, American International Pictures, Stockholm Film, and the *Nippon Herald*.

Known for his brilliance for soliciting funds, Gabriel Katzka entered the arena as the fourth producer—that was three too many as far as I was concerned. Therefore, when I signed my contract, a stipulation was made that only one of them could be on the set—Arnold Orgolini.

A major obstacle stood in the way of production. Sandy had no script! In an attempt to get something on paper for the backers, he'd asked Edmund H. North, whose credits included *The Day the Earth Stood Still*, to develop a story. No one seemed happy with it, so we agreed to begin again—a recurring theme in my life!

Stanley Mann started writing and three months later we had something to work with. But just at that point, my main ally, Bill Creber, left me in the proverbial lurch when he departed the production over a contractual disagreement. Perhaps it should have given me a hint about what lay ahead.

We began assembling an all-star cast, à la *Poseidon*. Sean Connery accepted the role of Dr. Paul Bradley, an American astrophysicist. Also a young actress who could speak Russian fluently was required for the part of Tatiana, the interpreter. Leslie Bricusse suggested Natalie Wood and she signed when she realized that, although it wasn't a big role, it was a good one. Brian Keith was cast as Connery's Russian counterpart, Dr. Alexei Dubov. He didn't speak Russian, but in a short time he learned his lines phonetically turning in a bravura performance. Martin Landau played Air Force General Barry Adlon, the villain—and I was delighted when Karl Malden joined us in the role of Harry Sherwood, head of NASA.

Karl Malden: I had known Natalie ever since we were both under contract to Warner's when we made a film *Bombers B-52*. She was fifteen and played my daughter. Later, I did *Gypsy* with her. She had grown up, and had this wonderful part, which she did brilliantly. Ten years later, I was working with her again on *Meteor*. She and I used to hang out in her trailer and just talk. She spoke Russian, and I speak Serbian, and we could understand each other.

Trevor Howard's agent phoned from London asking if there was anything for him—he wanted to make an American film. The part of Sir Michael Hughes, the longtime British scientific associate of Dr. Bradley, was open and Trev came over for a three-day cameo. Henry Fonda also did a two-day piece as the President of the United States, delivering a heartfelt two-and-a-half minute speech to the Washington press corps. Unfortunately his scene was deleted in the final print, but on the day we filmed it, he had received a standing ovation from our two hundred extras.

In order to portray the various potentially disastrous effects of the meteor heading towards earth, we were scheduled to shoot on several locations to which visual special effects would be added. The first was in the Bavarian Alps, but when we arrived there there was no snow. I made an immediate decision to switch sites. Within twenty-four hours the unit was settling into snowcovered Chamonix, where, by pure coincidence 12,000 cross-country skiers were holding their annual marathon. It was a stunning sight and an opportunity not to be missed—the superimposed effects would show them being swept away by an avalanche. It would have been a spectacular moment if all had gone smoothly. But . . .

We went to Hong Kong to film people racing away from the shoreline for higher ground before a giant tidal wave struck. But . . .

Returning to the studio I directed the dirtiest scene I've ever had to do— our heroes fighting their way through a ruptured subway tunnel virtually filled with mud and water. Natalie Wood had the roughest time; ironically she was terrified of water. It was a ghastly experience reminiscent, on a much larger scale, of the goo the cast had had to endure on *In Which We Serve*.

The only pleasant memory about filming this sequence is that Donna came to the studio and reintroduced herself. I wiped mud off my hands to help her onto the subway set and, in the midst of this chaos, began a friendship that would one day culminate in my second marriage.

Another unforgettable event during *Meteor* occurred in December 1979. Alfred Hitchcock received the Man of the Year Award from the British American Chamber of Commerce and I was asked to present it to him. We had met socially through the years with our mutual friends Eric Ambler and his wife Joan Harrison who produced Hitch's television series.

He was very old and frail in a wheelchair when I approached him for a quiet word before the ceremony. "Hitch, it's Ronnie, do you remember me?" I asked. Smiling tentatively, he placed his hand on my arm, "Of course I remember you Ronnie. You're one of my boys." His extraordinary life ended within four months. Years later, in 1994, I felt very nostalgic and honored to be given the same award from the British American Chamber, presented by Dennis Storer, the organization's Executive Director.

Filming had taken longer and cost more than anticipated, but was eventually completed. To mark the occasion T-shirts were issued to the unit with the line "There Is Life after *Meteor.*"

Once edited, a great film, costing over ten million, was beginning to emerge. Only the special effects were needed to replace the "scene missing" sections.

What changed the film from being something I could have been proud of to a horror were these special effects. The head of that lamentable department had insisted on taking his own camera on location. The producers accepted his request, despite the advice of our cameraman, Paul Lohmann, who wanted him to take a guaranteed steady Panavision camera. He assured us his own was equally as steady—but it wasn't. Consequently the footage he filmed could not be "married" precisely to our shots. No amount of lab work could ever put it right. Another $5,000,000 gone and still no viable special effects!

Arnold Orgolini and I scheduled a meeting in Sandy Howard's Sunset Boulevard office to discuss what could possibly be pulled out of the bag to save the picture. I suggested we needed to spend more money to get usable effects material, Sandy didn't agree. The meeting began in a gentlemanly manner, but it wasn't long before it took on another tone. Accusations were hurled back and forth. People in the outer office could hear the yelling. Realizing there was no compromise other than to cut around the effects, thus destroying the film, I wanted out and walked away.

Sandy had hired an inexpensive special effects man who delivered a mediocre meteor shooting across an unbelievable sky. Adding insult to injury, he recut the film to suit himself, and, despite my best legal efforts, my name still appears as director. *Meteor* cost $16,000,000. The result was a terminal disaster and an unhappy experience for all concerned.

• 30 •

Walter Matthau

I said "No" to a screenplay by Brian Garfield and Bryan Forbes entitled *Hopscotch*. Two weeks later, producer, Ely Landau asked if I'd be more interested if a new script was written. This was certainly worth pursuing, so we arranged a meeting. Apparently Garfield, whose book had won an Edgar, the mystery writers' equivalent of an Oscar, and Landau had spent more than four years getting the project to this point. It would have to be rewritten without Forbes' input, since he had departed to direct a play in England.

But still I hesitated.

When Ely contacted me for a third time, he opened with, "What would you say if Walter Matthau played the lead?"

"That would make a big difference," I replied, "but I can't think why on earth he would want to do it."

I re-read the book with this casting in mind and then told him for what I thought would be the last time. "I'm afraid I still don't see it working—it's just not very good."

Less than a week later he was at me again, sounding desperate.

"Ronnie you just have to make this picture because Walter Matthau won't sign unless you direct."

Something didn't sound kosher! Matthau and I had never met so why would he impose this condition? Nevertheless, a meeting between us was arranged in Ely's Century City offices.

Immediately, I was impressed by Walter's intelligence, his big personality, and his great sense of humor. And we both had the same opinion about the script.

"What made you say you would only do the film if I directed it? You don't know anything about me."

"Because I grew up in New York with Ely," he said in a deliberate voice, "and he's in a spot. I wanted to help him, and in a moment of weakness I agreed, then immediately regretted it and wanted out." He laughed, adding, "I could only do that by saying I would take the part if Neame directed and I knew you wouldn't."

So, I was his excuse for backing off!

"Let's do it anyway!" he grinned. "We'll work with Garfield on a new screenplay and treat it lightly."

By the second week of January 1979, I was set to direct *Hopscotch*, which, despite its unusual genesis, became one of my most favorite films. Walter was to play an old CIA veteran named Kendig, who writes a tell-all book exposing the Agency's dirty tricks department—his revenge for being fired.

Before we began, Walter's long-time agent, Leonard Hershan, phoned to say Walter loved Mozart and it would please him greatly if, somehow, this music might be incorporated in the film.

Being a Mozart fan myself, I spoke to our arranger, Ian Fraser, who thought it could work as the basis of the whole score. Mozart was interwoven into the story to the extent that the music was even used during chase scenes between Kendig and the CIA. Deciding to go one step further, we made Matthau's character a classical music aficionado.

Ian Fraser: I bought every Mozart record I could lay my hands on, and one of them was this wonderful Rondo in D [K382], which became the main theme. I was particularly proud of the chase music—the Post Horn Serenade. We recorded the track with the Los Angeles Chamber Orchestra and pianist Ralph Grierson. We used a little Puccini and Rossini too, but it was mostly Mozart. Who would have thought he would become a movie composer? It fitted the picture like a glove.

During scripting, *Hopscotch* was transformed from a serious screenplay into a comedy—with Walter's help. Once we'd made a one-line continuity of the story and discussed how to flesh it out, Brian would adjourn to the typewriter and bash out the scenes. I've never known anyone type so fast—this was long before computers!

Brian Garfield: I think Ronnie should have his name on the credits as screenwriter, but he refused. We may have started with the script Forbes and I had written, but it changed so much because of Ronnie's direct input. If any screenplay deserves to have a director's name on it, along with other writers, it's *Hopscotch*.

Walter's contribution was invaluable. Occasionally, however, he came in with material he had written which wasn't very good. Brian and I would tell him so and he'd just say "Okay" crumple up the pages and toss them in the waste bin. There was never an ego problem.

But when his material was good, he was his own best writer.

There's a scene in which Kendig arranges to re-meet his girlfriend, a former CIA agent. "But it's far too plotty," we told Walter. When he came in the next morning and asked for some unusual research material, one couldn't help suspecting that he was trying to come up with a solution.

"What could he possibly want with wine catalogues?" I asked Brian.

Two days later he brought in his new pages. Having created an introduction to Isobel, a woman of a certain age, his previous relationship with her is cleverly established by talking about wine—every line giving an insight into both characters.

Their reunion takes place in Salzburg. Kendig is sitting at a table at Winkler's Café as Isobel approaches. She asks him what kind of wine he prefers "Red? White? French? Do you prefer a young or an old wine?" Kendig moves in closer to Isobel as he says, "As a general rule, the older wines are better."

He then asks her if she is a wine salesperson and she replies that she's a widow living off her husband's generous endowment. As they speak about the effects of wine on the liver and cholesterol, they move in closer still to each other and then embrace.

Walter had given the scene everything we needed to know about them without being obvious. He cleverly buried the plot in what appears to be frivolous talk.

Once we had a completed script, we needed an actress to play Isobel. Walter suggested Glenda Jackson, his costar from *House Calls*.

A wonderful idea, however would she be willing to play a role of less than twenty minutes screen time?

Walter contacted her and she accepted without a moment's hesitation—because she adored him.

With these two key players attached to the project, we were able to cast other excellent actors including Ned Beatty, as Meyerson, the head of the CIA's dirty tricks department, who is determined to silence Kendig at any cost; my old chum Herbert Lom as Yaskov, the Russian spy; and Sam Waterston, as Cutter, both an antagonist and protégé of Kendig.

Sam Waterston: I was doing *Heaven's Gate* in Montana. Every morning we were driven miles and miles to the Canadian border where we would sit parked in a field all day, and then turn around and come back to where we were staying—usually without having shot anything. I got a message from my agent to call Ronnie, who I'd never met. He said, "John Gaines, our mutual agent, tells me you are in an unpleasant situation." And in that inimitable Neame voice and with a chuckle he said, "I've got a little film for you. I don't know whether it will revolutionize cinematic history, but I can promise you a very good time." I accepted, and, as promised, he delivered.

We had a budget of about $8,000,000, and a start date of September 24, 1979 in Munich. This was when Walter suddenly threw a spanner in the works announcing he had no intention of going to Germany for the short period of location work and, referring to a key sequence at the Oktoberfest, he added, "I'm certainly not going into a marquée with all those beer swilling Krauts!"

I found this difficult to understand, as he had known for weeks the opening scene took place at the festival. But he explained that too many of his relatives had suffered in German prison camps. His final comment, "You'll have to do my stuff in the studio here."

Although that was a possibility, it represented enormous extra cost, and wouldn't be nearly as good, however his feelings had to be considered.

About two weeks before we were due to leave, he came to me with a suggestion, "The part of Ross, the junior member of the CIA team, I think my son David would be good casting." My response: "Send him to see me tomorrow." David was, without doubt, right for the role and I told Walter I'd cast him. "With one proviso."

He narrowed his eyes.

"You come to Munich."

He thought for a moment, then reluctantly agreed. Nevertheless, he said he would not go into the marquée. And that was final!

I accepted and thought somehow we'd have to manage.

A few days later he came to me saying, "Ronnie, I think my stepdaughter, Lucy would be excellent for the lady pilot who flies me to the Bahamas at the end." I said I would see her. Lucy Saroyan arrived for the audition in leather flying jacket and pants. Not only did she look the part, she also read it well. I told Walter she was on, "But with one proviso."

He knew what was coming. "Well, I suppose I'll have to go into that damned marquée won't I," he said grudgingly—and I sighed with relief.

The unit consisted of two other old friends, production designer Bill Creber and lighting cameraman Arthur Ibbetson. Arthur's sense of humor complemented Walter's and quickly they became great buddies, with Arthur reverently referring to Walter as "guv."

While on holiday several years earlier, I had been to the Oktoberfest and thought what a great setting to use in a film. Each year, thousands and thousands of people come to the city to drink from the largest steins of beer in the world. Each major brewer puts up a marquée to sell what it claims to be the best brew. Never have so many consumed so much in such a short period of time!

For exterior shots of the opening parade and scenes with our principals conversing amongst the crowd, a concealed camera was essential. Arthur's excellent suggestion was to hide it inside a moveable kiosk—a lightweight affair that looked like an advertising post. The art department designed it with a disguised hole large enough for the lens to peer through. Trying to remain inconspicuous outside, I couldn't shout "Action." Instead I stood in front of the lens until we were ready and then waved a handkerchief as the cue. With each shot finished, we moved the kiosk to the next area.

A similar difficulty inside the Oktoberfest marquée was solved when one brewery, for a substantial fee, permitted us to film inside their tent—the other *braumeisters* would have nothing to do with us. Arthur, his crew, and I went in at six A.M. and set up three cameras on a balcony and placed lights on either side aimed towards the crowd below. If anybody looked up at the balcony all they would see were bright lights.

Fifty extras split into five groups (each with a captain) and were seated at our principals' tables.

The main action was rehearsed while the marquée was still empty and then, at noon, it rapidly filled with two thousand beer drinkers—all singing and swaying to the accompaniment of an oompah band. I gave the cue, this time by walkie-talkie to each table captain, and the lengthy sequence was shot in a matter of hours. And Walter had made good on his word participating without a hitch.

Walter and Herbert Lom had several scenes together in Salzburg. Herbert appeared on the first day wearing a leather trench coat to keep out the chilly weather. Although it was not part of his official wardrobe, it was the perfect accompaniment to his character and I asked him to wear it during filming. Sam later ad-libbed, "Yaskov must have seen *Casablanca* twelve times!"

After a week of shooting in Bavaria Studios, the management treated a few of us to an evening at the Bayerische Staatsoper, the Munich Opera House. Appropriately we saw a performance of Mozart's *Die Zauberflöte* and sat in the Royal Box. For Walter, it made his visit to the city worthwhile.

Shortly afterwards he said he wanted to pay homage to the six million Jews who had died in the Holocaust by visiting Dachau, the internment camp situated not far away. On his return he appeared deeply shaken. His anguish was worsened by tourists who had callously asked for his autograph.

Typical of Walter, he turned his grief into a lighter anecdote, explaining that he and his wife Carol had been fighting before their visit to the concentration camp. Once they had completed the tour she had taken Walter's hand and said, "Let's not quarrel anymore, it's so senseless." But Walter replied, "It's too late for apologies Carol, you've completely ruined Dachau for me."

He and Glenda made my life extremely easy throughout because they liked each other so much. Both were spelling fanatics and very competitive. So often, while waiting for a setup, they would challenge each other, "I bet you can't spell . . ." and one would give the other some incredibly difficult word. This interplay between them continued nonstop.

Working with him was never dull. We were constantly laughing to the extent that it was difficult to get anything done. He tended to joke right up to the clappers and sometimes after. As with Shirley MacLaine, on more than one occasion I had to be firm and say, "Walter, will you please behave yourself." "Yessir! Yessir!" he would reply good-naturedly, jumping to attention and saluting. Then he would behave seriously for, maybe, fifteen minutes.

Walter Matthau: When people ask me when am I going to do a serious part, I have to smile because my comedy is my serious stuff. The more humor something has, the more serious it is. Writing comedy is very tough. In the lives we lead, there's a lot of tragedy, but there's a lot of comedy too. There can't be one without the other. There's a fine dividing line between the two—if you step over that line, it shows.

After filming in Germany and Austria, we moved on to England.

Two days after our arrival in London, I received a telegram from my brother: "Am dying. Can someone come immediately?" I had been down this street several times before in our lives, but this time it was impossible for me to leave the production. I phoned Christopher to see if he could help. He was in preparation for a television series *The Flame Trees of Thika*, and had some flexibility.

Christopher Neame: I left immediately for Nice, not knowing quite where I was going to find Derek, as he'd given no clear address. By midday I'd tracked him down to a furnished room on the top floor of a sorry apartment building. We set out the next morning for Bordighera in Italy. He knew of a nursing home there, but no beds were available. Eventually I got him a room in a hotel and arranged for a doctor to see him straight away. The conclusion was that he was certainly ill, but there was no danger of him dying. I stayed close by for twenty-four hours to make certain the doctor remained available and then returned to London where I explained my uncle's condition to my father. Both of us kept in contact with him over the next few weeks.

Funds were made available to secure Derek's accommodations and further medical treatment. Believing that his condition wasn't grave, I was able to concentrate fully on the scenes to be shot in London.

There was virtually no studio work but even so weather cover was essential. Bill Creber found a former bank building near Trafalgar Square and obtained permission for us to build and shoot interiors there.

During our several weeks in England we filmed on an airfield, in various country lanes—and at Beachy Head where the climax of the story takes place. Good naturedly the British weather cooperated.

Then, back to the States, Atlanta and Savannah, Georgia.

Atlanta stood in for Washington, D.C., where we matted the Capitol into the background and used federal-looking offices for the interiors.

Savannah was the backdrop for one of the best sequences in the film. In it the head of the CIA, Meyerson (Ned Beatty) owns a second home that Walter rents under a pseudonym. Meyerson finds out and is livid, immediately calling the FBI for assistance. His intentions are clear—he wants Kendig dead or alive. In an overenthusiastic effort to nab him, the house is shot up and virtually destroyed to the panic-stricken consternation of Meyerson.

Numerous potential houses were seen for this location but none was right. It looked as if we were going to have to build our own, so Creber was asked to sketch a plan.

Consulting with a building contractor, Creber informed us that it would cost forty-five thousand dollars to build. "But why bother?" he asked, "There's a house just down the road that matches the description."

We went to look at it and as we pulled into the drive I was amazed. It was the house in Bill's sketch! I was sure he must have seen it before and was pulling my leg—but he swore not!

The woman who owned it was flattered that we wanted to use her home. She was told that because of the weight of the cameras and lighting equipment, the foundations would have to be strengthened where necessary—and, for story reasons, the verandah enclosed. As part of her compensation we built her a permanent gazebo.

It was unanimously decided not to mention the shoot-up sequence—no point in risking the possibility of being turned away before we'd even started.

The day before the scene was to be filmed, I tactfully informed her what was planned—"Simply shooting out the glass panels around the verandah. But," I clarified in my most reassuring tone, "we won't be using real bullets and the glass isn't real either."

I don't recall her saying anything, but do have an image of a blank stare. I suspect she was too stunned to comment. And I was too busy to notice her or her family's reactions.

Shooting Ned's facial expressions and general reaction to the demolition of *his* house was a joy. In fact, when we edited the sequence, I had difficulty cutting away from him because he was so good!

As promised, we didn't cause any damage. The crew swept up the debris, and we left everything in the same condition in which we found it. Handshakes all round.

When I look at the film today, I am constantly reminded of what a joy *Hopscotch* was to make. The cast and crew were exemplary and all the locations fun to be on. There's little more a director could ask for!

Except perhaps to work with Walter again.

While I had been editing, Beryl phoned with the sad news that Derek had died in Bordighera. The doctor's diagnosis of his condition had been inaccurate. There had been so many previous dramas, but this time he hadn't been exaggerating the severity of his symptoms. Colin Colahan's family made the funeral arrangements at an English Cemetery.

Over and over, this lovely man had attempted to destroy himself. Whatever I had tried to do for him hadn't been enough. And now the only gesture I could make was a small yearly contribution for the upkeep of his grave.

My younger brother didn't have much in the way of possessions—a few books, an unfinished manuscript. The mementos I have of him, besides a couple of photos, are some of his poems—one of which was published in *The New Yorker* in November 1937.

> *The New Order*
> Clerks and typists end their toil
> And don eccentric clothes to go
> For coffee at the Café Royal
> (Only nine pence each, you know),
> And they romanticize their lives,
> Weirdly garbed, in Soho dives,
> Posing as Miss So-and-so,
> A poetess from Pimlico,
> Or, incognito, "Mr. J",
> An artist sent by Night and Day.

This faction in fantastic suits
With females smoking black cheroots
Is not, as you might think, the seamier
Side of London's gay Bohemia,
Nor dress reformist's cranks,
But honest city men from banks
And office girls, who hope to be
Described as Wits from Bloomsbury.
The bona-fide artists wear
Their fifty-shilling suits with care
And even budding poets dress
Aided by a trouser press;
For now that fast decreasing few,
Who once above this realm held sway,
Like Gusty John and Wyndy Lew,
Are seen no more, gone with their day!

After I had taken a few weeks finishing *Hopscotch*, producer Paul Heller offered me *First Monday in October*, a title that refers to the opening of the Supreme Court for its yearly sessions.

I had met Paul years before at the Venice Film Festival and have known him ever since. Previously he'd produced the classic *David and Lisa*. He is a warm, intelligent man, a gourmet chef, with eclectic tastes in art, food, and friendships. He and his wife, Kathy, are often in my home and vice versa.

I had seen Jerome Lawrence and Robert E. Lee's exceptional stage production in New York with Henry Fonda as the irascible Supreme Court Justice Dan Snow—a character based on William O. Douglas. Jane Alexander had played opposite Fonda as Ruth Loomis, the first woman Supreme Court Justice. The two characters are at constant odds with each other over Ruth's gender and the story's theme, censorship—Justice Snow is liberal, Loomis is more conservative.

Fonda was set to star, but first Paul and his coproducer, Martha Scott, had to get the finances in place. I pointed out that Walter Matthau was very bankable, and I thought he would play the part beautifully. I went so far as to say if Paul were prepared to cast him, I would agree to do the film.

But Paul had committed to Fonda and I understood his position. Not long after our conversation, he found some backers.

Paul Heller: I told Hank, "I think we've got it together." Then he dropped a bomb by telling me that Jane had just asked him to do a movie with her—*On Golden Pond*. Ronnie contacted Matthau, but he was wary.

"That's Hank's part. I wouldn't do it unless he tells me it's all right," So we called Fonda who said that was fine with him and gave Walter his blessing. It was gracious on both their parts. They were both real gentlemen.

When Walter and I first looked at the screenplay together, he felt it was too wordy.

"They're good words, though, don't you think?" I responded. "However I won't try to persuade you if you don't want to do it."

"Oh, I want to do it," he countered. "They're Academy Award words, as far as I'm concerned. Not only do I want to do it, Ronnie, I'd do it for nothing. But don't ever tell anybody that."

The screenplay retained many of its theatrical origins and it couldn't really have been otherwise. Nevertheless we would be able to open up the story with scenes in and around Washington. Among them Arlington National Cemetery (most cooperative), the Smithsonian (lots of permits required) and a Chinese restaurant (a free meal).

The problem came with the Supreme Court Building—they would only grant us permission to shoot on the steps, no movie cameras were allowed inside the hallowed halls.

Production designer Phillip M. Jeffries had to replicate the interior down to the last detail on a stage; the corridors, barbershop, offices—all built with absolute accuracy from the still photographs we had been allowed to take.

Walter suggested Jill Clayburgh be cast opposite him. That year she had been nominated for an Oscar as Best Actress in a Leading Role for her performance in *Starting Over*. In fact, it was at the awards ceremony where Walter first met her. Paul and I considered her a bit too young, but because Walter's instincts were good and also because Leonard Hershan represented both of them, we decided to pursue the suggestion.

The result was that my agent, John Gaines, and Hershan were able to generate such interest in the package that a bidding war began over *First Monday* between MGM, where David Begelman then reigned, and Paramount, where Michael Eisner was head of production—we chose Paramount.

Our schedule called for eleven weeks of principal photography to begin on August 18, 1980, in Washington. The start date was approaching just as a press agent's dream came true. President Ronald Reagan nominated Sandra Day O'Connor as the first woman Supreme Court Justice and we counted on Paramount to capitalize on this bit of luck.

Then bad news.

The Screen Actors Guild called a strike, beginning on July 21 to last for ninety-five days. There was nothing to do but wait.

During the hiatus, Jill announced she and her husband, playwright David Rabe, were expecting a baby. She was maybe three or four months pregnant by then, so we had to adjust the schedule to accommodate the event. Unfortunately some complication with her pregnancy set in, though her doctors assured her she'd be fine by the time production began.

On Sunday October 26 we were having a preproduction meeting when the news came through that Jill had had a miscarriage.

Paul Heller: I called Eisner (who is Jill Clayburgh's cousin) and told him Jill's miscarriage wouldn't have an impact on the production in any way, because we had plenty to get on with without her. He went ballistic. "I'm shutting down tomorrow." Not once did he ask, "How is she?" I've never had anybody yell at me like that before. After Ronnie's agent, John Gaines, called him, the dust settled. And since nobody told us not to shoot, we went ahead.

We did everything we could in Washington without Jill and then returned to Los Angeles.

One of Justice Snow's sequences was to be shot in the mountains and this gave Walter's doctor some concern because of recent heart surgery. He said he could go up to eight thousand feet, but not an inch higher. The trouble was there was no snow at that altitude and we needed it. Defying orders, Walter climbed an additional five hundred feet and lived to tell the tale!

When Jill was well enough, about ten days later, she joined us at the studio for the interiors.

The core of the story is the battle between Walter and Jill over a porno movie, *The Naked Nymphomaniac*, which the Justices must consider banning. For this it was necessary to have actual pornographic footage, glimpses of which would be seen during a key sequence. Ruth Loomis (Jill) is determined to view the entire film; Dan Snow (Walter) refuses to go even to the projection room. We know she'll be the one to cast a negative vote while he'll cite the First Amendment to support freedom of speech.

Paul engaged an "adult film" production company to produce a ten-minute movie to our specifications. For reasons of good taste, I played the scene mostly on the justices' horrified reactions, cutting in just a minimal number of shots of the adult reel and later adding a suitable sound track to give the impression that more was happening than actually was. When the time came, we escaped the X rating from the MPAA and received an R.

Ian Fraser and I worked on the music together, deciding to use pompous Baroque to establish the tone of the piece under the credits, while selecting some of John Philip Sousa's marches to underscore the lighter side of the story.

On the whole, Paul and I thought Paramount sold the picture incorrectly. We objected to the poster showing Walter and Jill in judicial robes, back to back, with the scales of justice between them. This gave the impression it was a serious film. Consequently we may have lost out on the potentially large audience who enjoy comedies.

The publicity man on the film was fellow Brit and dear friend Jerry Pam.

Jerry Pam: I fault Paramount for missing an opportunity to take advantage of O'Connor's appointment. It was so perfect for the situation, but they never generated any excitement about the picture. Nothing!

Nonetheless, I am proud of it, and working with Walter again was as comfortable as wearing an old shoe.

Walter Matthau: Translating a play into a film is tough for the writer and the actors. When something is written for the stage, the action is moved by words, something written for the screen is moved by action. A movie has to be successful, not just prestigious. *First Monday* was a successful translation as far as my critical faculties are concerned, but it wasn't a success financially. It's one of the best pictures I've ever done.

First Monday in October's lack of recognition reinforced a growing antipathy towards the type of films that were in demand—high concept, big names, wall-to-wall special effects blockbusters that have to make millions over the first weekend. The ones I liked to make, and think I was pretty good at, were the art house pictures—good stories with interesting characters. However those kinds of projects are almost impossible to finance these days and the studios seem unwilling to devote time to building an audience. I was ready to hang it up but wasn't quite sure where to find the hat stand.

• 31 •

Donna

$\mathcal{R}$ichard Burton as Gulley Jimson and Elizabeth Taylor as Sarah Monday, his ex-model and wife, was a tempting combination. *Herself Surprised* is the first in Joyce Cary's trilogy that ends with *The Horse's Mouth*. Mike Todd Jr. wanted me to step into familiar waters to direct it on location in Ireland.

I lunched with Burton, who was persuasive and enthusiastic. He advised me to visit Liz to make further arrangements. The next day, I flew to Florida and saw her at a health spa where we enjoyed reminiscing. She was equally persuasive and enthusiastic.

Without returning home I flew directly from Miami to rainy Dublin for location scouting. Todd Jr. joined me and leveled me dumbstruck, "Financing has fallen through! There isn't going to be a film." With various excuses, followed by a polite handshake, he took the next plane out.

Suddenly left with a schedule wide-open, I made reservations for London, treating myself to a stay at the Berkeley to figure things out. After a lot of soul-searching I felt it really was time to step away from directing.

Back in Los Angeles, I threw a sort of retirement garden party to celebrate my fifty-seven years in film. On the hottest day of the summer my friends abandoned the tables that had been placed around the pool and congregated in the kitchen, the coolest room in the house. Guests included Pamela Mason who I had met years earlier at Wembley when she and her husband cameraman Roy Kellino welcomed her soon to be next husband, James Mason, into their home; film critic Charles Champlin, childhood chum Jack Davies and his wife Dorothy, screenwriters Fay and Michael Kanin, Walter and Carol Matthau. Roddy McDowall videotaped the event as he often did at such gatherings—dashing about, camera in hand, capturing everyone but himself.

Another of the guests was Donna (aka Dona, claiming it's shorter to write with friends). Since our second introduction during *Meteor*, we had kept up our friendship. Pretty, diminutive, with long, blond hair, she has a twinkle in her eyes to match her enigmatic smile. She is someone who has an understanding and wisdom about the world.

I learned that after leaving the University of California at Santa Barbara, she had spent a year at the Sorbonne, and then went to Cornell to do her graduate studies in theater. She had worked for novelist James Clavell before relocating to Montreal, where she became a film researcher on several features. She later segment produced television programs in the States.

British journalist Roderick Mann was also present at my party and talked about how he had always wanted to turn his novel, *Foreign Body*, into a film but, among other obstacles, could never find the right Indian actor to play the lead, Ram Das. His wife, Anastasia, came up with a suggestion. Through her travel agency, she had recently booked Victor Banerjee on a flight back to India from Los Angeles where he had come on a publicity junket for David Lean's *A Passage to India*.

"Victor is perfect for Ram Das," she announced, "and Ronnie, whether you like it or not, you are going to be our director!"

"But I'm retired, I answered firmly."

In the process of supporting my conviction, I had somehow consented to do it—part of me still wanted the challenge.

Agent Paul Rosen helped line up the financing, contacting my old ally Arthur Krim who was now running Orion, while French Canadian writer Céline La Frenière worked on the adaptation.

The film, a romantic piece of fluff about an unemployed Indian posing as a doctor, was shot in England where my son Christopher joined me as producer. We engaged Colin Brewer as the line producer.

One of the only difficulties arose over casting the part of Ram Das's cousin, I. Q. Patel. From the people we saw, finding an Indian with the right comedic appeal proved problematic. We ended up signing the witty cockney, Warren Mitchell.

Warren Mitchell: There was a scream of protest from the Asian members of British Actors Equity. "Why is this European playing an Asian? Were there not enough Asian actors out of work willing to play the part?" Ronnie's forthright reply to the press was, "This is a comedy and I thought Warren would add the dimension I wanted for the film. Why can't he play an Asian? He's an actor." I think he added, "This is all bollocks," but I can't vouch for that.

We also cast Trevor Howard as the decrepit Doctor Stirrup. He was old and ill and found it hard to remember his lines, but he made a brave effort.

Principal photography began in November 1985 at Wembley Studios—the days there constantly bringing back memories of the "quota quickie" era.

My grandson, Gareth, was on a break from school and joined the crew in his first professional job. He was so smitten that Christopher and I had some difficulty in persuading him to continue his studies for a final year at university. Three generations of the same family working on one film must be a rarity and it couldn't have been more fun or more satisfying.

Variety gave the film a good review and it did well especially outside of the US where it was considered too British. And after all these years it is still shown on television bringing in steady residuals.

Back in California, Donna and I met often. Although we are from different cultures as well as different generations, we share similar temperaments and interests. She has an understanding of British film history and is familiar with England, having spent many summers there. We both enjoy traveling, particularly through Europe, always gravitating towards London.

Recently she had returned from a trip to India and joined Columbia's legal department. I got into a routine of driving each day to meet her for lunch at a little French bistro near the studio.

Around this time, Sydney Samuelson, the first British Film Commissioner and a brilliant film historian, gathered up bits and pieces about me while shuffling through some ancient archives. He kindly organized and narrated a retrospective both in Los Angeles and in London. I owe a large debt to Sydney for the recognition I have received in my later years.

Sydney Samuelson: In 1991 I found myself researching Ronnie's life and times for the BAFTA event "Salute to Craftsmanship—Ronald Neame." I was charmed to find out that, although he is hugely (repeat hugely) older than I am, we are both sons of pioneers in the business, and ones who had their early successes during exactly the same period of time. How pleasing it is to know that both our mums and dads were actually British filmmakers in the Edwardian era.

In the early '90s, Peter Beale, a founder member of BAFTA/LA, headed ShowScan, a company that produced a technical process in which 70 mm film is projected at sixty frames per second on a surround screen. He had been commissioned to produce a short film for Lotte World, an enormous indoor Korean theme park.

It was basically a goodwill travelogue using children as its centerpiece—a fourteen-year-old Japanese girl and a ten-year-old Korean boy. Peter asked me to write and direct the seventeen-minute short—then he sweetened the offer, "You can choose any locations you want."

As interesting as this sounded, I declined reemphasizing, "I'm retired." But Donna tipped the scales, "If you decide to do the film," she offered as bribery, "I'll take time off work and join you on location."

Peter, with his wife Francesca, ran several ShowScan films for us and what we saw was thrilling—even the seats shook and tilted in synchronization with the action. The idea of working in this new medium was another temptation. So, of course, I said, "Yes." Although *The Magic Balloon* was a small project, the unit was impressive—Jack Cardiff agreed to work as cinematographer and was completely at home with the wide screen, and *Poseidon* set designer, Bill Creber also proved invaluable. Frank Langella (of *Dracula* fame) was engaged as our evil magician and Henry Gibson became his sidekick.

The children encounter the magician, who chases them in their hot-air balloon around the world—Langella, dressed in black with a jeweled turban and cape, is on a bicycle-like flying contraption invented by Creber. Besides Venice, Italy I also wrote in Honolulu, Lake Powell, Arizona, and Seoul, Korea. A second unit filmed other locations around the globe.

In Venice, I made the mistake of giving Donna a walk-on part with Langella. Once again I had the ever-unpopular task of telling them to stop joking around. Frank is a great wit and, other than Donna, I've never met anyone who can chat on the phone longer. After *Magic Balloon* we flew to London.

David Lean had died earlier that year and Donna and I had been invited to the memorial service set for October 3, 1991. We shared a taxi to St. Paul's cathedral with Tony Havelock-Allan and Valerie Hobson, who, despite earlier predictions, were now divorced, but even so had remained close. Valerie had subsequently married John Profumo. As we approached the steps of the Cathedral, photographers lined us up along with other surviving figures from David's life. The Royal Philharmonic Orchestra also assembled in front of the church playing "Colonel Bogey" and the themes from many of his films.

Out of the corner of my eye I noticed Alec Guinness, who, in his usual fashion, slipped inside the cathedral incognito. I also spotted Ann Todd.

Once we were seated, Johnnie Mills read from *Great Expectations*, John Box delivered a moving tribute and Robert Bolt, assisted to the microphone by his wife Sarah Miles, made a short speech. Tom Courtenay and Omar Sharif also said a few words.

It had been an immense tribute, but the acoustics in that chilly, enormous place made it difficult to understand the speakers. I couldn't help thinking David would have been more aptly honored in an intimate church—perhaps St. Martins-in-the-Fields as Noël had been. Noël's words came back to me that day, "One doesn't know whether to be unhappy that someone has died or whether to be grateful that one is still alive."

Donna and I returned to California and continued seeing each other.

Early in 1932 I worked on a musical entitled *Maid of the Mountains* with Friese-Green shot on location in the South of England. Lately—more than sixty years later—the words to one of its songs kept replaying in my head.

> At seventeen he falls in love quite sadly with eyes of tender blue.
> At twenty-four he gets it rather badly with eyes of a different hue.
> At thirty-five you'll see him flirting madly with three or four or more.
> But when he thinks he's past love it is then he meets his last love
> and he loves her as he never loved before.

So Donna Friedberg and I were married on a boat in Santa Barbara on the morning of September 12, 1993—surrounding us was a small group of friends. Wearing orchids fashioned into leis around our necks, we sailed out into the harbor for the ceremony.

Over the next two months there were more celebrations. And then on New Year's Eve we drove back to Santa Barbara where we toasted in 1994 in high spirits, looking forward to the future. After the festivities, we started back to the hotel bungalow beneath a clear sky. And there it was, heavy in the air—the distinctive scent of California's night blooming jasmine.

In Los Angeles seventeen days later, at 4:31 A.M., our world changed.

Donna Neame: A thundering freight train raced through our bedroom, shattering glass, overturning bookshelves, vanity tables, scaring us frozen. Our alarm system blared at deafening pitch, then silence—electricity was cut off. Several moments later we started to breathe more evenly as we faced the dark. We stumbled barefoot downstairs to the study, the only cantilevered room in the house, making it, unbeknownst to us, the most dangerous. With bleeding feet, we searched for and lit candles, not an intelligent move in the event of broken gas lines. We were not prepared for this catastrophe and did everything wrong.

It was an eerie feeling looking out to the valley on the right then the city on the left and not seeing any lights whatsoever. We were alone in the quiet above a black terrain.

At dawn we saw the damage inflicted by the 6.8 Northridge earthquake.

The cliff on which our house is situated had split down the middle and a section had dropped eight inches towards the ravine below. The upper terrace built a few feet from where we sleep had cracked off, reaffirming the words "death is a hair's breadth away."

Donna Neame: Geologists told us, "Get out now!" But Ronnie would have none of it. He had lived through two World Wars, including the Blitz and he wasn't about to leave his home simply because we had no electricity, no water, and we might at any moment slide down the hill into Coldwater Canyon!

I have always known in life there are credits and debits, one pays for the pluses with minuses. Donna and I had been handed the bill. The earthquake tore away the underpinning of our home as well as our lives. It took a long time to rebuild both. But when we did our home was stronger—"bullet proof," the contractors were to assure us. And, through adversity, the foundation of our marriage also became indestructible.

While the rebuilding took place, we traveled throughout Europe, including Monte Carlo where I was asked to be president of the jury at its annual Film Festival. Our cosmopolitan friends Bill and Jacqui Saunders were responsible for my appointment. We met the Prince and his heir and while I worked hard viewing entries; Donna and Jacqui drove past Casa Jolanda (which had been sold years earlier) on their way to Ventimiglia's open market. We often visited London, welcomed each time by former *St. Trinian's Girl* and socialite, Sally Bulloch, who now manages the Athenaeum Hotel.

Returning to Los Angeles frequently, we supervised the reconstruction of the house. Every time a room was finished it became our territory again. Then one day, going upstairs to our top floor, I found myself catching my breath. I attributed it to lack of exercise or to the stresses of rebuilding, but when it became worse Donna insisted I consult a doctor.

"Your aortic valve is letting you down," the heart specialist said, "We must do a replacement or I can't guarantee the time you have left." Clearly an operation was unavoidable. Surgery was scheduled a few weeks later in July.

The night before, Donna stayed with me at the hospital—the procedure was to start at 8:00 A.M. the next morning. She walked beside my gurney as I was wheeled down a corridor towards the gray double doors leading to the operating theater. As we said goodbye, we did so not knowing if we would ever see each other again. When I awoke almost twenty hours later I felt that I had been given some borrowed time.

The earthquake and my aortic valve were only part of the debt life had handed out. Once my surgery was completed I thought we had paid in full; however, there was another hit coming!

As I grew stronger, Donna's younger brother Jerry, forty-four, became ill. He was in the same hospital as I had been and sadly he succumbed to a rare lung disease leaving a wife, Pam, and three children, Zac (eight), Jake (two), and Matty (only five months).

Donna and her family were inconsolable and it was also tremendously upsetting to me. Jerry and I had been close. He was rusty haired, talkative, smart (VP of a computer company) and fun-loving, not to mention a superb bartender and film buff. Here I was, more than forty years older and I was getting better while he had been cheated out of his best years. It wasn't right. I sank into a depression common after heart surgery, but once recuperated, I have, in a way, become a surrogate father to his boys and love playing with them when they come to our home.

Recuperation would have been more difficult without two of our favorite people, Alan and Meredith Silverbach, who were instrumental with their support throughout our troubling times.

Eventually I became well enough to accept an invitation for BAFTA's Fiftieth Anniversary to be held in London in October 1996—Her Majesty Queen Elizabeth would be there.

The evening was hosted by the Academy's Vice-President, David Puttnam, and Chairman Eddie Mirzoeff. Maggie Smith, and Tony Havelock-Allan were also present. The highpoint of the evening occurred when I was given the opportunity to say a few words to the Queen.

"Ma'am, I want to take you back more than fifty years."

"Good gracious," she said.

"Do you remember when you came on the set of *In Which We Serve* with your mother and your sister? You were fourteen and Princess Margaret was eleven?"

The Queen smiled. "Yes, I remember, and what a lovely day it was."

The trip was tiring but worth it, and at last we were getting a bit of credit.

More pluses were to follow.

Two months later we returned to London for my investiture. Close friend Merrick Baker-Bates, the British Consul General, had informed me that I was to receive a CBE (Commander of the Order of the British Empire).

When Donna and I arrived at the palace on a frosty morning we had to smile upon hearing the orchestra in the minstrel's gallery playing—"Oklahoma." Those of us waiting were given instructions on exactly how to pro-

ceed when we were called. As I neared the stage, a gentleman held an arm
out in front of me to make sure I didn't move until the right moment. The
person ahead was given his medal and certificate, and, as he left the stage, I
moved into the next spot. There was a mark on which I had to stop and then
turn to the left and walk four paces towards the Queen and bow. It was a
treasured moment—over in a flash!

The next evening at Piccadilly, BAFTA presented me with a Lifetime
Fellowship Award and I was pleased to see so many friends and colleagues
including Cornie Lucas, Lord Brabourne and Countess Mountbatten, Lord
Putnam, Sir Sydney Samuelson, Freddie Young O.B.E., and Ossie Morris
O.B.E., as well as my son, grandson and many others.

Credit and pluses continue!

Christopher remarried and lives with his wife Sally-Ann near Canterbury—the city the Neames migrated to in the fifteenth century presumably
from France. In addition to his career as a film producer, he has written the
book and lyrics for two stage musicals. With drive and energy, my grandson,
Gareth, continues to gain accolades in the industry. My eldest granddaughter, Shuna, is a trained physiotherapist and married to a successful businessman, Jonathan Atack. They have two sons Alexander and Oscar. And my
youngest granddaughter, Emma, is an artist married to another artist, Andrew Price. Their children, Thomas and Isobel make me a great-grandfather
four times over. I am proud of each and every one of them.

Our Los Angeles home turned out to be more beautiful than it had
ever been and there we have entertained many interesting people in and out
of the creative world. Jean Louis and Loretta Young became frequent visitors.
Ossie Morris also comes over when he's in California. On his last visit he
brought *Mr. Moses'* line producer Dick McWhorter—again we teased him
about the "cheap gas."

Maureen O'Hara often joins us; we had met her years earlier at a Carol
Reed festival in Santa Barbara. With Bill Saunders at the piano we've enjoyed
evenings in our living room starring Johnnie Mills and the rest of us singing,
"My Old Man Said Follow the Van and Don't Dilly Dally On the Way." One
evening Bill played while Mel Brooks belted out his rendition of "Mammy."

The teenager who used to come over to play my piano in La Mortala
did rather well for himself. Not long ago, Donna and I were in England for
Lord Lloyd-Webber's fiftieth, celebrated at his country estate in Sydmonton,
Hampshire. Five hundred people were entertained at a sit-down dinner in a
huge marquée attached to his home. At the front, above the stage in neon
was written, "Happy Birthday Andrew and Imo" (Andrew's daughter Imo-
gen was celebrating her 21st).

The next morning a smaller group of us attended a church service followed by a lunch for another 500 people in the marquée. It was elegant beyond imagination—Andrew's wife Madeleine had thought of every detail.

Johnnie Mills was seated next to us and Donna was particularly impressed to meet Tom Stoppard. His play *Arcadia* is one of her all-time favorites and deals with the distortion of history. Bearing that theme in mind, writing this autobiography, I have relived experiences and revisited friendships trying to straighten out some misconceptions and inaccuracies concerning my own life, hopefully without creating new ones.

The happiness I have attained in my latter years is not taken for granted. Thus far there has only been one dark cloud. Even though it could only have been expected, it was difficult to accept.

Beryl died on the morning of October 8, 1999. She hadn't been unwell; it was just that her ninety-six years had finally caught up with her. She had remained cheerful until her quick and painless death. I made immediate plans to leave for England.

Christopher had made the arrangements and the funeral was held at Selling Church, near Canterbury, close to where she had spent the last three years of her life. After the ceremony, the coffin was taken out of the church to the music of "I'll See You Again." I had hoped she would see the new millennium, but it was not to be.

Taking the bitter with the sweet, the new century brought with it my ninetieth birthday. No one could have had a better celebration. The three-day event started with a phone call on Thursday from my grandson confirming that he was flying in the next day. During the conversation he asked us if Saturday could be set-aside for a lunch at the house with Prince Edward.

That Friday night Gareth arrived and we were sitting in the living room just before dinner when we heard the front gate bell ring. My grandson went out then reentered with a man who walked across the room and sat beside me. He was slightly in shadow, but as he spoke I thought he sounded like my son. In fact, after I had gathered my senses, I comprehended that Chris had flown over to surprise me. Looking at him and then at Gareth I was aware of my father's legacy—three generations of Neame men resembled Senny—fair haired with bushy eyebrows, and that slightly protruding chest.

Saturday's lunch with Prince Edward and some of his colleagues was tremendously entertaining. The Prince couldn't have been more delightful. And the next day we had another party with friends.

On Monday April 23, 2001, a 300-guest celebration was organized by BAFTA/LA and Donna at the Four Seasons Hotel in Beverly Hills. The British Consul, Paul Dimond, presented me with a resolution from the Los

Angeles City Council proclaiming my birthday as Ronald Neame Day, the Queen Mother sent a signed copy of a photograph taken of us over fifty years earlier on the set of *The Magic Box* and I was also presented with a lovely commemorative book filled with remembrances of friends and colleagues.

Guests included Ernest Borgnine, Stella Stevens, and Carol Lynley, as well as Michael York, Glynis Johns, Anna Lee, Karl Malden, Carl Reiner, Maureen O'Hara, Phyllis Diller, Juliet Mills and her husband, actor Maxwell Caulfield and many others. Also in attendance was long-time chum, reporter Army Archerd from *Daily Variety*.

Army Archerd: "I'm not 90, I'm 60; the '6' got turned around," laughed Ronald Neame at the lavish party. You could fool anyone about Neame's age; he's as spry as ever, singing "I Can't Give You Anything But Love" to wife Donna and beaming as Estelle Reiner sang "Happy Birthday" to him, à la Marilyn Monroe to JFK! Tuesday Neame drove (in his brand new silver Mercedes) to his Santa Barbara house to activate his birthday present—a digital camera—in his computer.

Bill Saunders, who had flown in with his wife Jacqui from Monte Carlo, played the piano while Loretta Swit sang a provocative version of "You Do Something to Me." Then I belted out a few more tunes. Later that night, as people were leaving, Red Buttons handed me a note, "Did you save me from drowning in *Poseidon* only to kill me with your singing?"

At the conclusion of the evening, I gave what I considered a brief speech, relating a few anecdotes and thanking everyone for giving me an unforgettable party.

Alec Guinness: Ronnie has a sentimental streak, which one has to fight against. He always wants things to be kind and gentle, a happy ending kind of attitude. He is a sweet fellow, but given an audience he is inclined to go on too long. He doesn't know when to draw the line, which sometimes makes me cross. He is a very genial man; he wants to be loved and, indeed, he is loved!

· A ·

The Films of Ronald Neame

ASSISTANT CAMERAMAN OR CAMERA OPERATOR

Adam's Apple (1928)
Blackmail (1928)
The Maid of the Mountains (1932)
Fires of Fate (1932)
Mr. Bill the Conqueror (1932)
For the Love of Mike (1932)
Happy (1933)
A Southern Maid (1933)
Girls Will Be Boys (1934)
Radio Parade of 1935 (US: *Radio Follies*, 1934)
The Old Curiosity Shop (1934)
Once in a Million (US: *Weekend Millionaire*, 1935)

DIRECTOR OF PHOTOGRAPHY

Drake of England (US: *Drake the Pirate*, 1935)
Invitation to the Waltz (1935)
Joy Ride (1935)

Honours Easy (1935)
A Star Fell from Heaven (1936)
Improper Duchess (1936)
King of the Castle (1936)
The Crimes of Stephen Hawke (US: *Strangler's Morgue*, 1936)
Radio Lover (1936)
Scarab Murder Case (1936)
Reasonable Doubt (1936)
Strange Experiment (1937)
Café Colette (US: *Danger in Paris*, 1937)
Brief Ecstasy (1937)
Against the Tide (1937)
Feather Your Nest (1937)
Keep Fit (1937)
Second Thoughts (US: *Crime of Peter Frame*, 1938)
Murder in the Family (1938)
Who Goes Next? (1938)
The Gaunt Stranger (US: *The Phantom Strikes*, 1938)
Penny Paradise (1938)
The Ware Case (1938)
Cheer, Boys, Cheer (1938)
Trouble Brewing (1938)
It's in the Air (US: *George Takes the Air*, 1938)

I See Ice (1938)
Let's Be Famous (1939)
Come On, George! (1939)
Four Just Men (1939)
Young Man's Fancy (1939)
Return to Yesterday (1939)
Saloon Bar (1940)
Major Barbara (1941)
A Yank in Oxford (1941)
One of Our Aircraft Is Missing
   (1942)
In Which We Serve (1942)
This Happy Breed (1944, also
   co-screenwriter)
Blithe Spirit (1945)

PRODUCER

Brief Encounter (1946, also
   co-screenwriter)
Great Expectations (1946, also
   co-screenwriter)
Oliver Twist (1948)
The Magic Box (1951)
Passionate Friends (1949)

DIRECTOR

Take My Life (1947)
The Golden Salamander (1950)
The Card (US: The Promoter, 1952)
The Million Pound Note (US: Man
   with a Million, 1953)
The Man Who Never Was (1956)
The Seventh Sin (1957)
Windom's Way (1958)
The Horse's Mouth (1958)
Tunes of Glory (1960)
Escape from Zahrain (1962)
I Could Go On Singing (1963)
The Chalk Garden (1964)
Mister Moses (1965)
A Man Could Get Killed (1966)
Gambit (1966)
The Prime of Miss Jean Brodie (1969)
Scrooge (1970)
The Poseidon Adventure (1972)
The Odessa File (1974)
Meteor (1979)
Hopscotch (1980)
First Monday in October (1981)
Foreign Body (1986)
The Magic Balloon (1990)

· ℬ ·

Awards and Honors

Academy Award nomination for *Brief Encounter*, writer 1946
Academy Award nomination for *Blithe Spirit*, special effects 1946
Academy Award nomination for *Great Expectations*, writer 1947
Governor of the Academy of Motion Pictures Arts and Sciences 1977–1979
Governor of BAFTA/LA, 1987 to date
Man of the Year 1994 from the British American Chamber of Commerce
Lifetime Fellowship Award BAFTA, 1996
CBE (Commander of the Order of the British Empire), 1996
Founder Member and Chairman of the British Film Academy
Founder Member of the Association of Cine Technicians (ACT)
Founder Member of the British Society of Cinematographers

Acknowledgements

𝒯hanks to Anthony Slide for his talent, patience, and incredible knowledge of film history. Who could have believed that someone of his age would know about George Formby, and even more astonishingly Betty Balfour, both stars of early British films. Having my autobiography associated with Anthony has been an exceptional pleasure.

A strong acknowledgment to production editor Kellie Hagan, who, despite a few challenging moments, brought the whole thing together.

Tremendous gratitude to three dear friends whose memories and power of observation are often sharper than mine: Sydney Samuelson, whose father was working in films even before my parents; lifelong friend Ossie Morris, my director of photography for several years; and Kevin Brownlow, perhaps the most experienced film historian of our generation.

Thanks to Sheridan Morley and the Noël Coward Estate, who were kind enough to grant permission to use Noël's lyrics and quotes from his diaries.

It would be impossible to list all those friends and colleagues who took their time to add their contribution to this book, but here are some of them: Malcolm Arnold, Peter Beale, Ernest Borgnine, Colin Brewer, Red Buttons, Michael Caine, Phyllis Calvert, Jack Cardiff, Jane Carr, Christopher Challis, Petula Clark, Anne Coates, Bill Creber, Clive Donner, Bryan Forbes, Frederick Forsyth, Freddie Francis, Ian Fraser, Brian Garfield, Judy Geeson, Guy Green, Alec Guinness, Tony Havelock-Allan, John Hawkesworth, Paul Heller, Anne Hutton, Glynis Johns, Jack Klugman, Bryan Langley, Anna Lee, Mort Lindsey, Carol Linley, Herbert Lom, Andrew Lloyd Webber, Cornel Lucas, Shirley MacLaine, Karl Malden, Terence Marsh, Pamela Sue Martin, Dick McWhorther, Johnnie Mills, Warren Mitchell, Jerry Pam, Marion Rosenberg, Alvin Sargent, Jean Simmons, Norman Spencer, Stella Stevens, Audrey Totter, Wendy Toye, Lawrence Turman, Sam Waterston, Shelly

Winters, Googie Withers, Susanna York, and, last but certainly not least, Richard Zanuck.

Special mention to *The Poseidon Adventure* Fan Club, James Radford and Jak Castro, Lovetta Kramer of the RMS Queen Mary Foundation, the Judy Garland Club, and the George Formby Society.

Karen Stetler of the Criterion Collection was kind enough to promote this book in a newly released DVD of *The Horse's Mouth*.

Finally, thanks to the Margaret Merrick Library of the Academy of Motion Picture Arts and Sciences, the British Film Institute, BAFTA, and BAFTA/LA.

—Ronald Neame

Index